contents

contents

mix

ten years of creative writing at
Bath Spa University College

First published by MA2 in 2003
Ipley Manor, Marchwood, Hampshire SO40 4UR

For information about the contributors, please contact
Mike Martin at mixanthology@aol.com
telephone: 07703 333004

Copyright rests with individual authors.

Art direction: Wendy Ashley
Cover and text design: Gemma Gorringe and Rachel Mountifield
Bath Spa University College, Sion Hill, BATH BA1 5SF

Printed and bound in Great Britain by Bookcraft,
Midsomer Norton, Bath.

ISBN: 0-9540526-2-5

A CIP catalogue record for this book is available from the British Library.

contents

acknowledgements

We should like to thank the staff at Bath Spa University College for their help in putting this book together, particularly Richard Francis, Tessa Hadley, Richard Kerridge, Colin Edwards, Philip Gross and Lucy English from the School of English and Creative Studies, and David Beaugeard and Michael Soderberg from the School of Art and Design.

We are grateful for financial support from the college and from the literary agents PFD, particularly Simon Trewin who has been so active in encouraging new writers. PFD also provides an annual prize for the best work of fiction produced each year on the MA.

Sarah Duncan, Sue Swingler, Rachel Bentham, Barbara Bloomfield, and Linda Ewles have also been very generous in passing on advice and the benefit of their experience of compiling last year's anthology.

We hope to make a modified version of this edition available on the internet later this year and we thank Alison Kelley for masterminding the project.

As this edition reflects ten years of the Creative Writing MA at Bath Spa, we asked for contributions from previous graduates, and acknowledgements are due to the publishers and editors of the books and journals listed below in which the following work first appeared:

The Better Part by Deborah Gregory was published by Solidus in 2002. *The Treatment* by Mo Hayder was published by Bantam Press, a division of Random House Group Ltd, in 2001. Jennifer Hunt's poem 'Fossil' first appeared in *South* (23) in April 2001, 'Pebbles' in *Acumen* (38) in September 2000 and 'September' in *Poetry Wales* in January 2002. Elizabeth Kay's poem 'Metrophobia' appeared in her book *The Spirit Collection* (Manifold, 2000). Simon Kerr's short story 'Firefighter' was published in *The Black Mountain Review* (2). Sarah Rosenfeld's poem 'The Smell of Grass' first appeared in *We Write in Water*, the 1999 anthology of Bath Spa's Creative Writing MA. Julie-ann Rowell's poems 'Corruption' and 'Return' first appeared in *The Reader* magazine (8), 'Cargo' in *The Reader* (11) and 'Stay in Touch' on The Poetry Society's

acknowledgements

website. Mary Taylor's poem 'Departure' appeared in *Freewheeling* in 1995, 'The Nunnery, Iona' in *Acumen* (39) in 2001, 'Pasture of the Geese' in *Coracle* in 1998, 'The Barnakle' in *Other Poetry* in 1996, and 'Pomegranate' in *Eating Your Cake... and Having It*, Fatchance Press, 1997. Mimi Thebo's short story 'Taking it With You' was first published in *Mslexia's* 1999 'death' issue.

The editors:
Paul Meyer, Stephanie Boxall, Mike Martin, Wendy Ashley, Cassandra Keen, Morgaine Merch Lleuad, and John Pemberton

foreword

Creative writing at Bath has come on apace since I first became involved with it some five or six years ago. It is now a major league player and is consistently producing writers of outstanding quality with finely honed voices and page-turning momentum. As book deal follows book deal, the word is being spread throughout the English language and in translation that Bath Spa really means business. At PFD we also believe in nurturing new talent – it is crucial to our business and vital to the creative wellbeing of the publishing community we are at the centre of. Therefore, it gives us great pleasure to be able to sponsor this anthology for a second year and to continue to be part of the extended Bath Spa family.

In this volume, which celebrates the tenth anniversary of Bath Spa's Creative Writing MA, you will find an extraordinary group of students who are producing work that will be read widely in years to come – of that there is no doubt. Among them is rising star Holly Atkinson who is the recipient of last year's PFD/Bath Spa Prose Prize. Many congratulations to her and everyone else featured herein.

Read, enjoy and spread the word.

Simon Trewin
Literary Agent, Peters, Fraser and Dunlop

strewin@pfd.co.uk
www.pfd.co.uk

introduction

Suspicious people occasionally suggest that creative writing courses are likely to turn out standardised writers all using the same house style. It couldn't happen. Writers are the most cussedly individualistic people you'll meet. In order to succeed, they have to keep on trusting the stories and symbols that excite them. While thinking honestly about the criticism they receive, they have to be able to hold on to their vision, keep their nerve and finish the book. It's exceptionally difficult, and they wouldn't have got as far as starting the course without being extremely stubborn. Often their stubbornness is used to guard the place where their writing flows freely. And that goes for the teachers as well. Any good MA course will have a team of tutors comprised of working writers of various kinds, each with their different vision and taste. They could never agree on a single house style, much less impose it on the students.

The best piece of evidence, though, is the wonderful diversity of this anthology, and of all the work students have produced since the course began in 1992-93. They have published realistic fiction, magic realism, suspense fiction, comic fiction, strictly metrical poetry, free verse, modernist poetry, bluegrass poetry, radio drama, science fiction, erotic fiction, television drama, chick lit, lad lit, travel writing and nature writing. Many of these genres are represented in this collection. I remember a novel about civil war in West Africa, so cruelly observant it screamed; a darkly funny novel about growing up in Frome; a delicate corona of sonnets; a novel about a man who doesn't leave his house for fifteen years. Among the publishers who have accepted books by our students are Cape, Weidenfeld, 4th Estate, Abacus, Picador, Pan, Sceptre, Allison & Busby, Hodder Headline, Bantam and HarperCollins.

Graduates of the course who now teach for it include the novelists Lucy English, Tessa Hadley, Mo Hayder and Mimi Thebo. Richard Francis, Philip Gross and Steve May continue to be wonderful teachers and to help the course develop its professional connections. Recently they have been joined by the novelist Nicola Davies (who writes as Stevie Morgan), the children's writer Julia Green and the poet Tim Liardet. The course now enjoys support from many literary agents, publishers and BBC producers who visit each year, talk to students and read manuscripts. Peters, Fraser and Dunlop, the literary agents, who have helped several of our students secure good publishing contracts, now award an annual prize for the best novel by a student. They have also provided generous sponsorship for this book.

Les Arnold set up this course when there were few in the country and the academic and professional worlds were largely sceptical. The first students arrived only a month before Les's sudden death. Our first Course Director, Jeremy Hooker, an inspiring poet and teacher, led the course for four years and established its practice of meticulous and sympathetic close reading. Richard Francis came as Professor in 1999, from the successful novel-writing course he had built at Manchester University, and has done more than anyone to help us become one of the leading courses for novelists in the country. We are now developing poetry and scriptwriting, and designing a new MA course in Writing for Young People.

The results are here in this volume, thanks to the students and staff, and to the quite exceptional work of this year's editors.

Richard Kerridge
Course Director

the space between waves

from a novel **by daniel allan**

He had hoped to have the house to himself when he got back, if just for an hour or so. Despite his brother having only been staying a little under a week, he was already finding everything too crowded. Suffocating. Whereas before he and Hana could finish their meal and perhaps push the plates to one side, leave their wine glasses until the morning, they now found themselves having to clear away almost immediately. *Excuse me*-ing around Simone or Nicholas in the kitchen as they prepared their own meal or something for Andy.

With Andy on the prowl, *such an inquisitive toddler* (Simone's assessment, not his; he preferred meddling, nosy prying), the house – which to them had always been a sanctuary, a place of comfort and safety, of cushions and soft corners – had subsequently been disclosed by Simone to be a veritable nest of danger: of furtive eye-gougings and scoldings; of avalanches, burns, trips, impalings and smotherings.

Their domestic idyll – the snow dome cottage replete with wisteria and climbing roses, cosy front-of-fire winters seemingly never more than a wrist-flick away – had been demolished by Andy within hours of his arrival. Reaching for everything dreaded in the house: knives, buttons, glasses, corkscrews, screwdrivers, film containers, batteries and fuses; he and Hana, at Simone's insistence, now found themselves teetering on the brink of domestic tragedy. A horrific abyss into which they might, at any second, be hurled by as little as an errant spoon, a carelessly tossed shoe.

"It really isn't hard to make the adjustment, honestly. We found it tricky at first, didn't we darling. But we soon got into the swing of it. I hope you don't mind. It seems such an impropriety, what with Nick not having told you about us. But he really is such an inquisitive little boy. He really is."

"It won't be a problem, I'm sure." Hana had replied smilingly while Simone, chased the boy for a cuddle. *It won't be a problem*, Michael found himself repeating aloud as he passed the farm, and made his way back across the fields. To his dismay, the house wasn't still sitting battened down for the night, curtains drawn and chimney barren. Instead he clearly saw the kitchen lights on, the back door open and figures moving round the house.

"Well hello, early bird." Simone was in her silk dressing gown, a black Japanese-type kimono with pink magnolias and white satin trim. She cradled Andy, who straddled her waist and stared suspiciously at the stranger who had just stepped into the kitchen. "Catch any worms?" He smiled but said nothing. He looked at Andy, source of all the recent tension.

He regarded the boy staring at him, so innocent-looking in blue pyjamas. He recalled being told that one should always assert authority over a dog by staring it down, making it look away first. He also remembered Hana saying that a cat stares back until it feels comfortable enough to blink, only then can you know it trusts you. He gazed back at Andy who neither looked away nor blinked. Just stared with the cold dead eyes of a reptile.

Michael was reminded of a photograph of Rasputin, the Svengali at the heart of Russia, harbinger of doom. With a jealousy he resented, he was fed up with Andy's childish solipsism, disgruntled with being frowned at and hidden from. He felt victimised by the child's apparent amnesia, his never entreating him, never growing to trust him. Just the frowns and the hiding. And always, despite Hana's insistence to the contrary, his hysterics at being directly spoken to, or attempts at being picked up. He tried his hardest to stay looking and not to blink.

"I'm just making coffee. You want some?" Simone turned round to him, swinging Andy out of view for a moment. A victory he took gladly, however small.

He only nodded. He slid his bag from his shoulder and took off his jacket. The day was barely two hours old yet it was already hot and humid, threatening a day like yesterday, of hot heads and temper and discomfort.

He went through to the conservatory and put his bag on the table, before collapsing down into a chair. Simone rattled around and babbled in the kitchen. He wanted his space back. That was the thing. He wanted to come into the house and for it to be empty and quiet and peaceful. He wrestled for the right word: tranquil, and mouthed it silently. He wanted it back the way it was.

With a masochism he was convinced thrilled Hana, he liked the resentment dawn brings, with its weight of expectations, its chores, its demands. Whereas their late-night talks in bed were mostly a fug of conversation, planning and good intentions, morning always brought with it the rancour of having been woken, a churlishness that plans are only that unless to put into action, and that good intentions are worthless in the diffidence daylight brings.

He enjoyed coaxing Hana out of bed, of running the gauntlet her waking mood might bring: grumpy, desolate, and obdurate. He enjoyed the martyrish nature of having to get up and make her tea; of soothing her into consciousness with cooings about the weather and with things they had discussed they intended to do. He liked snuggling back under the duvet with her, drinking in her smell; maybe even falling back asleep curled up with her. He loved squandering much of their little time off together with decadent snoozing or lovemaking; waking later to find early morning long gone, its note the cold tea on the side.

Simone compounded all this. He already loathed her cheerful morning demeanour, the alacrity with which she rustled up breakfast and coffee or tea. But most of all, the keenness with which she narrated every move she made for Andy's sake. *Mommy's just boiling water for the coffee, isn't she darling. Look Honey, Mommy's buttering her toast, yes she is, she's buttering her toast.*

What had begun as acute curiosity for him and Hana, a source of wondrous discussion – *A child, could you imagine? All day every day, needing you, depending on you* – had rapidly become little but a spring of annoyance for him. And the inquisitive empty vessel, hungry for information, for stimulus, for knowledge, seemed little served by the wittering blow-by-blow commentary delivered by his mother.

"There you are, coffee white with two." He went to thank her but stopped as he looked straight down her dressing gown and at her breast. Hanging full and heavy. He felt a flush of embarrassment but was also a little thrilled. She stood up and instinctively adjusted her gown. *Had she seen him? Did she see him looking?* He looked quickly away, engrossed suddenly by something some distance out of the window but the image had burned itself onto his retina, flickering on the hills when he blinked. She seemed not to have noticed.

"White with two, Andy. You hear Mommy? Uncle Mike has white with two sugars!"

He gathered up his coffee and continued looking out of the window. If Simone had wanted conversation, she was out of luck. She hovered for a moment before turning and walking away, burbling on to Andy. "Uncle Mike's got his coffee, hasn't he Andy? Do you think Daddy's ready for his now?"

He sipped slowly and noisily, enjoying the noise his gasps of breath made in the gradually emptying mug. Beneath Simone's constant garbling in the kitchen, he made out the birdsong in the hedges, watched one of the feral cats draw and pounce into the long grass. When he was done he ran the mug under the tap and went upstairs to rouse Hana.

She woke up crabby, more than usual. His adjectives about the day, blistering, fresh, gorgeous, were ignored and he ended up sitting at the foot of the bed apologising and trying to find one of her feet to rub, although she kept withdrawing whenever he came close.

They had rowed last night. A tired, flamboyant fight that caught suddenly and without warning, before quickly burning itself out and smouldering throughout the evening. It culminated, for them, in a meal conducted under exam conditions: all harsh whispers, significant looks and glances at the clock, while Nicholas and Simone sat, apparently none the wiser, as silent invigilators.

He had hoped that they could awake to a fresh day with it all forgotten, water under the bridge. He even said as much, ferreting around for one of her feet. But however much he thought they might have got away with it, that they could wake up and pretend it had never happened, that the whole of yesterday had never happened; a creeping realism set in. As with most of the rows they had nowadays, significantly more than a night's rest was required.

"Well this should make the next few days swim by, shouldn't it?"

It had started as soon as Nicholas and Simone took Andy out for a stroll, escaping to their own thoughts and from the growing atmosphere in the house. Michael watched them walk up the lane and disappear round the bend.

In a way, he was grateful for their exit. Although it had meant a certain row, he felt weary from the fanatical pleasantness he had been showing Simone since their return from the beach; compensating her for the distress Hana had caused. Now, self-consciously at first, his tone of voice and mannerisms exaggerated as if projecting into a darkened auditorium, he let his sense of indignation swell into anger, remembered his helplessness waiting on the beach.

"No, really. Make strangers feel welcome in your home by abducting their children for half the bloody day!"

"They're not strangers. In case you've forgotten. Again. Nicholas is your brother and the brunette with him is his wife."

"You know what I mean. Don't try shifting this on to me. Four hours you were gone, Hana. Four hours. No wonder she was worried sick."

"Honestly Michael, I was only up the beach." Hana was laying out a towel and some loose clothes to follow her bath. "Anyone would think we'd set out to sea on a pedalo, the way you're going on." He followed her across the hallway and into the bathroom as she set the plug and began running the taps.

"Oh, I'm sorry, is this all a bit tedious? No, don't look at me like that and don't make out I'm going on, either. You're in the wrong and you know it."

She went to raise her voice too. But chose rather to keep it low and calm, deliberately pacing her sentences and choosing her words carefully. She would make him see how silly all of this was, what a fuss he was making. She certainly wasn't troubled by something so small, so insignificant. No, she would take the mature position: temperate, controlled, even. Besides, she knew this would infuriate him even more. "I lost track of time."

"Yeah right, and the tide coming up the beach wasn't a bit of a giveaway then?"

"I didn't notice the tide. Excuse *me*." He stepped back a little. "And anyway you should have known I'd be back. What did you think, that I'd run off with him or something?" And she laughed.

There, she'd said it. And at once the thoughts that had lurked just beyond her recall, had remained hidden out of the corner of her eye, stepped out into view. *He could have been hers.* She ducked under his arm and scurried to the bedroom for some clean underwear.

She opened her dresser and rummaged through the drawer; kept her flushed face turned, not wanting to give anything away. She recalled her conversation with the elderly woman by the rock pools. Why hadn't she cleared up that Andy wasn't her son, that she was only watching for him? But still no guilt came. She glowed anew when she remembered how the woman had talked to her: mother to mother. Not with pitying condescension or polite assertions such as those made by Simone: *You'd make a good mother, you're a natural.* But with a mutual understanding and respect. *You know what it's like; I've no need to tell you. You're still here aren't you?* As a woman of the world. As someone who knew.

Michael watched from the doorway. Re-assuming the position he'd taken up at the bathroom door, leaning against the frame, crossed-armed and lounging. He caught the reflection of himself in her dresser mirror and tensed his biceps a little. Fixed his face with a furrowed brow, slightly curled lip. Authoritative and stern.

"You might have. I didn't know what to think really."

"Well, I didn't run off with him. Nothing happened and we came back a little late. That's all. No panic, no drama. No headline stuff, I just lost track of time."

"But you only went down for a paddle and a look at the rock pools.

What took four hours?"

"He's only a toddler, Mike. What was I supposed to do, drag him there and back within the hour?" She looked for a reply that wasn't forthcoming. "I didn't realise it was such a brief mission, I'd have synchronised watches."

"Yeah, yeah, get clever. Where did you go for four hours?"

"To the rock pools, I've already said."

"Not for four hours you didn't... "

"I told you I lost track of the time... "

He watched her. Why wouldn't she look at him?

"Hana. Hana!" She looked up. "What's going on?"

"Nothing. Really, nothing. Honestly."

"Then why won't you look at me?" She finally looked up. Her eyes were red. "What's going on?"

"Nothing." But she couldn't keep up the pretence, and turned away. He stayed watching her, saw her in the dresser mirror, wiping her eyes. His breathing deepened. He no longer felt angry; a new instinct took over. Fear. Scared to touch her, to walk over and put a soothing arm round her, frightened she might dissolve and tell him something he didn't want to hear, he instead became bullish. Relied on battering the truth from her.

"Look, this is stupid, tell me now. What's going on... "

"Nothing... "

"*Hana!*"

"I fell asleep. Okay? I fell asleep, happy now?"

"You what?"

"I know, just stop it... "

"Where was Andy?"

"He was fine. It was for a split second, honestly, he was fine he was just... "

"Jesus, Hana!" His volume stopped her dead; she even flinched a little. "You fell asleep while you were supposed to be watching Andy... "

"Only for a second... "

"And you want kids? Shit, you can't be trusted to have kids; you can't even look after someone else's." He stopped, his breath scraping hoarsely from his lungs. Something in her look told him that was enough, that another word might snap whatever fragile thread of composure she was clinging to.

"That's not fair."

"Fuck fair, can't you see what you did? Anything could have happened... "

"I know, but it didn't... "

"Anything could have happened, can't you see that? You can but you can't admit it. You're too pig-headed."

"Me pig-headed? You must be joking! What about you today? Not talking to anyone and sulking all bloody morning with your book and your *Where's my fags?*" She had screwed up her face and dropped her voice in imitation of him. "Honestly, you're like a child half the time. As a matter of fact that's not fair on Andy. He's more reasonable than you are." It was a cheap shot but it worked. His face switched from furious to quizzical in the split second it took to shift his eyebrows.

"What on earth are you talking about?" He stepped into the room his face screwed up in antipathy. *What was she going on about?* "How come you're in the wrong and suddenly I'm the bastard in all this. And what's wrong with me reading on the bloody beach all of a sudden?"

"Nothing." She nudged the drawer closed with her leg, where it remained slightly open, wedged with bra straps and a garter belt. "Absolutely nothing. I loved it. No, I really did. Sat there for three fucking hours while love's young dreams half-shagged in front of me all morning. Don't look at me like that... "

"I hardly think... "

"Too bloody right you hardly think. You barely talked to me all morning, so when I eventually find myself something to do and leave your sight for five minutes... "

"You fell asleep!"

"... for five minutes, find something for me to enjoy by myself, without your help or fucking approval, you have a fit about it."

"This isn't a fit!" He found his voice soaring in volume to match hers. It felt good to finally really cut loose and shout and scream. To do whatever he wanted without feeling their guests' presence, listening for a child's cry, feeling as though he was treading on glass. "This isn't a fit. You walked off with someone else's child... "

"It's Nicholas's child. Your nephew!"

"... with someone else's child for half the day, during which you fell asleep. I mean, Jesus Hana! He could have drowned; he could have been taken. No wonder she's so upset. You're going to have to apologise so we can get on... "

"I did apologise!"

"You didn't, not properly. You left everything hanging. Simone's got the right arse-ache about it and I've had to bend over backwards to make out you're not some kind of nutter." She leapt up from the bed and began hastily undressing, her voice dropping in volume whenever she stripped clothing up over her head or looked down to a stubborn fastening.

"You self-righteous bastard! How fucking dare you. Bend over backwards? What do you think I've been doing since they got here?" She pulled her vest over her head. "It's your brother Michael, not mine. It's your brother and his fucking wife and his fucking child. I've cooked for them, I've cleaned round them." She dropped her sarong. "I've sat there listening to her inane chatter for I don't know, fucking hours! Purely because he's your brother. I mean, who turns up at someone else's house with a family they've not mentioned to anyone. It's just rude, let alone whatever weird level it must reach. Does that seem even remotely normal to you? 'Hello All, I've not seen you for ten years, here's my secret fucking family!'"

"You said you didn't mind."

"Jesus, Michael, I don't mind." She unhitched her bra. "What's wrong with you? You're blind to everything around you. Of course I don't mind. I love you. But I can't take the pretence much more." Kicked away her knickers. "Stop pussyfooting around him and find out what he wants."

She stood naked in front of him, apparently unknowingly, as though she'd simply run out of clothes to remove. He barely noticed, however, his breath shallow as he took in what she had just said.

"What do you mean, *what he wants?*"

"Well doesn't it strike you as just a little odd that he turns up after ten years, with a family no one knows about, a wife he's completely unsuited to and a child named after your dead father? Not strange to you? At all?"

"I don't know. Perhaps he was homesick and, anyway, I think they do suit each other."

"Michael!"

She scooped up her towel and clean clothes and pushed past him. Rushed into the bathroom and slammed the door before he had a chance to wedge his foot in.

"Hana, open the door." She didn't answer.

"Hana. Hana! Open this bloody door."

Her voice was strained and distant behind the door. Sounded close to tears. "I can't hear you." She turned up the taps.

"Hana... Hana!"

"The water's too loud. I'm just having a bath."

He thumped the door turned and away.

"Stay in there all bloody night, then." He stalked down stairs to the kitchen, muttering. His head already ached and now his hand was sore.

the ninth wave

from a novel **by wendy ashley**

The park was a surprise. She had forgotten it was there. Erin and Joe brought her, the first summer they were all together. It was a hot and muggy summer, the days long and oppressive. There was little respite from the heat, and the stink of the river permeated everywhere. But the park was separate from all that. The trees seemed to create their own breeze and kept the smell of the city out. They'd spent most of that summer enjoying the shade of the park – lying on the grass chatting, getting to know each other. Erin would bring along some stage costumes to mend and Hope would help sew on the sequins. Then the autumn came and the weather shifted, and somehow the place was gradually forgotten. Things changed, she changed. It was a long time ago. Except here it still was, the gates and half the railings still missing, the battered trees still alive.

Hope hesitated, aware of the return journey. She grew breathless at the thought of it and she did want to be back before Joe. But this felt special, as if it was a reward for all that effort. Now she was here she couldn't not go in, if only for a minute. Perhaps she could bring Joe back. It might help both of them.

There were people in the park. She didn't know why she'd expected the place to be empty. Just because she'd forgotten, it didn't mean everybody else would. Someone had even taken time, recently, to trim back some of the overgrown shrubs and weeds, keeping the main path open and visible. Life continues, even when you're not there, she thought. It was oddly comforting.

A few people sat around a smouldering campfire on the opposite side of the dirty pond. They looked peaceful and relaxed – their limbs unbent. Two brindled dogs leapt in and out of the small group, licking hands and faces and snapping at twists of smoke. Makeshift bivvies of cardboard and plastic sheets nestled under the trees behind.

The pond was bigger than she remembered. The edges were muddier and less defined, and water had slipped over sections of the old pathways. But there were still ducks, and a few seagulls squabbling over scraps of food. An old, bald-headed man was throwing chunks of bread on to the brown water. His blue-black skin absorbed what little sunlight fell on him. Hope wondered if he should be giving away food when he was so thin. A light wind rippled his overcoat and there seemed no resistance beneath, it might as well have been hollow. But the man was smiling, a wide broken-toothed smile. One of the ducks waddled out of the water and lightly pecked at his shoes. The man chuckled, bent down and let the duck take a crust from his fingers.

She made her way around the flooded pond, pushing through swathes of wet grass and the occasional bush where the paths had been eaten away. There was a bench up ahead, near the bent shape of a small tree. Things were hanging from the branches. As she got nearer they revealed themselves to be mainly strips of coloured cloth. But there were also pieces of broken mirror and photographs dangling from thread. The photographs were sad. The faces in them were creased and scratched, and some were barely there at all. But the overall effect was strange and beautiful. She stroked the rough trunk and wondered about tying something to the tree herself, but realised she had nothing except Joe's scarf. Would he mind? she thought.

Touching the scarf reminded her. A brief flare of panic jolted her into realisation. She wanted to push the scarf up over her mouth and nose, to shield her marked face and stop herself from screaming. She was totally alone and Joe didn't know where she was and she still had to walk all the way back. She held a hand over her mouth and tried to stay calm. She had forgotten, she really had forgotten. Maybe that was a good thing? No, of course that was a good thing. If she could forget once, she could forget again. It would be okay. There were people around; she had been here before. It would be okay.

The edge of the bench pressed against the back of her knees and she sat down with a thump. The tree was now several paces away. How had that happened? She looked anxiously around the park. The man was still feeding the ducks. The group across the pond was still around the fire, the dogs now stretched out asleep. On another bench, further up the path, three women sat crammed together chatting while their children ran in and out of the nearby shrubbery. Everything was fine.

The hand on her mouth felt very cold. It shook a little when she took it away. She rubbed the palm hard against the rough material of her coat, until the skin burned hot with friction. She felt better for it. The sun was growing brighter. There were rainbows on the oily surface of the pond and parts of the sky seemed to have more colour. Perhaps she should just rest for a while. Panic attacks were only natural, but they would go away. The hardest part had already been done; the walk back was only that. She should be proud of herself for coming so far. Hope let herself relax and leant back on the bench. The seat's wooden struts creaked and shifted, then relaxed with her. She'd stay a little longer, just until the old man had run out of bread. She was smiling when the wooden struts creaked again and someone sat down next to her.

"I didn't think I'd see you out again so soon," the man said, settling back. "Not alone, anyway. I'm pleasantly surprised. This can't have been easy."

Hope stared at him. At least she must have been staring, because she didn't seem able to blink. He wasn't looking at her. His attention seemed focussed somewhere over the other side of the pond – his sharp profile half-shaded by that hat. But he was talking to her, wasn't he? There were things she needed to sort out in her mind, things that just wouldn't keep still. This wasn't right. It couldn't be the same man, not again. Coincidences don't work like that.

"The weather must help, of course," he continued. "Such a change after all that rain."

What was he trying to do, have a friendly chat? Laughter contracted in her throat, but she clamped her lips together and managed to suppress it. No, this really was very wrong. She had to do something. Could she just get up and walk away? It sounded easy enough. There were people around, surely he wouldn't dare do anything. She could go and join the group with the dogs, there were enough of them.

She tensed her leg muscles and scanned about her for the quickest, most visible escape routes, but it was too late. As she prepared to push up from the bench, the man casually stretched out an arm and laid a hand on the back of her neck. His touch was light but it was enough, stilling any movements. She had seen what his hands could do.

"So, how are you doing, Hope?" He glanced down at her, his expression unreadable. "I hope your face isn't too painful."

He smiled slightly, as if he'd made a joke, or maybe it was concern. Hope couldn't tell. She was finding it hard to think. His fingers were working their way under her scarf, their touch dry and smooth against her skin. She clenched her hands and tried to stay calm. His grey eyes narrowed. He was still looking at her, waiting for something. Was it her turn to speak? Maybe that really was all he wanted, a 'friendly' chat.

She swallowed hard and forced her mouth to move. "I'm fine. It's fine," she said. "Thank you." Her voice sounded odd, very small and hoarse. She could barely get the words out. But he seemed satisfied, because he nodded and smiled again.

"Good. I'm sorry for the bruises. He was unnecessarily brutal. Some people have no contról."

The dogs started barking, chasing a seagull away from the campfire. The bird had something in its yellow beak. She should say something else, humour him. *He did save you, Hope.*

"Thank you for helping me. I'm... I am grateful."

His thumb gently rubbed at the top of her neck. "I'm glad I was there. It could have been very nasty."

"Yes," she said.

The women from the other bench walked past, their children running off ahead. A little girl threw an object at the ducks. It made a hollow splash and the birds scattered, quacking loudly. Hope watched the ripples move across the water. Her back ached from holding so still.

Her forehead felt damp.

"I'm sorry, but I do have to go now." She fought hard to keep her voice steady. "My friend is expecting me soon. He'll worry if I'm late."

"Well, that's understandable."

"Yes, so I should get going."

He sighed and she almost expected him to take his hand away. But when she made to stand, his fingers flexed and tightened, urging her back.

"I'm sure Joe won't mind if you stay a little longer," he said softly. "He seems a reasonable kind of man."

Fear began to shiver through her body. Or was it anger? She wasn't sure. This man, he had no right. One hot tear squeezed its way out and ran down the side of her nose. It caught in the corner of her mouth.

"Why?"

The grip on her neck relaxed. "We have things to talk about, Hope."

"How can we have things to talk about? I don't know you."

He smiled, pushing his fingers up into her hair. "Do you know how long it took me to find you again? I think we have a lot of catching up to do."

She closed her eyes. He was confusing her. She didn't know him, she really didn't. He'd be very difficult to forget.

"I really am very sorry, but I think you've made a mistake." She breathed hard, carefully forming each word. "We met for the first time, only two days ago. I'm not who you're looking for. I can't be."

Fingers twisted in the hair at the base of her skull, pulling strands free from her ponytail. She opened her eyes. His smile had gone.

"But you are, Hope."

Another tear ran down her cheek. He wiped it away with his free hand, the stiff oilskin of his sleeve brushing her chin. Her clenched hands felt cold again, the palms slippy. Not now, please not now.

"You really shouldn't worry, little unda. I'm concerned about you. I don't want to hurt you."

"Then why don't you take your hand off me?" she hissed.

"I don't think you'd listen to me nearly so well if I did that," he said reasonably.

"But you're not telling me anything!"

She wanted to scream. She hated the touch of his fingers, she hated him. She wished for a knife, something sharp she could jab into his leg and shake his cool demeanour, if only for a moment. And she guessed it would only be a moment. Would he even cry out, or would he just laugh at her? But most of all she hated the smell that came from him. She hadn't noticed at first but now it was unavoidable, wafting from the cracked material of his long coat. It wasn't an unpleasant smell, it was fresh and brackish. But it was familiar, too familiar. She couldn't pinpoint why, and she wasn't sure she wanted to know.

"Please, I don't know what you want from me."

"You do. Come on Hope, you can't hide all your life." The man stared hard at her until she had to look away. "Think about it. There is something quite special about you."

Blobs of light shivered on the ground at her feet, thrown by the mirrors in the tree. She thought of Mama Sparkles, of Erin. Erin had called her special, but his voice had never been so empty.

"No," she whispered. "There isn't."

"I will lose my patience eventually." He grabbed her left fist and pulled it up from her lap. "Open it. Open your hand."

She didn't want to, but there was no choice. Slowly she uncurled her fingers and the drops of water began to fall.

"There. Do you really think that's normal?" He shook her hand and the water fell faster, splashing on her coat. "Do you?"

"Stop it!" she begged.

"But I'm not doing it, am I?" he said. "You know that." He gently placed her hand back down. "You can taste salt, can't you?"

Hope began to pull her coat sleeves over her hands, but then changed her mind. "That's none of your business," she replied shakily.

"Your dreams aren't going to go away. Not now. You can't control it, Hope. They will only get stronger. I can help you, but it's your choice."

His fingers slipped from her hair and rested again on the nape of her neck. She fought back a wave of nausea and made herself look into his eyes. The grey had become a cold black. They frightened her, but the fear seemed irrelevant. She'd been frightened enough. Slowly she said, "I will never need your help."

This appeared to amuse him. His eyes lightened a little and he cocked his head to one side, as if to examine her more closely. "I think you might change your mind, unda. But it is your decision."

He pulled his hand from under her scarf and away from her neck, but the tension stayed. She watched nervously as he untied a feather from his hair.

"What do you think Joe would think about this?" he asked suddenly. "Could he handle it, do you think? Would he want to?"

Her tongue stuck itself to the roof of her mouth and she couldn't answer. He smiled at her expression and began twirling the feather in his hands.

"It must be very difficult to lose someone you love. Yes, I think so. A bad thing to go through." The feather stopped moving and he looked almost thoughtful. "Erin had the true strength in that relationship. It's a pity."

An icy weight had settled in Hope's chest. It was horrible to hear him say Erin's name. It was all horrible.

"Perhaps you should consider your decision more carefully." He tapped the feather on her nose. "I'd hate for you to make the wrong one." The man stood up, his tall frame slowly unfolding, and walked to the tree. He tied the feather to one of the dangling strips of cloth. "For you, Hope," he said, looking back at her. "A little encouragement." He bowed his head to the tree then quietly moved away, disappearing among the overgrown shrubs and bushes.

The feather twisted slightly in the breeze.

title card: 'opportunity knocks'

from a novel **by max ashworth**

Okay, before we start. This isn't gonna be nice. We'll have shitloads of fun anyway.

You'll get to join in.

Something's gonna happen to someone. But when? Ooooooh.

Maybe now.

No.

Not yet.

Soon.

Trust me.

After his English Lit. 4-5, my housemate Alex knocks and redundantly tells me to keep my eye on Emily. She's my girlfriend. Well, sort of.

"That Jezzebel tart's been stretching his muscles in her direction, man." He almost sounds apologetic.

Everyone knows Jezz and his groupie just split. Both parties made it clear round campus that they were the dumper, not the dumpee. You know how it goes.

Cut to **EXT. AMEHURST VIEW—NIGHT** and what's happening right now is Jezz walking through the strangely warm night. He's wearing a white tight-fitting T-shirt. He has that cocky 'I'm gonna get it' grin, and he will. But not the way he's expecting.

Right now he's passing the faded 'AMEHURST VIEW' sign. He's kicking at weeds and he loiters, and this gives him opportunity to check the street. He grins to himself. I'm not sure why.

Now he's at the gate, glancing with the standard-issue lack of interest at the house, the windows – stuff like that. Whatever. Now he's grinning. Now he's ducking and diving under low branches waving... like... say, amateur actors pretending to be trees.

Okay, scrap that.

His eyes are livid – you know, trying to focus on darkness and stuff, and his neck remains rigid, almost as if he now trusts his eyes less. Slowly he mounts the stairs. Looking for Emily's room?

He doesn't know which one it is, but he figures he'll know it when he sees it, he's Jezz, he's a geezer. His friends call him Gezzer.

Course they do.

And right now Jezz's looking up, detects soft light drifting on motes of dust... say, made angry with identification.

Okay, scrap that, too.

'Emily's' door is ajar. Now I emphasised it cos it's not really Emily's door – oh, you got that. Anyway, there's a vertical band of light seeping through the jamb like... say, sunlight reflecting off a polished lamppost, or... say, like a yellow-white band in an abstract painting.

I know what I mean, and, anyway, you can fuck off. I can't help the purple prose. See, the house keeps dishing out these strange highs from time to time. Tagline insists he's stopped playing 'You've Been Spiked', yet whenever something weird happens or when suddenly we thought it was yesterday, when it was three weeks ago, bang, we're talking to the carpet, and Tagline's having inane epiphanies about consumerism, religion, and Bananaman, every five minutes.

And one of these random highs is happening right now.

Ghostly Connotations: 1

Video Nasty: 0.

Soon Jezz will be able to see the black-bin-bag wallpaper/carpeting effect. This is an area strangely neglected in home decorating programmes.

And after the break, 'How to Prepare your House for a Blood Bath', featuring our own home make-over guru, Jeffrey Dahmer.

Jezz won't see the bucket meant to stop his blood seeping through the floorboards. And now, don't get me wrong, that'd be a wicked thing to see happen, but think about the clean-up, man: blood – gooey and elastic as bubble-gum – dripping through the house like acid defying a sieve. Me no thinkee so.

The stairs creak a bizarre syncopation. And, somewhere in the house, footsteps reciprocate.

Ghostly Connotations: 2

Video Nasty: 0.

Now at first I'm not sure, but I think Jezz's singing 'Things Can Only Get Better', but then I realise my mistake and I slap myself a good one on the forehead. Of course it's gotta be 'Let Me Entertain You'. I'd dance, but I can't move because of the rustly carpeting.

I do have a plank of wood though. Clever me, eh?

I play the wood like it's a guitar.

As you do.

And right now his footsteps are creaking closer and I'm imagining dirt and long dead insects sifting through the floorboards, fine and pure as dead skin. And now I'm imagining the whole house shaking itself, like a snake removing its skin, and the dust settling back again into the foundation and ready for redistribution.

You're gonna have to go with me on this one.

Now the technical term, I think you'll find, is Haunted House Osmosis. Okay, the house feasts on recycled layers of skin prematurely shed through isolation, through withdrawal. It grows taller, invites dogs and cats to crawl under it to die and then, seeking moisture, the roots of the house gulp at dying nutrients. This strengthens its foundation, its facade: its defence, preparing for lean, cold months of hibernation.

Or…

Anyway, the floorboards never creaked before.

Ghostly Connotations: 3

Video Nasty: 0.

And if a tree falls down in a forest and there's no one there to hear it... yeah, yeah, shut up. I get enough of that 'do not read this sentence' pop-philosophy from Emily.

Now, initially I plan on screaming, "Yaaaaaaaa*aaaaaaaaaa*hhhhhhh!" as I swing the four-by-two, and right now I'm thinking that maybe I should've hammered a six-inch nail through it.

But that'd end things way to soon. So scrap that one. Another for the cutting-room floor. Goodie, even more kindling.

As always, what you're getting is edited highlights.

He's at the door jamb now. My left hand's on the handle, ready. There should be edge-of-your-seat music, too. Frenetic violins, the percussion section high on crystal meth.

The door swings wide. Jezz looks up.

And *now* he notices the glossy carpet. He looks decidedly vexed to see me, but he just stands there stupidly.

Disappointing.

And as you'd expect, I'm seeing everything in slow motion. So there's the dull thud of the wood hitting him in the face, and him swooning back. Now he's doing the slumping gracefully bit; his knees buckle and his eyes stare ahead, frozen. All this happens in silence. And now I'm imagining that we're kids having play-fights, painstakingly choreographed, thanks to The A-Team.

Jezz's eyelids flutter. Then close. Now still.

And what's happening right now is Jezz coming to. Vexed again.

He's confused. He doesn't know where he is.

All say, "Aahhh."

No, don't.

"Emily?" says Mr Soon To Be Cut Into Teeny Tiny Pieces and singing, 'What Are You Gonna Do With *That* Nail Gun?'

Now he's starting to get up.

Now I kick him down.

Whumph.

Soft thud, rustle. What you'd expect.

And right now I'm getting bored with kicking him down. I don't need to take advantage of his grogginess. I can 'have' him. You know, kick the shite out of him.

Now the typical way of doing this is to create Jezz as a likeable character, then you feel sympathy, and tension. But he's not a likeable character, as you've gathered, and if so you get one of my Special Gold Stars. Well done to you! So instead I'll go into overkill. Yep, pun intended.

Yeah, I know. Lame-o.

Before he starts getting rowdy, starts 'giving it large', I time a knee into his stomach. This produces the desired effect. And his face turns slightly purple. Now I've got time to tie his arms and legs together and round the legs of the chair. Oh, and Mr Gag. I want to take a photo of his purple face.

But I don't.

Now I'm finding the cassette player, inserting tape labelled 'Laughter Track 3' and my finger waves eeny-meeny-miny-mo over the play/stop/record/rewind buttons. And what's happening right now is me being cunning as Dick Dastardly.

I look over my shoulder and ask Jezz if he agrees on my choice of background. I press play and gradually laughter builds.

"Sorry, Jezz. But Emily can't make it tonight. Now I hope I'll do."

Fade out.

You see, Jezz, Emily's would-be suitor, fancies himself as a bit of a karaoke singer. So what's happening right now is me giving you the low-down on Jezz.

Karaoke's a typical 'lad' thing to do, as of course you know. He's a Stars In Their Eyes wannabe. Getting shags by singing songs by gay icons, and ultimately finding a girl to wank into. Maybe he hopes to emulate the Pretty Boy acts marketed for teenage girls moistened by

Aryan wannabes. This is why Jezz is gonna make a great murder victim.

And he had a guaranteed celebrity-based future. Maybe hosting Saturday morning TV. Chuggie cockie, snortie snortie, Betty Fordie. He's got it written all over his face.

Now he also says "Top" which means 'great', by the way, and whenever someone says it in a pub I just wish I hadn't brought a switchblade along. What with me and my Dr Strangelove arm and everything.

And he thinks Emily, my Emily, *our* Emily, is interested in a fuck like him. Thinking she wants him – and, ooh, do you want it, sir? – he mistook her politeness and natural coy nature as a come-on.

Well, Jezz, glad to say: you will get your big break tonight. Sorry, pun intended again.

Ta daaaaaaaaaaaa. And tonight, Matthew, I'm gonna be Cut Into Teeny Tiny Pieces, singing 'Now What Are You Gonna Do With *That* Nail Gun?'

(Grateful and enthusiastic audience applause.) Now if you want to clap, you know you'll have to put the book down first.

But – wait – don't clap too loudly. You don't want people knowing you're strange.

Matthew Kelly:	Don't be shy, folks, pick up and phone:
0891 20 30 40 (1)	If you want to see Jezz's thigh sliced into little teeny pancakes.
0891 20 30 40 (2)	If your bag is more facial deconstructive surgery.
0891 20 30 40 (3)	If you want to know more about the consistency of eyeballs.
0891 20 30 40 (4)	**If DIY is more your thing, moving into nail-gun territory. (I endorse this. Matthew Kelly's still thinking about it.)**
0891 20 30 40 (5)	If you'd like Jezz to sing, '(Hit Me Baby) One More Time'.
0891 20 30 40 (6)	If you'd like me to sing a little song. It's your time.

0891 20 30 40 (7)   If you'd like to sing a little song. An apt one, obviously.
Yeah, go on, join in.

And what's happening right now is me noticing how much Jezz's tone has evolved amidst the evening's party games. We've jumped forward about half an hour, by the way.

Here are my guesses why he's not such a happy bunny right now. Well, considering that right now he's tied to a chair (a) inside a large metal bucket (b) and way up high in the top room of the house (c) – the 'Look Out' – it's to be expected. Oh, it's 'Look Out' as in, "Look out, he's got a hammer." Just in case you weren't sure.

Ghostly Connotations: 3,

Video Nasty: 1.

Close up: He's still wearing his cone party-hat (d), but then again, his hands are broken (e) and tied (f), so he's no way of taking it off (g). I keep reminding Jezz of this.

And just to reinforce my childish malevolence gig that I've got going, every so often I flick the elastic and this adds to the thin red whip-like marks under his chin (h). And, continuing with the theme, he cries like a child who doesn't want to be the centre of attention any more.

So what's happening now is me pressing stop on 'Laughter Track 3'. I'm shushing Jezz, my finger to my lips, and when it's finally silent I spray some of Emily's perfume about and little droplets of fine mist shiver in the warm breezes.

Now I have to gag him again. He's stopped being sorry and wanting to be my friend. Do I need a partner in crime, he's wondering.

This is to be expected.

We can do rape and mutilation sessions, he's suggesting.

We can fuck body parts while singing 'Hi-Ho Silver Lining', he's coaxing.

We can tie people's arms and legs to the axles of two cars and drive as fast as we can in opposite directions.

Necrophilia, he's suggesting, in a tone convinced of likely popularity.

Ghostly Connotations: 3

Video Nasty: 2.

"Can't you be more original than that?" I'm saying. "Say something fresh and exciting for the folks at home. This is not just your time you're wasting. Spice it up, or you'll hit the cutting-room floor."

What's happening now is Jezz getting angry, cursing, using nasty words. Shouting. "Help!" and stuff like that. After a while you can blank it out.

He fidgets wildly in his chair.

This is to be expected.

And I was hoping for such a shiny happy pretty pop-celeb thing. Well, back goes Mr Gag. "Say 'hello' to Mr Gag, Jezzy-poos."

I have to think about the noise level you know. I don't want to piss the neighbours off when we haven't even moved in yet.

And what's happening right now is me slapping Jezz about the face with a wet fish. Yeah, I brought a fish. And right now is about half-an-hour later; the blood splatter level is rising up the bin bags.

I don't know what's been happening for the past thirty minutes, but apparently right now I'm reciting all this stuff from 'Religious Oppression 101' and "... thou shall not... " slap "... harvest and distribute... " slap "... the pleasures of the sacred... " slap "... fish, you fiend... " slap.

And what's happening right now is me thinking maybe bringing a fish wasn't such a good idea.

"Oh, one last question. Okay, the first question, Jezz the Swiz," I ask. "What's your PIN number?"

Anyway, maybe it's just me, you know, but I don't think the Barclays cash machine will accept, *"Help, oh God please help me, he's crazy. Help. Heeeeellllllllllllp! Yaaaaaaaaaaaaaaaaaaaaaaaahhhh."*

What they will do, however, is approve your overdraft increase. Isn't that nice of them?

* * *

And thank you for just informing me, Matthew, of the viewers' most popular choice. And there's a drum roll, so what's happening right now is the viewers' favourite.

And it is:

(5) Jezz is gonna sing, Britney Spears, '(Hit Me Baby) One More Time'.

(Fanfare.)

And I gave the nail-gun option a personal endorsement, too.

I wrote a song and everything.

So what's happening now is me switching over cassette tapes. I think it's time to let Jezz have his way. What d'you reckon? Let him have his little moment? His big shot at stardom? Fame? A chance to prove he's not Jezz the Swiz?

He can't resist the temptation, I'm sure. And with such a captive audience as well. What a golden opportunity.

More fanfare? Or would that be just too much?

Now as I'm fast-forwarding until I find the song, I'm also waving a shiny hammer in front of his mouth, and telling him to pretend it's a microphone, but – heed – *a special* microphone.

A punishing-unenthusiastic-or-out-of-key-singing microphone.

I press play. The song starts and I dance. And now I'm doing my beckoning-friends-to-the-dance-floor bit, but Jezz can't get up. He tries, but I think he's more likely trying to free himself.

Rascal.

"I must confess," I sing, then encourage him to continue the line, and I say, stilted, as though a line from a 'poem': "In-my-loneliness." And I sigh, wave the hammer some more.

I'm dancing with the groove – all the time holding out the hammer, swaying it, trying to tempt, coax our star into song.

"Okay, here comes the chorus. It's quite apt, don't you think?"

The music builds. There is that strange burble, burble sound as before and I wonder whether it's on the tape, so insistent it seems. Now

I realise it's his mobile drowning in a pocket of blood. I kick him in the kidneys again. And – again – it eventually stops.

Ghostly Connotations: 3

Video Nasty: 3.

Jezz braces himself. Takes a deep breath.

And what's happening right now is Jezz screaming, "Heeeeeeelllllllppppppp." So I hit him on the head with the hammer. (Tommy Cooper voice:) Just like that.

I sigh, rewind the tape.

I find the place, wait, gesture for him to get the fuck on with it this time, wave the hammer provocatively and stuff.

And in a big burst-watermelon-face effort, he goes. "Mit be braybe mon bloor pine."

Now I can see his heart's not in it, so I oblige and smash the hammer into his right cheek.

Just like that.

I hear a satisfying crick-crack, and for obvious reasons, I have to put Mr Gag back quickly.

So, folks at to home. Did Jezz achieve the most claps in your clapometer?

No?

Well, that's not very good news for Jezz.

So, as I expect, his closed eye doesn't come free when I insert a corkscrew, twist, and yank out, and right now I'm imagining that it's like trying to separate the yoke from a fried egg. And as I reach for the melon-baller he faints.

Ghostly Connotations: 3

Video Nasty: 4.

From somewhere comes a heavy banging sound, regular, impatie

Dun dun derrr!

Ghostly Connotations: 4

Video Nasty: 4.

What's happening right now, despite Jezz's unconscious state, is I'm sawing his feet off. You just missed me removing a few toes with secateurs. I could have pulled the toenails out with pliers, but I think, what's the point if he's out cold? What's happening right now is me remembering that that didn't stand in the way of me sawing his feet off.

Ghostly Connotations: 4

Video Nasty: 5.

And now his remaining eye opens just in time to catch the end of my Rolf Harris impression.

There's me panting and flicking the saw as if it's a wobble-board and – flash – I'm making a thin dotted line under his hamstrings. I leave an inch space so I can draw a pair of scissors on his thigh and, using my switchblade, I'm carving CUT HERE with an arrow pointing to a matchstick pair of scissors fast thickening into red obscurity. I'm even considering perforations.

The sawing's getting real difficult on the football-developed thigh muscles. And I'm forever getting the teeth of the saw lodged in stubborn bone. Sweat drips create clear streams through the blood getting crispy on my face. But don't worry; it's not my blood.

Ghostly Connotations: 4

Video Nasty: 6.

Now who's the rascal? Eh?

The banging continues, getting louder, more impatient.

More canned laughter ebbs and flows. And what's happening now is a camera zooming back.

It leaves the room in the house as though through the upstairs window. The laughter from the tape is still audible and falls into steady syncopation with the thundering wind. The camera swirls anti-clockwise around the house as though caught up in a whirlpool. It spins around faster, occasionally wavering from the house, slightly out of control, out of focus.

Below, the street speeds, fading into segue, the tail lights of passing cars bleed into the orange trails of the streetlights. Everything's a drunken whirlpool, and the colours marble, lingering in the swirls and —

And cut to **INT. MY BEDROOM—EARLY EVENING** and what's happening now is Alex exploding into my room. He's getting Tagline disease, he says.

"Hey man, so you finally woke up?" he also says. "I been banging for *ages*. Anyway. Listen, man. It's Jezz on the phone for Emily."

And his eyes are saying, "I told you so."

Pretending to be groggy from sleep, I take the phone and wait for Alex to leave.

What's happening right now is my tone is bright and friendly, chatty.

"Yeah, Jezz... Em and I split... Yeah... No biggie. I'm cool about it... She wants to meet you at the house she's moving into next term... Oh, you already know where it is... What? Yeah, she's great in bed... No problem; I'll tell her you'll be there in an hour, then.

"Oh, Jezz," and I add finally: "Break a leg."

the accidental hermit

from a novel **by holly atkinson**

Estella Mullen is killed in a car accident. Daniel, her husband, retreats into their house for comfort and begins a strange, reclusive existence. Estella's parents, James and Celeste, blame Daniel for the accident. Here, they are preparing to visit his house and remove all of their daughter's belongings.

Celeste didn't want to go. She wasn't ready, not yet. She honestly felt it was too soon for everyone involved, particularly since emotions were still so raw, and her own state could only be described as delicate. And, furthermore, there was still a lot of pent-up, unresolved anger which in such a volatile environment could be potentially and irrevocably damaging (Brian, her therapist, had used those exact words during their last session, which she had copied neatly into her white leather notebook for reference, along with other such useful phrases like "needing a little me-time", "revelling in your own cry-hour", "searching for your mother-child" and other similarly helpful hyphenations). Celeste told all this to James as he knotted his tie in one smooth meticulous wrist-flick in front of the mirror, explaining her main points clearly and concisely without resorting to hysterics or emotional manipulation, even though she was painfully aware from that familiar look on James's face that he was, in fact, not listening. Somehow, the most important thing was that the words were said.

As she stood there in the master bedroom talking to his back, she noticed how her own face fitted exactly into the remaining space in the mirror; how her chin seemed to rest on his left shoulder and her painstakingly coiffed pile of blonde hair nestled neatly into the curve of the gold frame, as if it were a space made just for her. She watched her lips mouthing the words and thought how small and pale she looked in comparison to her tanned, life-sized husband, and how peculiar it seemed to make a sound from one mouth and see it come out of another. Standing behind James, a good six feet behind, along the Persian rug, she realised that if she just bent her knees a little, just a couple of inches, her face would completely disappear. She tried it, to make sure.

As James dribbled spit onto his fingertip and smeared it along his eyebrows, ensuring all hairs arched at the desired angle, he noticed Celeste's face sliding up and down behind his back. She is an odd creature, my wife, a funny emotional thing, he thought; but he chose to ignore that fact for now. He wanted to focus on the matter in hand, and so he spoke to her eyes, when he could see them, rising and falling like a slow-motion seesaw. He tried to believe that her mirror image would listen, even if the real Celeste would not.

"Darling. I don't want to go either, but it's not a question of – darling, will you stop that?"

Celeste stopped, wobbled a little, then like a good child returned her face to its rightful place, resting on his shoulder.

"Thank you." James was trying to be patient, but these days he was finding it increasingly difficult to deal with Celeste, and to disguise the words he didn't say: as if twenty six years of conversations through mirrors had worn down the glass until it reflected their blood, their bones, his secrets.

"Yes, it's not a question of want. It's a question of rights. We owe it to ourselves. We both deserve this." James spoke slowly, rhythmically, as if he were reciting the words to a song, or quoting unarguable truths. With one last definitive tweak of a nose hair, he stepped away from the mirror, keeping his back to his wife, and closed his eyes. This seemed to him the only way to escape, for even a moment, that shrunken, bewildered expression Celeste had adopted recently; it appeared from nowhere and lurked behind him like a sick puppy. Or, perhaps more accurately, he thought, like a bad spy – an undercover agent who hadn't grasped the concept of undercover. It was becoming rather disconcerting.

"Maybe we could do it next week. I think I could do it next week. Maybe that would be better?" Celeste said quietly.

James spun his shining shoes round to face her, twisting the rug into ruckles. Celeste winced, but decided this would not be the appropriate time to mention it.

"Celeste." It took him a second to find her. It was actually quite alarming if he thought about it, the way his wife blended so perfectly into her surroundings: how her hair matched the gold light fittings, the dado rail, the picture frames, how her cream silk suit appeared to match exactly the material of the curtains, the embroidered bedspread, the Persian rug, the cushions on the window seat. All of which she had bought, of course. Even her skin was pale to the point of blending in with the paintwork. He tried to recall when this strange phenomenon had happened, when exactly his house had become the complementary backdrop to his wife's own decorated body. It was as if she had designed it purely to avoid the horror of clashing with her surroundings as she swanned from room to cream silk room. He couldn't pinpoint a specific time.

And then, more alarmingly, he wondered whether Celeste had decided one day to model herself on her own soft furnishings, as if she were just another design feature, an extra fitting; as if she were trying to blend in and disappear. *Exactly which came first?*

He located his chameleon wife and grasped at the arms he knew must be lurking somewhere beneath the silk. His fingers dug in a little too hard. He felt the muscles in her arms tightening, and she shrank back, subtly, but enough for him to notice. He was noticing a lot about her these days. Or perhaps he was just noticing her. This entire episode was giving him one of his headaches.

"That man, Daniel, had Estella to himself for the last four years of her life. He has everything she touched. He has everything she made. He has everything we bought for her. She was ours for twenty-five years but what do we really have? Nothing. Old photographs, memories, an extra bedroom for visitors, that's all. Twenty-five years and that's all we have. We want more, Celeste. We deserve more."

Celeste examined the carpet, humming under her breath. He tried again, with something he knew would work if he could just time it right.

"You will never be a grandma now. Stelly was your one chance. No little rug rats calling you Nana, no paddling pool in the garden, no Lesty the glamorous granny. Think of that." And then, stepping back and measuring the careful distance between them, he said what they had both been thinking for months. "This is all your family now. Right here. Just you and me."

They didn't even try to hide the looks on their faces: that shared recognition of the small desperate horror of just the two of them, for ever. It just wasn't, in any way, enough. At least they agreed on something.

"I know. You're right. I know. I just don't know if I can bear it."

It didn't occur to Celeste until much later, after her weekly consultation with Brian in fact, that for James, the word 'we' really meant 'I'. And, although Brian explained that any couple suffering such a loss would experience these feelings of crisis, and would inevitably have to reassess and reaffirm the boundaries of their relationship, learn each other anew as it were, Celeste just thought: no. No. Stuff that. I just don't think I love him any more.

Celeste hadn't worked since the accident, or "The Day", as it was referred to in their house, said always with a slight bow of the head, a dropping of the voice and a swivelling of the eyes to the corner of whichever room they happened to be inhabiting. She said to her friends, I've hardy slept a wink since The Day; I seem to have lost my purpose since The Day.

"It sounds callous, Midge," she said one day to her best friend Marjorie, over a glass of wine and a guilty cigarette, "but I had hoped that The Day would have brought James and me closer together, but it has done exactly the opposite. I think he only liked me because I was Estella's mother, and now I can't even be that. I don't know what I am."

Midge lit another cigarette, nodded wisely.

"Actually," Celeste continued, "do you know what? I don't think he liked me even then. I think he blamed me because Stelly chose to follow me instead of joining his precious law firm. He had dreams, you know: Hattersley and Hattersley incorporated. He used to practise writing that on bits of paper. I saw them in his study. All different styles like he was inventing a new signature. He thinks interior design is frivolous and pointless. I don't think he's noticed all the work I've done on this house."

"Lesty-love, peach tree," Midge said, blowing smoke through her nostrils, "I've told you a thousand times before. Your husband is a fuckwit."

"I know, darling, I know," Celeste said, sighing, giggling, pouring another glass of wine.

But Celeste had lost her desire to make things beautiful. Where once she could look at a house and see instantly how to enhance and exaggerate the available light, how to create an elegant yet functional area for entertaining, how to make it nice enough for even her to live in, now all she saw was a house. She left the answer phone on all the time, and if it was a client calling, she let the tinny voice speak into the empty room. She would not return their calls because, quite frankly, she thought they ought to have bought a decent house in the first place.

Her own house, the house she had named after much deliberation and indecision *Ellamwood Grove* – after rejecting *Ellam Lodge* (too like an orange-stained log cabin in some godforsaken part of America), *The River House* (stylish, but too like a restaurant), *Ellamsage Meadows* (too like a flowery perfume for rich old ladies) – would always be her sanctuary, her place of beauty, her show-home of dreams. For twenty years she had nurtured it, altered it in accordance with her own moods and the fashions of the time, restored every inch of the crumbling red brick and, in the early days when a gardener was an extravagance, even hacked back the unruly ivy with her own gloved hands. It had grown with her, and she had grown with it.

But now, since The Day, it had become so much more to her. Now she realised how much she *needed* it, how it housed her own sanity, her own history, her own self. She felt it was part of her flesh. In *Ellamwood Grove* the light, the colours, the fabrics, the space, the view of the hills, and the sounds of the river, all created for her a kind of soft, feathery blanket, wrapping around her, keeping her calm and contained and warm. The daily dose of Valium helped, of course, but she preferred to forget about that, because it lacked poetry. Every morning when she looked at herself in the mirror and saw her ageing face staring back, she thought: at least I have my home to be proud of. At least I have this one, perfect thing.

She spent her days walking slowly like a ghost through the rooms, smoothing, tweaking, touching her hair and her make-up in mirrors. Each and every day the same, since The Day; pottering, pruning the roses, feeding the peacocks and the cats, sitting by the river at the foot of the garden and listening, not thinking about anything at all. She cooked things she didn't want to eat, ironed things she would not wear, collected the dry cleaning, distributed wafts of ylang-ylang and honeysuckle air freshener randomly throughout the house. She wasn't sure whether she did this because she enjoyed it, or was just trying to make James happy when he arrived home from work, complaining, smelling of suits and business and sour aftershave, pouring himself a large gin and tonic. When she allowed herself to think, she strongly suspected she was just trying to make him appreciate her. My God, I've become a housewife, it sometimes occurred to her, mid-vacuum. But it didn't matter, because it wouldn't last for ever. Something would change, it would have to, as soon as she allowed herself to think about the future.

Since The Day, two months ago, everyone had established their own new realities, their own ways of fumbling blindly through the days, and this was Celeste's. That was why she didn't want to visit Daniel. Not because of pain or grief at seeing his house, at touching Estella's things, but because it meant an interruption to her careful numbing rhythms. She was scared it would jolt her into change, force her to make the decision she suspected she was going to make. And she just wasn't ready, not yet, please, not yet.

Daniel felt physically sick when he saw them. He was the kind of man who experienced emotions as ailments. Fear, happiness, love, all brought with them a side effect: a lurching stomach, an itchy palm, a sneeze. It was Delilah the mouse, Daniel's friendly and compact alternative to a guard dog, who first spied their car sloping up to the curb. She was taking her daily run along the bedroom window sill, a place she had taken to scurrying because she liked the feel of the sun on her fur and the challenge presented by the curtains, and she warned Daniel with a louder than usual squeak and a frenzied scratching of claws on the window pane. He couldn't prove it, but he was convinced that her subsequent fall from the sill was not entirely accidental, and that the trembling in her tiny body was not just due to shock. She was a very perceptive creature. Lurking behind the curtain, Daniel watched them approach the house, and he slipped Delilah into his top pocket for comfort. For a moment he considered pretending to be out, but that, he quickly realised, was not a viable option for a housebound hermit. He was constantly, unavoidably, available.

He was always prepared for the knocks at the door, but it was usually a friend, a neighbour, the vicar, or Shelley. He was lulled into a rhythm of days spent expecting, of the comfortable beat of soft words and false smiles. It was what made the day tick, what made him get out of bed, what reminded him to eat and sleep and to cover his body with clothes. It was a comfortable rhythm, easy and unthreatening in its repetitiveness, which meant, day after day, week after week, he did not have to leave. He was not prepared for this. Slowly, wasting time, he went down the stairs and opened the door.

"Daniel."

"James. Celeste."

Nods. Controlled voices. Eyes looking at the ground, the door frame, not meeting.

"How are you?"

"Yes," James said.

Yes? Yes what? Daniel wondered, as he stepped back to let them into the house, pressing his body against the wall to avoid the embarrassment of touch. There were too many things that could be said for him to know where to start. And so he said nothing.

They stood at awkward angles in the living room, the curtains closed, the air heavy and hot. Daniel motioned for them to sit. He fidgeted with his shirt cuffs as if he were standing trial in court. Right then, Daniel would have given anything to suddenly acquire the power to reach out his arms and hide the living room from their view, shuffle it all into a big pile behind his back like a cartoon character would, and whistle and tap his foot as if it wasn't there at all. He didn't want them to see him here, living and breathing in a place where every colour, every piece of furniture, every stroke of paint and decorative touch displayed so clearly and unavoidably the evidence of their daughter. He felt like he was squatting in a museum exhibit, trespassing in a preserved replica of the past. He wanted to blindfold them, or create a diversion to somehow prevent them from seeing it. Instead, he sat down in the armchair in the corner, the place where he always sat, the place that fitted around his body like a hug and gave him a perfect view of the room, and the crack through the curtains, and the television, and waited. And waited. He felt their eyes clawing at the walls.

the upgrade

a short story **by stephanie boxall**

It was raining slightly when Anna and Mark checked into the hotel around 7.30pm. It was smarter than the ones they'd been staying in; there were pale, moiré silk sofas, oak-panelled walls and bowls full of flowers. White. The doormen even smiled at you as you came in.

"You've been upgraded, sir," said the receptionist, who had perfect teeth and chestnut hair drawn into a neat, glossy ponytail. "We've put you in a suite on the 18th floor, which has its own whirlpool bath. Enjoy your stay!" She flashed them a dazzling smile. Americans were always friendly, especially in the service industries, but it was 21 September 2001 and tourism had taken a beating. It wasn't the best reason for getting the penthouse suite, but they might as well enjoy it.

Anna watched Mark put their bags into the lift: his long, straight legs, the broad, familiar back. They hadn't brought much luggage; there were only staying one night. On the way up, she stood beside him silently, planning the evening: the restaurant meal, the Jacuzzi they would have when they got back, the night ahead.

Mark unlocked the door and stood back to let her in. The room was pale and exquisite, like the reception area, and the view from the balcony was spectacular. As the sun slowly set over the harbour, lights all over the city twinkled shyly in preparation for the main show later on. Even the moon had put in a tentative appearance.

She opened the door into the bathroom. Beyond the sunken, semi-circular bath flourished a small garden of oleander: glossy, dark-green leaves covered with delicate white flowers and, beyond that, a smoked glass wall and the city laid out beneath it. Two fluffy white robes hung from a hook behind the door and a row of dazzling, jewel-coloured bottles stood on the glossy tiles beside the basin. Next to them was a television. And a remote. As the dusk grew purple around them, the starlight twinkled through the foliage, as though Christmas had come early.

Mark went back into the bedroom. "Did you bring the camera?" he called.

"Of course. It's in the bag." She followed him. "Where do you want to eat?"

"I don't mind. You choose."

Leafing through the guidebook, she picked an Italian restaurant that sounded as though it might be full of young people. She wanted somewhere noisy and lively; somewhere they could forget themselves and laugh.

"Why did you do it?" She couldn't help herself. They walked back through dark, unfamiliar streets still wet with rain. The restaurant had been noisy. But they were the ones making most of the noise. Even before the garlic bread crumbs had been swept away, the subject of Mark's infidelity had come up. They'd tried to make the best of it, but the pasta lay heavy and the wine was sour. They left without anything sweet.

"I thought we were supposed to be trying to forget," he said, his fingers gripping her arm painfully as they walked back to the hotel.

"I can't get these water jets going - what am I doing wrong?" Anna was suddenly overwhelmed with tiredness. She picked up a flower head that had fallen into the tub and laid it carefully on the edge of the bath. It was nearly midnight, but she wasn't going to pass up the opportunity of a whirlpool bath in an oleander-scented room on the 18th floor.

"I can't make it work," she called. "Can you help me?"

"Hang on a minute."

Mark couldn't do it either.

"You could just have a bath," he said.

"What about you?"

"I'm not bothered. I think I'll just go to bed."

Fifteen minutes later, Anna sank into the hot, scented water and felt her muscles relax. Two more flower heads floated tentatively on the milky surface, like tiny boats setting out on a journey into the unknown. She lay back. She could still see the stars, even when she closed her eyes.

It was late when she climbed into bed beside Mark, her skin soft and slightly damp. She lay for a moment, listening to his deep, rhythmic breathing. Then she turned out the light and laid her head against the broad, familiar back.

the good and the glamorous

from a novel **by gloria burland**

We are seated cross-legged on the floor, a perfect Lotus position – well, Mystica is. My thighs are not the flexible friends I would like, so my knees point uncompromisingly towards the ceiling.

Joss sticks burn in a corner and Buddhist chants and peace music play softly in the background. Neither is intrusive, but create a sense of wellbeing... or so I think.

"Before we start we must meditate for five minutes; this will clear any junk in our heads and help us to focus truthfully on the matter in hand," murmurs Mystica.

I close my eyes obediently, thankful that she's not suggesting we "Om". I've always regarded meditation as a last-ditch attempt to catapult wretches like myself, caught on the wheels of samsara, into some better realm – hopefully where thighs are always thin and Chardonnay flows through forests of couture boutiques, where everything is on sale half-price. Oh dear, this is so second chakra... forgive me.

As the Buddhists chant in the background I silently mouth my mantra: Hollywood... Hollywood.

"That was so beautiful," purrs Mystica. "Did you feel the power surrounding us?"

Did I what? Oh, yeah, sure... What I actually say in what I hope is a believer's voice, is: "Oh, yes." (Golden Rule: Don't upset your celebrity.)

Let us begin. I switch on the tape recorder, and prepare to take notes on how she looks.

"Could you tell me, Mystica, what it was that first drew you to seeking enlightenment? Was it a specific moment, or a series of events, perhaps?"

I have to say at this point that I am totally, and I mean TOTALLY unprepared for what follows.

"Oh, yes," she replies sweetly. "It was a Saturday morning. I know it was Saturday as that was my busiest time. When wives did the weekly shop and husbands came to me for sex."

My pencil hovers an inch above the paper... just for a moment I think I've misheard. Surely not? What! This is supposed to be an interview for chrissake, not *True* fucking *Confessions*. She's supposed to be telling me about her road to Chakra City.

"Go on," I manage to say. My voice is sounding sort of strangled. I hope she doesn't notice.

"Well, I s'pose that it was both a specific and a series of events. Shall we just say that my 11.45 john, was one john too many." She stops to light up a Silk Cut. "Sorry, d'you want one?"

I shake my head. "Go on," I urge.

"Right. Well, there he was panting away, slobbering in my ear, the usual scenario, while I feigned enjoyment, or at least participation." She takes a drag on her cigarette. "It was never a case of lie back and think of England for me, I always felt obliged to make an effort: you know, taking their money and all that. The sad sods, I felt sorry for them, really; they were all so pathetically grateful. Anyway, as I was saying, there he was plugging away, then he rolled off and that was it, literally, for him that is."

"What d'you mean?"

"He'd pegged it, on the job, so to speak."

Christ! She was so matter-of-fact, like the poor sod had been run over by a bus or something. Was this Enlightenment?

Commiseration didn't seem appropriate somehow. Still, I felt it necessary to say something.

"What a terrible shock that must have been. What did you do?"

"Well," she drew long on her cigarette, letting the smoke out in short lazy spurts – fascinating to watch. "I sat there looking at him, for ages. He looked quite sweet really, lying there smiling, with his todger poking out of his Y-fronts. I was so pleased that he was smiling, I mean, you know what they always say, but that smile made me believe that he really did die happy."

As she says this she smiles, like she's recollecting a fond memory. Shit. I feel that my approbation is required so I smile too. "What did you do next?"

She hesitates, frowning as she stubs out her cigarette.

"Yes?" I prod. She can't stop now!

"Oh, well, I might as well tell you, but turn off that recorder first." I did. She told.

"Of course, I'd already been paid – I insisted on it beforehand – and I almost put the money back. You know, conflicting emotions: guilt, if it wasn't for visiting me he might still be alive and all that stuff." She lights another cigarette. "But then I thought, no, I earned that, and, come to think of it, by the size of that smile I probably earned a lot more and I think I should be duly paid. So as gently as I could, (GENTLE? Why is she bothering to be gentle? She's just killed the poor sod... well, as good as.) I removed the contents of his wallet and called my neighbour, downstairs."

"Your neighbour?" I'm all agog.

"Yes." She takes another drag on her fag. "Daisy Way. She was all right. I slipped her a few bob and dragged the poor old bugger down to her flat. She told the police he was visiting her and, as she was ninety if she was a day, they suspected nothing. They even made her a cup of tea for shock."

"And? There must be more?"

"Too right," she chuckles. "The 'extra' payment was quite a tidy sum as it happens, enough to give me a fresh start. I moved here and that's when I became involved with the Centre."

Well...! Shit! Who'd have guessed it? She always seems so good, so pure in thought and deed, and I suppose she is these days. Well, it just goes to show, you can never tell... I need a drink.

The Ansaphone is flashing. For one wild and impossibly optimistic moment I think it might be Manny Soloman. Need I bother to tell you that it isn't? It's Candy.

"Hi, Julie. I'm *so* excited about your visit. Now, don't forget: bring plenty of black – it's a must. When you do those interviews you must swathe yourself in funereal threads. That way they will treat you seriously. (Can I take her seriously?) And another thing, your lips. (Lips?) Big lips are in. It was big breasts before and of course if you're lucky to have those too that's a bonus, but right now lips are more important believe me: think Liz Hurley, think Julia Roberts, think big, humungous smackers. Don't worry if yours aren't up to scratch; we can get 'em plumped up here. Remember, the Look is all. Look good and people will treat you better. (Good God, she's sounding like Tara.) Now, about Tony Blair... " At this point I stop the message and rush to the bathroom and scrutinise my offending and obviously totally inadequate labial(s). No! Not *Down There!* I pout. It makes no difference. Shit. As if I haven't got enough to worry about, now it's Lips! I spend the next hour pouting, pencilling and painting... perhaps if I keep biting them they'll swell up!

It's 6.30. I'll phone Roz, perhaps she'll meet up for a pizza or something. I need to share my intentions. I need advice, encouragement. I need approbation. I need a drink!

blooming nora

from a novel **by trudi cowper**

It's like I can't open my eyes to see again. Something soft and wispy
strokes my cheek. There's a whistling scream and then the soft stuff
brushes over my head as I move through it and stop so sharply that I'm
shifted forwards in my seat. I move off again with a mechanical clunk
and the whirr of pulleys and wheels taking me along. There's laughter
like a mean clown and some young voices behind me laugh too. Below
me I see some chinks of light and I know below that is the sea. The floor
creaks; I don't think it's that sturdy.

We must be getting nearer the entrance again because it gets
lighter. I can see that the cobwebs are thread or something and that the
skeletons are rubber. I'm only afraid that there might be real people
hiding in the sides who think it would be fun to grab me or whisper in
my ear or sit next to me. And then, as if he'd stepped out of my mind, a
big man in jeans and rolled up sleeves with dark fur all along his fat
arms appears in front of me and I hear a different scream, one that goes
on and on ringing in my ears. *Shut up Phoebe*, I think, *just shut up* but it
goes on until we are flung outside and I open my eyes to the bright white
day and close my wide-open mouth.

Be scarred out of your wits or your money back says the sign at the
ticket booth.

"Well no point me asking for my money back," Dad says looking a
bit uncomfortable. "Are you all right Levi?"

I nod and clasp Phoebe's hand tightly in mine.

"Let's get a toffee apple, or some other form of tooth decay on a stick." He takes my other hand as we walk past the booth. Two small boys who got off the train are at the window.

"Bugger off," the bulldog man growls to the boys. "She was scared, weren't she?"

Their shoulders sink as they walk away and one of them scowls at me.

Dad and I sit on a bench in the middle of the pier. He has a cup of tea and I have candyfloss. I like the colour of it. It doesn't taste of anything except pink wool but it looks so nice you have to eat it. The bits that get wet from your mouth go dark pink and sticky and get on your chin and your jumper and the stuff left on the stick at the end is hard pink sugar and Dad takes it from me and puts in the bin. He keeps looking at his watch and then out to the sea or back at the entrance to the pier.

"Levi, your Mum is coming to see you today. She'll bring you home, okay?"

So that's it. Maybe she's taking me away.

"But I want to come home with you."

He looks upward and his face tightens so that I think he's going to shout at me.

"Levi, don't make things difficult; it'll be nice to spend some time with your mum, won't it?"

I know I'm supposed to say yes, so I do.

I start to get cold on the bench once the sun begins to go down. People are still on the beach, there's even a couple swimming, but the empty deck chairs are being collected. I like to hang on to the railings, but I hold on tight in case the wind picks me up and carries me over, dropping me into the sea like a bird drops a mouse or a twig. Dad calls me over, throwing his third polystyrene cup into the bin. He tips his wrist again to check the time.

"Want to play on the slot machines for a while?"

He gives me a handful of coppers and I run inside, straight to the coin waterfall. I'm happy to not be waiting any more. I'm sure I'm going to win lots of money, there's stacks of it balancing just on the edge, but somehow my pennies and 2p pieces always miss it.

"I never win," I tell him.

"They're not designed for you to win," he says, but now I stare at a glass case full of fluffy toys and there in the middle is a Bugs Bunny with a carrot and a metal claw swinging over him.

"You'll never get one of those either; it's impossible to pick up anything."

I don't take my eyes off the rabbit.

"Look," Dad says, getting a 50p piece from his pocket change. "I'll show you."

I can hardly stop myself from jumping up and down to see Dad try to win Bugs Bunny. He never plays on any of the games.

"Watch, it won't drop down enough and even if it did it couldn't hold anything." He moves the lever and two other children come to watch, looking through the other side of the glass. The claw drops down towards Bugs' long ears and Dad presses the button to pick up. The claw hums as it moves and opens and all us kids gasp as it closes around the head and an ear.

"You see, now it goes up and it'll drop it."

The rabbit is rising up in the glass case; he's swung over to the drop hole and released. I dive down to the collect tray and pick him up.

"You did it! It does work!"

"Oh, great," he doesn't look pleased at all. "Now you're going to grow up to be a gambler."

I hug Bugs to me and the other two kids look at me with blank faces, as if I just won a million pounds.

"Don't bother," Dad tells them. "There's no way it'll ever pay out again."

The boys look cheated and I realise they're the ones from the ghost train. I try not to smile because I think that would be mean, but I feel one escaping from my mouth anyway.

I'm happy in the car but Dad is quiet all the way home. He's cross about something. Maybe because the claw machine *did* work and he said it wouldn't. I can't wait to show Mandy. We drive past fields and cows and tents and I remember again about what happened at camp and what Dad had said to me. I guess that's what he's still angry about. Not about the machine, about me. About me winning something when I didn't deserve to. I put Bugs back down on the seat between me and Phoebe.

When we get home I run out into the garden to see Joanie but her hutch door is open and she's not there. I call for Dad and we look around the garden until we find some dirt dug up by the fence.

"She's got out," Dad says and pulls himself up to look over into next-door's garden. "Can't see her, she'll be far away by now. Well, that's that then."

I can't believe that she's gone. I try not to cry. He looks at the hutch.

"You left the door open. I told you to be careful didn't I?" Dad strides back into the house in a bad mood. I'm sure I shut the door. Didn't I? Maybe someone came in and opened it. Maybe she was stolen.

It couldn't have been my fault.

Phoebe looks at the hutch too.

"It must have been you; you're the one who's supposed to be looking after her," she says in just the way Dad was talking. I feel a red rage boiling up inside me now everyone is turning against me. I grip my fists and clench my teeth and shake with a terrible mix of feelings that make my legs run into the kitchen and shout: "It wasn't me! It was her! It's her that's doing it!"

Dad turns around from the sink.

"Who are you talking about and why are you screaming?" He asks quietly as if he has run out of strength.

"Phoebe! Phoebe!" I stamp my feet and am crying without tears. I don't know why they don't come but they don't.

"Levi, I'm fed up with this. What is wrong with you today? You don't know anyone called Phoebe. You're making things up now; it's just silly. You made a mistake and now the rabbit's gone. Don't pretend it was someone else, that's lying. You don't want to be a liar, do you?"

I stop crying because the word sounds so horrible but my body still shudders as I shake my head.

"Good. Now go to your room and read or something while I get some dinner ready." He turns back to the sink and I do as he says while he mumbles to himself: "God, there's already one liar in the family; we don't need another."

It bites into me when I hear him talking like that. I know who he means and that he might be right but I still don't like it. I don't like it that he thinks I'm bad too.

I fling myself onto my bed. No one is ever going to believe me about Phoebe. Not now. It would be better if I never mention her to anyone ever again, otherwise I'll just get called a liar and I hate that word. It's something that the worst kind of person would do. An underground dirty place that some nasty thing would live in, that has no friends and that no one will ever like.

I pick up my book and wish that I could live in America where the weather is always sunny and everyone has bikes, wears sneakers and eats Twinkies. I see my photo of me holding Joanie in the garden one hot summer day with our faces against each other's and I wonder if something terrible has happened to her. I think of dark blood on her pure white fur and I squeeze my eyes shut. I think of Donna by the white china sink and I grip my quilt in my fists. I open my eyes and my hands and feel the soft yellow, like a baby's clothes. Maybe it used to be something of mine. One of my heavy tears drops onto it. I wonder what happened to Mum's rabbit; I never asked her. Granddad didn't know but Nan would. I could go and ask her. I could go right now. It would serve Dad right if he came upstairs and I was gone, just like Joanie. Everyone would blame him like he did me.

He didn't lock the door. He couldn't stop me from burrowing under the walls and running, far, far away and maybe never coming back.

I didn't take many clothes because I wanted to go quickly and I couldn't fit much into my vanity case anyway. I packed another T-shirt and my pyjamas and an apple that was going to be for Joanie and my purse with a 50p piece in it that was a birthday present from Nanna. She says that it is bad luck to give someone a purse without any money in it. I think it means that you will always be poor. Maybe I should not let my purse ever be empty but this is an emergency. I might have to spend that 50p before I get any more money.

It's easy to get out the front door without Dad seeing while he is in the kitchen. I run quickly even though I pull the door closed quietly, just in case he hears. Then I wonder how I will get to Nan and Granddad's. I've walked there and gone on the bus but always with Dad or Mum. I think I'd better walk in case I get the wrong bus. I could call for Mandy but her Mum might send me back.

I forgot about places looking different in the dark. Street lamps start to come as I walk past them as if they are lighting my way, as if they can see me. I know that after the traffic lights I turn left, but when I start walking down that street it's changed. The houses aren't the same and the front gardens like Nan and Granddad's have disappeared. It's some kind of nasty magic and fear grips my heart and I wish I'd never run away. If anything happens to me Dad'll be even angrier. Two people are walking towards me with a big dog and I hide my face as they get nearer. I keep walking and they pass me. I walk to the end of the street wondering if I came totally the wrong way and am nowhere near at all. Then I look right and see the tree that Granddad calls the monkey-puzzle tree. Its branches are like lots of monkey tails and it's at the top of their street. I run to their house and stand outside looking at the yellow light from the window. I knock on the door and Nan opens it.

"I lost Joanie," I tell her.

After Nan has sat me down and made me a sandwich and squash I ask her about Mum's rabbit.

"Yes she did have a rabbit, a black one, she called it Paul. After Paul McCartney from The Beatles. Do you know The Beatles?"

I nod. I've heard them on the radio.

"But what happened to it?"

"Oh, I don't remember sweetheart," Nan says standing up and leaning down to me. "Would you like a biscuit?"

"You must remember; Granddad said you would."

"Well rabbits don't live for ever do they dear?"

"So it died then?"

"Well, yes, of old age I expect. Poor old Paul. What about a crumpet? *Doctor Who* will be on in a minute. Granddad loves that."

"But what happened? Who found Paul?"

Granddad comes into the room.

"Lee-Lee! This is a nice surprise! Nan says you've come all this way looking for your rabbit."

"She wants to know about Paul," Nan tells him, fixing her eyes on his.

"Who's Paul?" he asks, puzzled.

"Ruth's rabbit, you remember?"

"Oh. Oh yes, *Paul*. Well Lee-Lee, I think he went to bunny heaven."

"I don't believe in heaven," I say, annoyed. I know that they are lying to me.

"It was a long, long time ago; you don't need to be worrying about that now. I'm sure your rabbit is far away in the forest by now with lots of other rabbits."

"There aren't any woods; this is a town. What happened to Paul?"

"This is all your fault Ted," Nan says going off to the kitchen. Granddad sits down next to me on the settee.

"Lee. Poor Paul got out of his cage, just like yours. But your one ran away, didn't it? I'm sure she's fine. We think that Paul got killed by a fox. Your mum was ever so upset. It's very sad but these things happen sometimes. And your rabbit got away didn't she? She's away on holiday, maybe she'll even come back!"

"How do you know he was killed by a fox?"

"Well, you can just tell. We had foxes around our way then."

"How did Paul get out of his hutch?"

"We don't know. Don't worry about it now. We can get you another rabbit. Or what about one of those gerbils, or a rat?"

"Ted!" Nan snaps at him from the kitchen. She comes in with a tray of tea and crumpets with honey and Granddad switches on the TV. Nan looks at him and cocks her head to the wall and he goes out into the hall to use the phone.

"Good news!" he says when he comes back in. "You can stay here tonight Lee, no point your Dad coming for you now. Look the programme's starting." He sits in his armchair and is about to balance a crumpet on the lacy white cloth draping one of the arms, until Nan frowns at him and he takes a plate from the coffee table.

I wonder if Mum had left the hutch door open just like Dad said that I had. And I wonder if Joanie has been killed by a fox and what that would look like.

After *Doctor Who*, Nan gets out her photo albums. She likes to show me pictures of me when I was a baby, and of Mum when she was little. There's Mum as a ballerina and on a horse with her riding hat on.

"I've got some of her rosettes somewhere," Nan tells me proudly.

There's more of her winning races.

"She was good at everything at school." That's what she always says. I suppose I'm not good at everything and I can't ride a horse, or stand on my toes but Nan does like to look at the pictures of me in my ballet shows.

"Oh look! Doesn't she look sweet? Doesn't she Ted?"

Granddad looks up from his paper.

"Yes dear, very nice."

I like to look at the ones of Mum when she is my age. She doesn't look just like me; she seems taller and her hair is different, in a long ponytail or a bun for ballet. I pick up a loose black and white picture of her standing in the garden, the sun in her eyes, and place it next to one of me, in our garden.

"Like sisters," I say.

"Yes," says Nan, and she takes the book from me and closes it. She slides it back on the shelf, tightly between the others identical to it.

"Can I look at some more?" I ask her.

"Not now, it's getting late. Come on, let's get you ready for bed."

We stand and Granddad looks up at Nan and gives her a look as if to say something without saying anything.

When Nan tucks me into bed I see a postcard on top of the fireplace of a dolphin flying over an ocean.

"Where's that from?"

"It's from your mum. It's nice isn't it?"

"Where does she live now?"

"Oh, I think she's just staying with friends now. She'll come and see us again soon."

"We were waiting for her today. On the pier."

Nan stops tucking and smoothing. She doesn't look at me.

"Perhaps she got the times wrong. She does that sometimes."

"We were there until the sun went down. Dad won me a Bugs Bunny!"

Nan's mouth smiles but the rest of her face doesn't.

"That's nice sweetheart. Goodnight. Shall I leave the door open a bit for you?"

I nod and Nan kisses my forehead and switches off the light. She pulls the door behind her, leaving a slice of light from the landing showing. I wriggle down into the sheets that bind me to the bed. I hear her and Granddad's voices murmuring into the night. While I'm asleep I think I hear a cry or a raised voice, but I open my eyes to hear better and there is nothing.

three poems

by cathy cullis

a norfolk church

It is not Christ's face with the long looks
of an Anglo Saxon hero
under-nourished by prayer

that captures my heart,
but the swirling mandalas
of sketched vines:

bright terracotta paintings
which have survived
years of neglect.

Like the wild bindweed,
the Spirit of Nature
refuses to disentangle

from its journey:
the passion
of light, space and dance.

Our voices lift in the cool chamber.
We pray for peace and friends
and babies and hundreds of flowers.

cathy cullis

winter solstice

A blackbird with its back to the sun
watches the spot where Jupiter shines.

This thin layer of snow, crystalline,
has unseamed earth and sky,

set us on a quiet course to dusk.
When I walk out upon the whiteness

I know snow has teeth to crunch against my spirit.
I think nothing, but walk a circle;

to walk a circle of light is our task.

july night

10pm and faintly dark –
the tallest pale sunflower looks over the garden
too demure to smile.
How many cats will tonight
come and dig around the lettuce?

Lavender has lost scent.
Pumpkin vines pause on a fringe of weeds.

Do flowers in their sleep mutter Latin names,
grope with their roots
for a glassful of water?

Imagine the copper red sunflowers
with weighty heads are dreaming of autumn:
how many tulip bulbs will be pressed into the soil
where their feet now grip.

soundtrack to a love story

a short story **by barb drummond**

Mum was late. She was always late. I should have brought a book, or chosen a window seat in the coffee shop so I could casually watch the world passing. Mum wanted to talk to me about my impending divorce. I couldn't decide which was worse: the break up or having to listen to Mum's advice.

'Play It Again Sam', the theme to *Gone with the Wind*: great love stories all have great music to remember them by. I always thought ours was a great love story. Fifteen years together, from university to almost middle age. In today's world, that qualifies as an epic.

I would like to be able to say it ended for a good reason, or at least for a definite one. Unresolvable differences, an affair, substance abuse, something dramatic. But it ended because of your socks. In fact, it began with them as well. So maybe we should have some sort of sock-themed music to waft through the following paragraphs.

I still remember how we met. I was dragged along to a party where I knew almost nobody, and after a couple of hours of cheap wine and cigarettes, I reached for my jacket to go home. I was squashed against the stairs in the hallway when I saw your ankles through the banisters. You were only wearing one sock, and it was a stripy, girly sort of thing. It made me laugh.

"I've run out of clean clothes, and I can't figure out how to work the washing machine," you explained, sheepishly "Not a good omen for a future computer programmer."

"Well, I'm hoping to get into public relations and I've discovered I'm not much good at relationships," I blurted out. I must have had more to drink than I'd thought.

We kept talking, hiding under the stairs while the party emptied. You walked me back to my door. We were both hoarse from all the talking, but I didn't want it to end so I invited you in. You declined, but promised to return with breakfast. It seemed like I'd just shut my eyes when you tapped on my door. You brought croissants – the first real ones I'd ever had. And fresh orange juice. God only knows where you got them, our corner shop sold only sliced white bread. Now all the shops sell them, but back then they made you seem incredibly exotic.

I taught you how to operate your washing machine, and you taught me how to blow smoke rings. The parties we went to probably didn't change, but they seemed so much more fun, knowing I had you to walk me home. Sometimes we stayed up all night talking, just the two of us in the kitchen and a bottle of cheap red wine. I can't remember what we talked about. It probably wasn't important. It wasn't really about words, just time spent enjoying each other's company.

We were made for each other. We both loved Italian food, French films and we dreamed of owning German cars. We collected brochures on exotic holidays, while all we could afford was to go camping in Cornwall or the Lake District. Even my aunt Evelyn liked you.

Over fifteen years we grew together from trendy studenthood to dinner-partying dinkies. Fifteen years of love, passion, and just enjoying each other's company. The lazy weekend lie-ins, hearing the neighbours yelling at their kids, getting ready to drive them to football matches or music lessons while we lay safe and warm in our blissful bubble of coupleness.

One day, we will talk about having kids, we said. One day.

Then we'd discuss whose turn it was to get the papers. And whether we wanted our croissants plain or chocolate.

When I moved in with you, the socks strewn about never bothered me. After all, it was your flat. And the place was packed with our combined belongings, boxes of books stacked against the walls, tapes and magazines roosting where they could, while we saved up to get married and buy our house.

But when we got married at last, had our own place and the space to spread out, I began to notice. How all your shirts and underpants and trousers found their way into the laundry basket, but your socks lay gasping on the floor. At first I just picked them up. After all, it's no effort, just to bend down and put them in their right place. But it started to annoy me, so I spoke to you about it. You shrugged your shoulders.

I stopped picking them up. But they still annoyed me.

Then one day, I found one of them in my briefcase, just as I was about to do a presentation. I'd noticed the smell earlier and assumed one of the reps had thoughtlessly kicked off his shoes. It was too much. I stormed home that night and hurled it at you as you were watching some Grand Prix race on TV.

"That went to work with me today!"

You glanced up at me, then at the sock beside you on the sofa. You shrugged, then looked back at the screen.

I grabbed the remote and the TV went black.

"Hey! I came home early so I could catch this semi-final." It was your turn to be angry.

"You almost made me look stupid in front of some really important clients!"

You muttered something I didn't catch.

"Was that an apology?"

"I didn't put it in your case. You should have checked before you went to work."

You lunged for the remote. I skipped out of your reach.

"Why is it so hard for you to put them away? It's only a little thing to ask."

"If it's such a little thing, why does it bother you?"

"I'm not your servant," I said.

"I never asked you to be. Where's the harm in leaving them on the floor? Nobody goes in our bedroom, they're not hurting anyone."

"They're annoying me. If you really loved me, you'd change."

"If you really loved me, you'd change."

I shoved the remote in my pocket and stomped upstairs. The sound of engines revving followed me. It was clear you didn't need me any more than you needed the remote.

That was it.

We were both determined to stand our ground.

And from this stand-off we each began our retreat. We each took to working longer hours, accepting invites to the pub after work that we'd always refused in the past. You started to like curries, I preferred Mexican. Our taste in movies no longer coincided so much, or at least we didn't work at it so hard, so we started going out separately. Since the source of our conflict was in the bedroom, we no longer went to bed early, unless one of us was home alone. We got out an old sleeping bag for the latecomer to sleep on the sofa. Strangest of all, or perhaps not, we both started getting headaches.

When did you realise it was over? Was it a sudden flash, a bolt of lightning out of a cloudless sky, or was it more like the take-over of the lawn by moss, after weeks of heavy rain?

One night in the pub, a visiting rep started flirting with me. I couldn't believe it at first – I had my wedding ring on display. When he got too insistent, I waved it in his face.

"Ever seen one of these before?" I asked.

He laughed. "Yeah, I saw it. But I thought you were one of those women who wear a ring for self defence."

"I wear it because I've got a husband waiting for me at home."

He frowned and emptied his bottle of lager. "I must be losing it. I can usually tell a single woman a mile off." He gave me a funny look, then turned his attention elsewhere.

He made a mistake, that was all. But then I realised I didn't have a husband waiting for me at home. I had no idea where he was that night, or any other night. A complete stranger had seen something in me I must have been ignoring for months.

Bloody socks. Maybe I should have cut you a bit more slack over them. But then, you should have listened to me. If only we...

No. I have to stop that. There's no 'we' anymore.

Oh, God, I knew I shouldn't have agreed to meet Mum here. This cafe always plays sloppy tunes; now it's Andy Williams singing 'Moon River'. Ah, the divine Audrey Hepburn and the gorgeous George Peppard. I'm just not in the mood for it.

And... no, I can't believe this. There's a man by the window who keeps glancing at me. He smiled, definitely in my direction. Rather cute, too.

Oh, my God, no. I have to get out of here.

He's wearing fluorescent yellow socks.

passionate pilgrim

from a novel **by lucy english**

Rose develops ME after a series of disasters. She loses her stepdaughters, her partner and her home. Then she loses her health. As she recovers, she decides to make a pilgrimage to Santiago de Compostella. What she finds there is unexpected and shocking.

In this part of the book, she has been involved in a train crash. She was unhurt but one of her stepdaughters was killed. Out of guilt her partner, Peter, decided to move to Suffolk to be nearer his other daughter. Rose refused to go because it would mean living close to his ex wife, Frances, who cannot stand Rose. Rose and Peter split up over this issue. The story continues just after their separation.

Living in the house without you is strange, but not terrible. Your shoes are still in the hallway. Your shirts are still in the cupboard. All around are remnants of you. Your fennel toothpaste. Your favourite jam. A hair I found in the bathroom. It's like you're away on a conference or a holiday. You could come back any time and occupy this space. But you're not coming back. Peter, you are someone who does not change his mind. You will go to Suffolk and I shall stay here alone.

At the end of January Peter collected his things. Rose didn't want to see him. Their last telephone conversation had been brief.

"Can I collect my things on Saturday morning?"

"Of course. Leave your key behind. I will be at Mimi's."

That was it. No goodbyes. No sentiment.

She didn't see him for nine years and didn't miss him once. She looked around the front room for the last time before Peter came. His books on India. His gardening books. They would be gone when she came back. In the kitchen she could see the winter garden, bare and sorry, and she felt the first tinge of panic. She would have to do the garden now and she didn't know how. She fled straight to her friend Mimi's. By the time she got there she was crying.

She cried all day. Benjamin offered his *Star Wars* videos. William said, "Rum business, this." And Mimi made chicken soup and shook her head. "I wish you two could sort it out. You're made for each other."

"I couldn't do it," wailed Rose. "I couldn't live near Frances. What if William had an ex-wife and he was always going round there sorting her out? How would you feel?"

"I'd give her a piece of my mind," said Mimi brandishing the soup ladle. "And I'd give William a piece of my mind." And Rose could see that, yes, she would because Mimi had that supreme confidence in knowing what was hers. But Peter had never been Rose's. They had bumped into each other. It was transient. She hadn't wanted it to be, but it was.

"You've got Benjamin. What if you didn't have Benjamin?"

"You can't play what if," said Mimi and gave Rose a bowl of soup. "What if Ellen hadn't died? I bet you say that every day."

"I bet Peter says that every day." And Rose stirred her cloudy soup. Cloudy with lumps of white flesh.

"He's acted out of guilt. I thought he was stronger." Mimi served up soup for the two men in her life. They sat cautiously at the other end of the table.

Rose dipped up a spoonful, but she wasn't hungry. She took a few mouthfuls, then apologised to Mimi and went upstairs to the guest room.

She lay on the flowery duvet. She was exhausted from crying. By tomorrow morning Peter would be gone, driving a van up to Suffolk. Now, he would be putting things in boxes, folding clothes into suitcases.

'Are you crying?' she thought, but she knew he wouldn't be. He would be stoical and quiet. Bleakly determined. That night would be the last he would spend in their bed.

Rose hugged herself. It hurt her deeply that now her body would remain untouched. Her body that Peter knew so well. She couldn't imagine anybody else being intimate with her. The thought sickened her. When had they last made love? Sometime before Christmas, and it had been unspectacular, unremarkable. A brief pre-sleep nuzzle.

'It could have been special,' thought Rose, and curled up facing the wall, closing her eyes tighter.

Peter was going to Jaipur. He was taking the train on Friday and coming back early the next week. Rose wasn't going. She was just getting over a fever, not serious but bad enough in the sticky heat of Delhi to make her not want to travel.

They were in bed together in the hostel. The bed was in a room not much bigger than the bed and they were lying by the open window looking out across a roof garden of washing. Sheets and saris flapped over a square of concrete. Pink saris, blue saris, bright as peacocks and birds of paradise. From the streets below, cars and motorised rickshaws honked at each other, and the wailing of slightly off-key radios melted into the background noise. The music of Delhi. The city that is never quiet.

They were making love. Quietly at first because the walls were thin, but then more passionately. Not caring who was listening or watching. Both of them moving to the strange beat of the city, rising and falling, slippery with sweat, tongues touching.

Peter's hands down her back pushing her against him and Rose holding him with her thighs, arching towards him. For a moment their mouths separated and Rose opened her eyes and looked at the man loving her. Peter, his eyes closed, his dark lashes on his cheek. His face like the face of the Buddha, totally calm, totally absorbed, feeling it all.

When he didn't come back from Jaipur she lay on the same bed and looked out of the window and waited. The moon rose over the city and stayed in the sky until morning. The doves flew in circles and the old men called. The washing was changed on the lines.

She waited for four days, then with some girls she met in the hostel she took the train to Bombay.

Before bedtime Mimi knocked gently on the door, "Can I come in?"

"I'm not asleep." Mimi brought in a cup of hot chocolate. "This is a very English thing to do. I used to do this with Benji when he was little. William said his mother always gave him hot chocolate. I'm sure it rots your teeth."

"I've been antisocial staying up here. I'm sorry."

"It's exceptional circumstances. Do you want anything to eat? You've hardly eaten all day."

"I'm fine." Rose sipped the sweet milky drink. Her mother used to bring her hot chocolate last thing at night and Rose would say, "Tell me a story." And her mother would wipe her hands on her apron and say, "Now, where shall I start? When the houseboy found a snake in the bathroom, or when my ayah took me to the bazaar?"

Stories of India. Her mother, the last of the colonials. Brought up in that stuffy society. Regimental dinners. Trips to the races. And mothers endlessly trying to marry off their daughters.

"Talk to me for a bit," said Rose, and Mimi sat on the edge of the bed. She was wearing pearly grey trousers and a black top. She was elegant, even at home on a Saturday. Rose's mother wore Crimplene slacks and shapeless cardigans.

"About what?" Mimi's ability to chat for hours to Rose had been recently impaired.

"About when you first met William. I was back from India, working in Cambridge and saving up to go to America... "

"And my brother was at Peterhouse and he got us tickets for the May Ball and you didn't go because you got sick at the last minute and I thought, Hell, I'll go on my own! That's right, I bought a new dress, turquoise blue, low neck and floor length. My, I'd never wear that now!"

Rose smiled. Mimi had forgotten her awkwardness at Rose's situation. She launched into her story like a liner on an Atlantic crossing, riding high above the waves.

"... There was champagne all night and a Jazz band and it was the warmest June I can remember in this country, like Carolina where my folks are or Darwin where Granddad is, and I was in the garden. My, that place was beautiful, the scent from those roses, you couldn't imagine it." And Mimi closed her eyes and imagined the long ago scent of the Peterhouse roses. "... Standing there was the shyest man I'd ever seen. He looked kinda lonely so I talked to him, for nearly an hour, and at the end he stammered and said, 'Excuse me, I don't know your name.' So shy."

She went on to describe their subsequent courtship and eventual marriage. Rose, who was tired now, listened to her friend. She was thinking of how she had first met Peter.

She was having breakfast in the hostel, scrambled eggs and naan bread. Instead of the cramped dining room, she sat outside on the scrubby rooftop courtyard. She liked sitting up there with the washing and the doves. Today another person was up there. A young man with shaggy blond hair. He was sitting with his legs crossed, looking out over the rooftops.

She said, "Do you want some food?" because that's what you did when you travelled. You shared food. He looked at her. He had grey eyes and long, long eyelashes. He wasn't that handsome. He had a beaky face but he had beautiful eyes. It was a peaceful face. He nodded and they shared the food, eating it silently. Eating with their fingers, listening to the slap of the wet washing and the whirr of the doves' wings.

"So here we are." said Mimi, "And if I hadn't gone to that May Ball it would have all been so different. Look at you, you're nearly asleep." She took the empty cup from Rose.

"Thank you," said Rose, not meaning the hot chocolate, but that Mimi had talked to her. She felt peaceful now. Sad, but not despairing.

"Be brave." said Mimi and gently shut the door.

Rose, in bed at Mimi's was at the station seeing Peter off to Jaipur.

I thought this time you were here to stay but it's the same as then.

We are both going on different journeys.

And as the train came in clanking and hissing, all the people who had been waiting got up off the platform with their children and their grandmothers and their parcels and their goats and moved towards the carriages.

Peter moved too. He swung his bag over his shoulders and shook his hair. He turned round to Rose and waved. She watched him squeeze into a carriage and he was leaning out of the window and waving. The guard blew the whistle and she felt her whole body tremble as it had done that morning. She could still feel Peter making love to her. And the train was moving and she ran after it along the platform as it creaked and steamed.

She could still see Peter waving and she was waving now at the last carriage as it disappeared up the track. She was staring at the railway lines shimmering in the solid heat of the air.

the last laugh

from a novel **by shane garrigan**

I nuzzle her palm. She offers me sugar. There's a sweet taste in my mouth. I run the tip of my tongue along her lifeline and stop short.

"Don't stop," she says.

"I've come to the end," I say.

Maybe I mention "life". Maybe I say, "I've come to end your life", but that doesn't sound like me.

"Let me see," she says, and stares at her hand.

She asks me to stop whistling, to spare her. What remains of her lifeline is perpendicular to her palm, dancing before us, teasing her with death. A snake – poisonous – spitting in her eye. And her eyes are beautiful. Terror instils a beguiling, seductive glint.

"More sugar," I say.

"Fuck?" said Kay.

She repeated the word, biting down on her lower lip before blowing this word-kiss-question my way.

"Excuse me?" I said.

"It's the way you said fuck," said Young.

Fuck fuck fuck fuck *fuck.*

I spit out each word closer and closer to his face. I scream the last.

"Headache?" I say. "Must be all the shouting "

He's on the rug with his back to the sofa. I stand over him. I place my foot on his face, force it back hard against the cushion and remove the axe from his head.

"Don't mind me," I say, flashing the blade towards Kay. "The man obviously has brains."

She laughs that inimitable distressed laugh. I hold the axe up to get a better look.

"Some people believe that you increase your own brain power by eating the brains of others."

Her eyelids flutter – have to do something about that – as if she's preparing herself to be disappointed in me.

"Don't be silly, silly." I make a face at the brain tissue to let her know I couldn't possibly. "What do you think I am?" I say. "Sick?"

I hear her sigh. She still loves me.

"I was thirteen," said Kay.

"You lost your virginity when you were only thirteen?"

"You're a sensitive bastard, Scott," said Young, turning on me. Ferocious. Like a big cat from a big gift shop in a big zoo. "Wake up. Kay lost her mum when she was thirteen."

"I"m sorry Kay. Really."

My face was sincerity itself. Inside I was killing myself. Good timing, Scott.

"It's okay," she said. "You just nodded off for a bit."

I stood up. For a second I saw the relief in Young's face as he assumed I was about to leave the two of them alone. He was about to speak.

"We need another bottle," I said.

No Scotch on the counter. I found two bottles on a shelf below, binned the packaging and placed them on top. Young and Kay were nodding at each other. Sympathy and empathy. Bosom buddies. Rock and a hard place.

So she'd lost her mother at an awkward age. Mother's love gone, father's love falls short. He turns to the bottle. She turns to whoring herself for cheap affection. Tragic. Ho hum. Stronger for it, I'd say.

Young was no doubt explaining the reason for my faux pas. Then again, no, he wouldn't. But it would come out soon enough. I requisitioned the bottle opener.

I left the bottles at the bar and went in search of the bathroom. I passed through Young's bedroom before I found it, a vast bedroom, fit for a king, or a knight.

I took my single malt piss, with so much pressure on my bladder I could've supplied enough hydroelectricity to power up a small country.

I unwrapped the complimentary soap and washed my hands. Looking back, I decided to run a bowl of hot water and pulled the lever between the taps to lower the plug. I raised the toilet lid. Then I soaped my hands several times, each time reaching across, leaving a trail of suds around the seat, which I wiped vigorously with sheets of tissue paper. The whole seat.

I repeated the process, left the lid up and the seat down. I scrubbed my hands and returned to the party, picking the bottles up en route.

They were still talking. Young seemed more relaxed. I had only just sat down when he stood up.

"Back in a minute," he said.

He was off to take a piss. It should have been Kay. I'd have to go back again.

"There's a bathroom this way," he said, walking and pointing to the reception area. "It's closer."

Lady Luck was smiling. Something was going my way.

I gave Kay directions to the other bathroom if she needed it. My eyes drifted down to her handbag and I began speculating – pads or tampons? As I pointed to the left and her eyes followed my fingers, I took the bottle opener from my pocket and pressed the metal against the camcorder. As I spoke, I disabled the red light.

"I wanted to apologise again for my slip before. Alan and I had been talking about our first times and I assumed... "

"Forget it Scott, honestly. Thinking about it now, it was actually quite amusing."

Amusing, not funny. Suddenly I wasn't laughing any more.

I was alone with Kay. For the first time this evening.

The thought had crept up on me like an assassin as one with the night. I was aware only when the blade was at my throat. Nothing made sense. Not the metallic taste in my mouth or the crimson breath spitting from my windpipe. And there's a kid with a shake blowing bubbles through a straw.

Music. I needed music. I wanted an orchestra, a big band and a voice in the background. That would complete the scene.

The flames swayed, dipping one way, twirling another, in time with the music in my head. Kay's feet were resting on the coffee table. She must have jarred it a little to manipulate the candles' dance card. Not the heels, though, but her insteps, pressed against the edge, her toes curling and stretching. I was trying in vain to separate each toe, trying to pierce the fabric of her stockings with my eyes. With her legs bent and her knees pointing upwards, she reclined on the sofa; her head nestled halfway down the rear cushion, her glass resting on her stomach. Her knees knocked against each other as she raised the glass to her lips. I stared into the distance. My thoughts were an avalanche, falling from her blouse into the darkness below, laddering her stockings, as I pulled this beautiful blanket behind me and wrapped it around us – a blank canvas on which to create something new.

I couldn't look at her face without looking through the point where her knees met. So my view of her was obscured every other moment. The light afforded me only a glimpse of darkness as her knees began to part and she watched as my eyes swept upwards from her seat cushion to her face and the smile upon it. My eyes were unable to penetrate this darkness, try as they might.

"Chess," I said.

Would Kay be a Sinatra fan? My mind was foxtrotting across the Capitol years.

"Huh?"

She shudders with a giggle and the Scotch spills over on her stomach.

"Stay still," I say, rising from my seat.

Her blouse has creased up about her body from where she has been slipping down the sofa. The whisky has collected in her belly button.

"Thirsty, Scott?" she says.

"Always," I say.

I ease myself in beside her and lean across, my head hovering over her stomach. She steadies the glass at her side. I pull her skirt down an inch or two with one hand and keep her blouse away with the other. I curl a rogue pubic hair around my little finger as I dip my tongue slowly beneath the whisky's surface and press gently against her skin. I taste the salt from her body mixing with the richness of the malt. I like the way she tastes. She is perfection formed over twenty years. What chance has a Scotch distilled for twelve?

"I'll never drink from a glass again," I say.

When I have finished lapping her button and her belly is empty, I look up. She smiles and pours more whisky from her glass.

five poems

by yvonne gavan

cherry blossom hill

Spring is warm in Sakuragaoka
And the cherry blossoms fall like pink snow.

On the way down the hill, to work;
A plum tree in the dust garden below,

Silk Kimono pouches in the shop-front
And in the grassy thrill cicadas have returned.

I remember last summer's thick sticky heat –
A maddening buzz from the bamboo mess

Outside my night-window: the sound of Japan.
And the moon's yellow light, a reflection

On its surface, a map of the rising sun.

yvonne gavan

temple song

"As a result of the painstaking, devoted work of the French archaeologists who restored Angkor, each element has been put in its place: the destructive invasion of the jungle has been checked, the buildings have been saved... "

Malcom MacDonald
Angkor and the Khmers

There's a sad music at Banteay Kdei
As if the stones moan with the weight of all the time.

Each slab stacked to an imagined place
Made to gauge for the lookers on.

Buttressed trees, they mumble, watch –
Those held with bars and brackets for an elapsed crime.
                "Let us slide and there be known,
a crumbling *once* a throne."

The song is different at Ta Prom,
Stones lie in peace and sigh,
               Sing of the shift of their load.

But who was here to hear them fall?

The measured creak of sway,
The crack of rock scorched in the sun,
The tumble of the sacred hall?

The *rain forest's* ears

Through reaching roots re-claiming.

There's even an echo of the harmony
In the wall that became a tree
And slopes, proud for the flash of fame,

now *crowned* with figs.

dusk

After the honey-light has passed
And the limestone crag is jet-jagged glass

Silver water ripples, rushing to the left
And patches smooth as glass slink, sliding through the dreft

A dragonfly skates the swirl
And the colour changes again

The sky has become a pearl.

midori

When the bamboo clacked like the sound of a harbor
I noticed you were there –
On golden skins

When the sky was a mystery of slithers of glass
You saw the blue above –
Feather-plumes

When the forest was a room in our story
I foot-traced your steps –
On tatami

When the wind spoke of windows and an end
I noticed you were gone
Midori.

new year's day

The sky lake-clear in the first sunrise
The world's edge arched by finger clouds
Black-green poplars still as shrouds.

four poems

by sue gibbons

the stars and the stripes
Dean's poem

And I now know –
What it is like
To drape oneself in
An American flag –

To feel each fold –
And every stripe lick
Against my skin

To lay there in the strange
Half-darkness of the
Moon's light –

clutching for eternity –
each and every one of
its stars…

a poem for shakespeare
*"Love, Death, Time, Beauty,
(the whole bag of tricks)"*

Not many have kept
Shakespeare waiting –

Though I don't suppose the
Audience sensed the irony as they –

sue gibbons

Waited for the poet who –
Did not show...

Unaware that for her there
was no lark –
Only the nightingale

Oh wasn't Shakespeare so right
To label all of life –
History, comedy or tragedy

Realising, perhaps, as she did,
That it's art, not life,
that ultimately destroys us

a poem for don and patsy

Thanksgiving day is
Almost over, so we take
Coffee by the telescope

Certain that we will see
The rings of Saturn on
This cold clear night

How far we've travelled
Since we realised that we
Couldn't actually fall off

And this prompts me to
Ask myself – will Earth
Become just another planet?

Or Saturn just another
Destination? As easily
Accessible as Russia or Japan...

for jeremy

Life engraves its
Own sacred space

Like the phallic figure
Chalked in white –

It's there to remind us
How fertile and full of
Grace we actually are

And having believed
That time couldn't be
Given back –

I now find myself
Proved wrong as I
Dancingly discover

Just how gloriously
Retrospective life
can be

back to the light

from a novel **by daniel gothard**

I met Jane the day after I'd broken up with Natalie. We'd been together for a while, I don't remember exactly how long. Just long enough for it to hurt when she told me: "I can't talk to you. You just don't take any notice of me any more... look at you now, still not paying attention. I can't do this, I'm really sorry, Phil." She knocked my wine glass over as she stood up to leave. I could see she wanted to apologise; she stopped for a moment and looked at the wine spill, grimaced and then left. Her coat was hanging off one arm and dragging the ground. She looked like a wounded animal, her dyed black hair looked wet and distressed, sticking up in all the wrong places. Her body, usually tall and slender, seemed crumpled as if her waist had collapsed; the black and white clothing she always wore was askew with hasty movements.

I felt like pond scum, as if I were an infection of some kind, causing pain, indecision and ultimate doom for other people.

We were having dinner in Bella Pasta on St Martin's Lane, always busy and particularly crowded on that evening. I sat with spatters of red wine across my side-plate, exposed as a failure in love. Other diners peered at me across candlelight and baskets of garlic bread. I noticed a group of four women. They were glaring at me, one of them tutting and sneering.

I looked at our plates; the pizzas had only just arrived. I was starving, so I sat there and ate all the food. I had forgotten how much we ordered. One large vegetarian pizza with extra chillis, and one large pepperoni pizza, two side-order salads, and garlic bread with cheese.

I paid the bill and waddled out of the restaurant into the London night, feeling bloated from the excess of food, a little bit drunk from the Chianti, and lonely.

I have to confess that I hated being without a girlfriend. Not just because of the lack of intimacy, but also because I love the company of women.

Natalie and I had already reached the stage of saying, "I love you". We did that on the South Bank, near the National Film Theatre – in the pouring rain. I suppose some people would call that romantic; I wouldn't recommend it to anyone. Unless you enjoy sitting around in soggy clothes for hours, shivering constantly, with your slow-drying hair stuck to your head one minute, and rising into something big and frizzy the next. I pretended that it was special to me. I hated every second.

On Valentine's Day I bought her a bracelet with adjoining hearts. She left it on the table, just before she left Bella Pasta. I honestly can't say whether or not it really was love. Was it just killing time, until I found someone better for me?

I walked up the street, away from Trafalgar Square, up to the corner of Long Acre. Then crossed over through to Leicester Square.

Leicester Square gave me what I needed. A fake sense of place and time, the bright lights of the cinemas and nightclubs and a buzz of something wild about to happen. A solid feeling of people and companionship. There were too many people, to be honest; the square full of gangs of young men with too much wet-look hair gel and no jackets on over their Ben Sherman shirts, shouting into mobile phones and eyeing up young women. Usually I would have felt claustrophobic and nervous, but I was desperate to be somewhere that didn't always end with me on my own. I shuffled through a crowd of people listening to a busker. He sounded out of tune to me, although I'm no musician.

I joined a group of people watching a mime artist. He was dressed like Charlie Chaplin. He threw shapes and contorted his face to give impressions of scenes. The crowd laughed. I thought it was sad and pathetic.

To me, he looked desperate. Like me, he was alone and silent. Isolated and stuck in the middle of a relationship he had no control over. He was at the whim of the group's laughter – they would make or break him.

I put a pound coin in his bowler hat and walked away. As I moved through the crowds towards Piccadily Circus I caught sight of my reflection in the darkened window of a shop. I looked destroyed. My features seemed to have dropped away into a hollow malice. I wanted to become lost, out of the open air and into the darkness, so far in that my features would completely disappear, and I wouldn't have to face myself again.

I walked straight through Piccadily Circus and turned into Shaftesbury Avenue; I seemed to be spinning by other pedestrians. This was the alcohol, which had become amplified in the crisp autumnal night. My head was buzzing and my eyes flashed surprises at me. More bright lights, leather jackets and T-shirts in shop windows, theatre neons and faces everywhere, faces looking right through me, avoiding me – I was that nasty drunk, a hooligan on the piss.

I'd never been to a peep show before, now it was something to do. I was too far gone into self-hatred for consequences. 'Legs and Lips', just off Old Compton Street, a dirty sex hole – perfect for the desperate loner.

A young woman with too much make-up on and poodle-perm hair grinned at me. She couldn't have been much older than me, and yet she looked haggard – falsely enjoying herself. She hung over a counter in the doorway, smoking a cigarette. Her bright purple spangly top barely covered her chest. She reminded me of a Victorian strumpet cliché. I gave her some money, sloped past her and made my way down the stairs. Her grin was filled with pity and contempt. She seemed to be judging me, looking at my clothes, my hair, the way sweat was building on my forehead and my fumbling for enough cash to get into the show.

"S'booth number five. Have a nice time, lover," she said.

I felt worthless and filled with shame, and yet also glad to be there, it felt like my worth. As my foot touched the surface of each stair, a bright red or green light flashed beneath me, and the theme from 'The

Stripper' began to play. I walked from the stairs along a narrow corridor, painted silver. There were posters on the walls. Adverts for sex videos, and sex toys. Some of the toys looked designed for maximum pain. There were other posters of women in degrading positions, pretending to enjoy their naked exhibitions, sticking their tongues out and off to the sides of their mouths, and half closing their eyes. Was that supposed to signify pleasure? I tried it myself, my tongue out, flopping against my cheek, hot and wet. I must have looked as deranged as I felt.

I could hear crashing music from a room at the end of the corridor. It sounded like The Prodigy or one of those other bands who use thudding drums and swooping screeches.

The booth was tiny and smelled awful. A combination of hash and cigarette smoke, disinfectant and semen; smells that were not only distinct, but also mingled together to produce a pungent nightmare. I couldn't see any window to peep from and assumed I'd gone into the wrong area. All I could see was a flickering light bulb, a wooden chair and the red walls around me. Even the ground seemed invisible. I felt suffocated by heat, stink and desperation. Would she, whoever she was – a dancer I thought – be able to see me, from behind the glass? Where was the glass to be seen from?

I stood quite still and tried not to breathe in. The light bulb dimmed and a widening square of white appeared on one of the walls opposite me. I sat on the chair and crossed my legs. I had expected to see other men, through other small windows around the stage, which lay empty in front of me. But it was just me and a black backdrop with gold stripes, behind the stage. Music sprang with a sudden jolt to my ears, from a speaker above my head. I focused on the stage and noticed a foot coming through the backdrop, and then the rest of the leg, a hand, an arm and then the whole person – a woman person, wearing a bra that barely held her huge breasts, and a thong, equally ill-fitting. She squinted for just a moment, saw me and then winked and blew me a kiss. I could feel myself getting hard and uncrossed my legs. It wasn't that I found her wildly attractive. She was tall, slim and blonde, an ordinary blonde, not Marilyn Monroe, but reasonably pretty. It was just that I needed to pretend she was there for me, only me.

She danced, pranced around, pulled faces and made loud grunting sounds. She pushed her breasts together, tore the bra off and tossed it over her head. She removed the thong slowly with her backside towards me. She made a peek-a-boo face while taking it off and then threw it in my direction. I felt embarrassed for both of us. I sat in quiet despair, wishing I wasn't there, or that, as long as I was there, the dancer would come to my booth and let me finish what I had started with her.

The window closed as suddenly as it had opened and I was left alone again. I breathed out, stood up and made for the door. I couldn't wait to leave. Shame had replaced lust as my emotional companion. I lumbered along the corridor, keeping my eyes towards the floor. The red and green flashing stairs seemed to go on for ages. I climbed quickly, as though I were being chased. I reached the entrance again and ignored the girl there and her questions about the level of my satisfaction.

"Come again soon; I'm sure you will," she said and let out a loud laugh. I imagined the whole of London hearing that laugh, and all their eyes burning me with contempt.

the better part

from a novel **by deborah gregory**

The Better Part is a black comedy based around a dire production of
Macbeth. *Against her better judgement the heroine, Nairne, agreed to
play The Third Witch when by rights she ought to have been cast in the
female lead. Since rehearsals began, she has been plagued by envy and
by desire; she is also hearing a voice from somebody else's past and
glimpsing scenes from the life this spirit led.*

The living room, lit only by the fire which had picked up and decided to
glow cosily, smelt of beer, feet and dope. Nairne, struggling to adjust to
the shadows, realised there were bodies in every corner. Somebody was
playing a guitar, gently and quite well. One very slim body rose from the
floor and Stephen Johns stood before her, offering her a joint which she
took gratefully. Then he led her to the kitchen where he poured her a
glass of wine. His wrist, she noted, was a wishbone, waiting to be
snapped. Nairne drank quickly, feeling that she had some catching up to
do. Next Stephen fed her, offering a dish full of vegetable stew. "I would
like," he announced, as if he knew Nairne far better than he did, "to be
debonair, or dashing, but I am simply thoughtful."

"There is nothing wrong," Nairne told him, "in being one of life's
kindly souls." He watched her as she ate, which she did slowly,
distinguishing tastes as if for the first time, peppers, onions, aubergine.
It was a seriously savoury meal seasoned with Marmite and chillies; it

proved to be precisely what Nairne needed. But when she looked down at her dish she saw fish where the diced vegetables had been. Tragic fish, some of which had disintegrated, while others, not prepared for cooking, had remained intact – one actually gazed reproachfully at Nairne. Then it blinked.

There was a crash. Nairne had dropped the dish and splattered her feet with stew. Stephen was already moving to the sink, for a cloth, as Nairne made for the back door. Then she was outside, under the misted moon. She ran towards the only path she knew. Even when the sound of the stream was foremost, faint guitar playing still followed Nairne into this disenchanted wood. Childhood terrors haunted her as she ran down the path; leaves brushed her face like the talons of the evil stepmother; roots were the claws of trolls stretched out to trip her; the wind was a man – big, close by, breathing down her neck; and moonlight, speckled by the trees, was the eyes of creatures who sneered as she stumbled.

Nairne was almost out of the woods, with the silhouette of the stone arch visible against the silvered sky. The bird was silent but for the whirring of its wings as it flew low over the stream. Then it passed so close to Nairne that the tip of a feather brushed her face. The owl screeched and the actress screamed, a marriage of sounds so eerie that the wood itself appeared to tremble. As the owl flapped its wings, Nairne's heart fluttered in fear. The bird was almost luminous as it flew on in the moonlight, crying in alarm.

Throwing her body forwards, Nairne managed the final few steps to the beach. Here she sat on a rock and peeped at the sea through her fingers. Pale light on the dark water. With a sigh, she let her han 's fall and allowed herself to be steadied by the constant tide.

"Might I tell you of my first visit to the ocean?" the voice wondered. "I ran away to find the shore. My life had been an in-between affair, un I saw the sea. My home was in the Borders, neither one thing nor other. I was the middle one of the three girls, not ragged poor, not rich by any standards. I wanted one extreme, to be the best, the youngest, dearest person in a room; to stand on a promontory with all of what you now call Britain at my back, all the New World before me. In one sense, not in the way that fate decreed, I wanted drama in my life."

"I guess you must be my familiar, are you?" Nairne snapped. "You seem to be, the number of times you've popped up recently."

"Is that modern wit? And speaking of modern, what was that weed you inhaled? I've not encountered it before."

"Root of hemlock digged i'th'dark," Nairne lied.

"No it wasn't. I've tried that, gave me a belly-ache."

"Marijuana then," Nairne said, resigned to being haunted by a know-all. "Look, whoever or whatever you are, I can't do this any more. These little talks may be cosy for you, but they're driving me insane. And the pictures, fish and naked women. I've got more than enough images of my own, thanks."

"I have no power to end them. Believe me, if the commanding hand was mine, I would be resting for eternity, my thoughts and memories taken with me to that void."

"Instead of which?" Nairne whispered.

"I am The Third Witch, Nairne."

"Well, pardon me," Nairne argued, "but I think you'll find I have a contract that proves otherwise."

"Let me rephrase that; we are The Third Witch. At present, you are full of doubts, but I shall allay all of these with proofs. Come, we shall rehearse together, practise how to be a proper witch. To do so we must travel with a dizzying speed. Westwards we shift, hand in hand, without the fabled broomstick but above the ground!"

Nairne felt her body lifted by the merest breeze, carried skywards like a piece of paper. She made no effort and offered no resistance; she simply held her breath in wonder. She was flying.

It seemed to Nairne that she knew how to brush the heather with her toes, to dip and ruffle the surface of a pond, to rise – letting the current lift her – over the roofs of hovels, squinting through the peat smoke.

"Fly, little hawking owl, learn this art, so often conceived but then miscarried by mankind, so frequently and easily achieved by figments, feathers, spirits."

"Here a river, shrouded in its early morning mist, hides the salmon as they swim upstream, homes the water rats that scurry through the purple loosestrife. There a stream, quenching the thirst of cattle, mirrors the heron on the bank. A fox, out hunting, eyes us with suspicion, but merely trots towards the hedgerow, while the hare, over whom we cast our shadows, drops its ears and sprints for cover."

"Three crows attack us as we fly, calling us names, flapping their threats in our faces. A goodwife, pummelling her bedding until duck feathers drift about her head, peers through her storm of down to spot five birds, ragged and black, a-squabbling in the sky."

"The goodwife would cross herself, if she dared, for her flesh is bumpy as a toad's, but these days the sky has spying eyes and, on its sighs, the wind carries insinuations.

"A sudden breeze teases us, lifting our skirts. Now it is insistent, a lover with his fingers in our hair, pulling back our heads, taking sharp bites from these stretched white throats. We billow like dark sheeting, struggling as we soar, higher than buzzards. The land below is nothing but a quilt of greens and browns."

"The wind changes yet again, a rough mistress now, slapping our faces, cuffing us hither and thither. She would rip the clothes from our backs and mark us with her lashes if she could. I shall bear such marks, in time, as human hatred writes its message on my flesh; but you, travelling companion, sister, saviour, you shall remain unscathed. For here is my arm around your shoulders, my shawl envelopes both of us. From the ground we must seem to be one shape, two-headed, with the wing span of an eagle."

"The hills flatten to a marsh, the grass toughens, whipped by a squall... "

"... which is, for me, the first taste of the long-awaited, the salty spittle thrown inland from the sea. The sea, my friend, the ocean of my imagination. Soon I shall espy this mystery, complete with ships from stories told to children in my Border village, foaming as it spews upon a beach, as it thrashes rocks to grains of sand."

"Under the spell of the sea, crows, rooks and ravens blanch, shocked into herring gulls, crying for their silver suppers."

"My nostrils itch with a fresh scent. Fish, dry-scaled, bloody eyed in my dish at home, never smelt of this."

"My own eyes wince at the brightness of the sun on distant water, a world of light approaches us."

"Hold me, Nairne, I find my senses reeling to accept a new eternity; not earth, not air, but water to the end of time."

"Along the estuary we skim, calling like curlews for the joy of being airborne, transported by the selfsame winds that carry sailors out to sea and bring them safe to port."

"I feel it now! The spray of waves, salt kisses, finally, falling on this landlocked cheek."

"A few yards more, with this rush of air on our faces, with the pebbles smoothing to sand below our open arms, and we are in the shallows, skirts soaked and heavy, lungs gasping with shock, dragged to earth by our waterlogged boots... "

"... but in the sea! Laughing together as we are sucked and shoved by its tides."

four poems

by heather lyn gupton

driftwood

Half lying
on the beige,
L-shaped couch
after a long day,
you'd wear white shorts
and bare feet
in our Florida split-level,
a can of beer on the coffee table
you made from driftwood.

Some years, happiness
was as scarce as driftwood,
treasure found only after
a raging storm had spat it forth,
and we wondered what stories
this driftwood would tell.

You, too,
are like driftwood –
worm-eaten and weather-beaten
to a pale, dry grey –
somehow the stronger
for having survived.

heather lyn gupton

fish

for d.b.

Guitar tab
makes all the sense
of Sanskrit sometimes.
My tiny fingers struggle.
No wonder they call it
the 'F' chord.

The offbeat
is so ingrained in me
that you say I'm like a fish
flapping out of water
when I try to accompany you on-beat.

Still, there are moments
when we connect
as tangibly
as two hands touching,
and I breathe the water,
swimming proudly,
scales glistening.

lark

I have given you
a pocketful
of attitude
all rolled up
in a defensive
little ball
so prickly
you immediately
roll me up
and spit me out
like dirt
from your mouth,
completely vexed.

Christ,
WhydoIputupwiththis?

She can sing,
this lark,
but she
can't dance.

the death of moonlight

The missus and I was just home
safe from the cinema when I heard it –
a mighty sound like a train a comin',
only there wasn't any tracks nearby.

Before you could say
"Fire in the hole,"
that twister had touched down –
Whomp! Whomp! Whomp! –
like a toad a hoppin'.
Then, a silence so eerie
it filled your head
with the memory of the roar.

Well, the wind had knocked
the door clean outta my hand
and me clear across the passage,
but the missus she done had time
to duck under the kitchen table.

We was counting our blessings
and pouring a shot to steady
our nerves when there came
a knock at the door.
It was the neighbours,
come to see if we was all right.

Seeing that we was,
Bob said I should go check the cows,
which was all a grazin'

heather lyn gupton

quiet and peaceful-like out front
when that twister touched down.

I told him, "Nosiree, Bob.
Them cows'll just have to wait
until morning" – and that not
but six hours away.
Come the dawn
they was all up at the shed
like normal, all of 'em
'cept the one we call
Moonlight, on accounta'
she's all black with a white face.

They found part of her
up by the trailer park
and her head was bobbin'
like an apple in the water tub,
cut off cleaner than you could've
done it yerself with a good knife.

There wasn't much left but what
they found up at the top of the town,
and that not much good to nobody,
but seeing that it was a Sunday,
somebody done cut out
Moonlight's tongue.

Couldn't blame 'em, really.
"Waste not, want not,"
my Mama always said.

the eggy stone

a short story **by tessa hadley**

We found the Eggy Stone that first afternoon of the school camp.

As soon as we had dumped our things in the big khaki canvas tents, each with eight metal bedsteads in two rows, the teacher took us down to the sea. We crunched in socks and sandals across a rim of crisped black seaweed and bone and sea-washed plastic: the tide was in, the long grey line of the waves curled and sucked at the cramped remainder of the beach, a narrow strip of pebbles. For the moment we weren't allowed to go near the water. Under our sandals the pale round pebbles rattled and shifted awkwardly. The boys began throwing them into the sea; we felt between them for treasures, the creamy spirals from old shells, bits of soft-washed glass.

Her hand and mine found the Eggy Stone at the same moment, our fingers touched, and somehow that sealed it; I was hers and she was mine for the duration of the holiday. We had never been friends before. I didn't deserve her; she had only been in the school for a few months, but her status was clear, she had been put to sit the very first day on the table where the charming girls sat. I was clever; but she was blonde with an elfin frailness and had a pencil case full of the right kind of felts and danced with the other favoured girls in the country dancing team that did 'Puppet on a String' instead of 'Trip to the Cottage'. Even her name was pretty: Madeleine. I was ready to adore her.

She was fragile but firm. It was she who named the stone and held it out on her palm for me to share. It was small and egg-shaped and dull black, with a ring of white crystal teeth around it at one end, just where you would cut the top off an egg to eat it. If it hadn't become, the moment we chose it, 'the Eggy Stone', it would have been nothing special: there were hundreds and thousands more pebbles just as interesting. Love can begin like this: as carelessly and accidentally as picking up a stone from a beach.

Madeleine began the cult, but I elaborated it. We took it in turns to hold the Eggy Stone, and the turns were decided by various ritualised competitions, including folded-paper fortune-tellers, and knocking the heads off weeds, and a kind of wrestling we invented, kneeling opposite one another with the stone placed between us and swaying in each other's arms, trying to force our opponent to touch ground on one side or another. Before each competition there was a form of words; something like "Eggy Stone/ On your own/ All alone/ Inaccessible light". I was probably the one who made it up (although it owed something to a hymn we sang at school). I had a bit of a reputation as a poet; whereas Madeleine was the kind of girl who chanted things by rote and knew all the skipping rhymes and all the variations for games like "Please Jack, may we cross the water?"

Whoever possessed the stone felt privileged and secure for as long as it lasted. The sensation of it, smooth and warmed and resistant in the hand, came to be an end in itself, a real pleasure; and whoever didn't possess it yearned for it, until the moment arrived for another challenge. Once or twice Madeleine cheated, pushing her hand into my pocket and filching the stone without any contest, showing me with her quick brilliant smile that any appearance of fair play was only ever granted by her favour. I was outraged and helpless then, thrown back upon a self no longer complete without her. But mostly the passing of the stone was kind between us, an extraordinary bond. We went about with arms draped round one another's necks, and all Madeleine's usual friends included me tolerantly in their circle. We took it in turns to hold the stone at night, in the dark, in our sleeping bags (we slept in different tents).

The cult of the Eggy Stone didn't seem any stranger than all the other strangenesses, in a week away from home. Misery and wonder were flooded together: gargantuan preparations in the kitchen where we took our turn at helping cater for the children from seven schools; Madeleine and I trailing hand in hand, ankle-deep in tepid sea-foam; cocoa made with water and served in tin mugs; dread of the publicity of the toilets and consequent constipation. Some of the girls (Madeleine, but not me) crept out at night to kiss the boys in their tents. We learnt new obscenities: "min" and "omo" among them (or at least that's how I heard them), which mystifyingly corresponded to the names of cleaning products. On the last night the teachers made a campfire and taught us songs with accompanying actions. *Indians are high-minded,/Bless my soul they're double-jointed,/They climb hills and don't mind it,/All day long.* Madeleine beside me touched toes and reached her arms in the air with a pretty equanimity, as if whatever she was doing at a given moment was the only graceful thing possible.

I asked her the next morning, on the beach, before we got on the coach to go home, what we were going to do with the Eggy Stone. She took the stone out from her pocket, holding it out reflectively on her hand for a moment; her face was quite clear of either malice or tenderness. I had a proposal ready, that we should keep the thing for a week each, changing over every Monday, dividing up the holidays: I was not foolish enough to imagine that the magical game was going to carry on between us, once school camp was over. But before I could speak, she turned and threw the Eggy stone, hard and far, with a confidence that made it clear she would one day be captain of the netball team; and I heard it land with a rattle among all the other pebbles and knew that even if I went to look I would never, ever be able to find exactly the same stone again.

blue earth

from a novel **by jules hardy**

Outside Spokane, Billy-Ray was picked up by a lone woman. Lucca smoked, she talked too fast, she drove too fast. She often looked at Billy-Ray and not at the road.

"Where you going?" she asked as they sped away from the town.

"Seattle."

"Why?"

"I'm going to the university." Billy-Ray was uncomfortable under her scrutiny.

"Why?"

Why? "Well, to study," he said.

"What? What are you studying?" Lucca dextrously lit a Lucky Strike Regular with one hand using a book of matches, tossed the spent match out the window. "Party trick," she said.

"I'm majoring in geology."

"Why?"

Billy-Ray frowned. He looked at Lucca. She was thin, probably quite short although it was hard to tell. Her hair looked darker than it should have been. She was old – forty-two, maybe forty-three, around the same age as his mother. "Because I like it."

"What's your name?"

"Billy-Ray Rickman."

"Lucca Barzini. Well, Billy-Ray" – the car swooped around a curve, threw up gravel, settled – "how can you like geology? I mean, you can like martinis or pasta or cats or sex but you can't *like* geology. It's not in the same league."

Billy-Ray had never heard a woman say 'sex' before but, then, neither had he heard a woman say 'pasta' before. He sat in the car, stunned, trying to work out why it was OK to like geology. "I think, in a way, it's all there is. It's like a… a starting point. Before we can do anything else. It's a starting point. If we don't know what we're standing on, what the world is, then how do we know what to do with it?"

Lucca Barzini, who was a journalist working for the *Tribune*, who had been in Spain in '36 and had seen the futility of trying to know what the world is, let alone what to do with it, smiled. "Where you from Billy-Ray?"

"Bow Regard, Blue Earth County, Minnesota." Billy-Ray was hugging his bag on his knees. He felt strangely vulnerable when Lucca looked at him.

"Ah – the Flatlands. What are you – Swedish? Dutch?"

"I'm an American."

Oh shit, thought Lucca. "Well, of course you are. I just wondered where your people are from."

"Germany and Poland."

"Have you visited there?"

"Nah. Never been outside Minnesota before now."

"I guess the Rockies must have been quite something when you saw them?"

Billy-Ray smiled and Lucca thought how charming he looked. "Sure were. I never realised how big they'd be. I mean, I guess I never thought about how they just go on and on."

Lucca lit another cigarette with her complicated routine of finger snapping. "If you've never been out of Minnesota, you've never seen the ocean."

"Can't say I have." Billy-Ray knew he sounded like a hick, like he had a straw in his mouth, hog shit on his shoes, but Lucca made him uneasy. She looked like something from a movie, with her black clothes and red lipstick. She almost looked like a boy.

"When are you due in Seattle?"

"You sure ask a lot of questions," said Billy-Ray.

"Course I do. It's my job – I'm a reporter."

Billy-Ray stared at her. "A reporter? A *newspaper* reporter?"

"Yeah. That's right. A *newspaper* reporter." Lucca smiled. "I file copy for the *Post* and *Tribune* in New York, syndicate a couple of weekly columns."

Billy-Ray considered the glamour of this. Everyone he knew was either a farmer, a store-keeper, a religious maniac or dead. "That must be great," he decided.

"Sometimes – sometimes not. I've been up around Kalispell for a few days, staying in a so-called motel. No hot water, dirt for a floor, rags hanging in the windows." Lucca shuddered theatrically. "Bears and snakes. Ugh."

"Why were you there?"

"There's been a few murders up in the back of Kalispell, way up in the hills. You know, where the nearest neighbours are ten miles away and the nights can get too long. Turns out they're all related. Not just the murders – the victims too. It's all the inter-breeding. Maybe there's more jealousy when it's just one big if not happy family."

"What? You mean they all, y'know? Cousins and all that?"

"Fathers and daughters, mothers and uncles, brothers and sisters. Brothers and brothers too. All of them."

Billy-Ray thought of what he'd done with Magde, imagined doing it with his mother. "Das ist widerlich. Wie koennen sie so etwas machen?" he muttered.

"What?"

"That's disgusting."

Lucca watched him for a moment. "I can't say it appeals much to me either, but they're a long way from anywhere. I guess they don't have too much choice."

"Abscheulich."

"You didn't answer my question."

"Huh?"

"When are you due in Seattle?"

"Anytime. School doesn't start until September. I thought I'd come out early and make some money. Can I have one?" Billy-Ray took Lucca's cigarettes from the dash.

"Sure. Light me one while you're there. So you left home already? Don't you have a reason to stay the summer? A girlfriend?"

Billy-Ray fidgeted with the matches. "Nah. Nothing like that." Thought of Magde crying quietly.

A road sign told them they were leaving Everett, twenty miles from Seattle.

"Would you like to see the ocean?" asked Lucca.

"Yah – I'm going to. In Seattle."

Lucca laughed. "That's not the ocean – that's just a big river. I mean the Pacific Ocean in all its glory."

"Yah. I'm hoping I will, one day."

"OK – well, I have to go into town to file some copy, deliver some papers. Then I'm heading out to the coast, south of the city. A friend of mine's got a cabin out there, near the Columbia River and she's loaned it to me for the weekend. I'm driving back into Seattle on Monday afternoon – I could drop you off then." Lucca drew smoke deep into her lungs. "If you want to come, that is. If you want to stay the weekend."

Billy-Ray Rickman may have been a hick from the Flatlands but he knew what was going on. "Can you see the ocean from the cabin?"

"I don't know. I think so. Maybe."

"OK, yah, I'd like to come."

Lucca dropped off the papers and then stopped at an A&P on the outskirts of Seattle. She and Billy-Ray walked the aisles, collecting together the ingredients for breakfast and some steaks, potatoes and salad.

"D'you like beer?" Lucca asked.

"Yah. And vodka."

Lucca picked up two cartons of Lucky Strikes, some beers, vodka, and brandy, along with a few bottles of red wine. Billy-Ray stood behind her, holding the groceries as she paid, trying not to register shock at how many bills she handed over. More money than his mother spent on food in a month. The woman working the till glanced at Billy-Ray and

Lucca, smiled an odd smile and Billy-Ray blushed.

"Do you want to go to the drug store?" asked Lucca once the bags were in the trunk. She shaded her eyes against the glare of the midday sun. Standing in the street, dressed in creased clothes, Lucca looked older than she did in the car. There were faint wrinkles on her neck and crow's feet by her eyes. Billy-Ray saw she was wearing trousers, black, tailored, high-waisted trousers, creased at the groin. He'd never seen a woman in trousers before.

"Excuse me?"

"Look, all I'm asking is if you need to visit the drug store. I'm a little too old to be a mother. Here." She held out two dollar bills.

"Right." Billy-Ray was sweating in his jacket. "OK. Right."

When he came back, two packs of rubbers rustling in his jacket pocket, Lucca was sitting in the passenger seat, smoking. "You drive," she said. "I've been at the wheel since six this morning and I need some sleep. Here's the map." She flapped a creased Rand McNally at him.

Billy-Ray slid onto the driver's seat, stared at the dash, not understanding it. "Where's the gears?"

"It's automatic."

"It's what?"

"The car deals with the gears. You just put your foot on the gas pedal or the brake. Simple. If you can drive a tractor you can drive this."

"What kind of car is this anyway? Never seen one like it before."

"You won't have done – it's a Cord 812. They only made a thousand or roundabout." Lucca folded a cardigan for a makeshift pillow. "Then the damn war came along you couldn't buy a new car or even parts for the goddamn old one."

Billy-Ray turned over the engine, slipped the stick a notch and grinned as the car slid forward. "Where are we going anyway?"

"Out past Aberdeen. I've marked it on the map. Highway 12, then south on the 105." Lucca laughed. "Can't miss it – it's called Cape Disappointment."

And Billy-Ray's stomach lurched when he heard that name.

But there were compensations – Billy-Ray loved driving the car, he loved the privacy, the *luxury* of the Cord 812. He'd only ever driven

ancient John Deeres and battered Ford pick-ups – and he'd never
encountered the idea of driving for driving's sake – to arrive somewhere
with the sole purpose of having fun. Not to load bales of hay or move
hogs or replace a rusted trough – simply to go somewhere because it
was somewhere else. As Lucca slept he floored the gas pedal, taking the
car up to sixty, the ragged verges flashing by. Then he slowed, lit a
cigarette, cruised along the highway at forty, fantasising about owning a
car like this, simply driving in a car like this with some girl. At a junction
he passed a hitcher, a tall blond boy with a bag at his feet, a boy who
looked hungry, who looked loose, who looked a long, long way from
home. For a moment Billy-Ray burned with shame (Siggy would have
stopped, reversed, picked up the boy), but then he thought, well... you
make your own luck. At the very moment Billy-Ray was considering luck
in all its guises, the Cord crested a rise outside Aberdeen and there it
was: the biggest ocean on earth. Billy-Ray coasted the car onto the verge,
climbed out and looked, breathed deep. He stood watching an
uneventful sea break on the coast, line after fractured line of foam and
spume rolling, snagging on sea floors, hidden rocks, weak sandstone
cliffs until the train of heaving water met the rising sandy bed. And
there the waves crowded each other as the train ploughed into land.
Billy-Ray knew that these waves had travelled thousands of miles to
break at his feet but it seemed inconceivable. He scanned the arc of
horizon, which extended as far as he could see – unending ocean, flat,
unbroken.

"So what d'you think Billy-Ray?" Lucca had woken and now stood
beside him.

He looked at the horizon, saw a tanker in the distance. "Do you
know what's across there? On the same latitude?"

Lucca lit a cigarette, with some difficulty given the stiff on-shore
breeze. "Surprise me."

"Japan."

Surprised, Lucca Barzini, ex-war reporter stared across the waters.
It was May 1946. "Japan?"

"Yah," said Billy-Ray.

"Jesus," muttered Lucca.

"It's OK," said Billy-Ray, putting an arm around her shoulders. "It's thousands of miles away." (A tall man putting his arm around his son as they looked across the rainbow counties of Minnesota.)

The cabin on Cape Disappointment was a two-room, timbered shack, shingled and weathered but well-built and sturdy, entirely functional. Functional apart from its location – inelegantly, unnecessarily but beautifully perched on a rise in the dunes, where the view from the small porch was of the wave-trains rolling in from Asia. Inside, the wood stove had been swept and cleaned, but there was a layer of fine pale sand on everything. Lucca found the linen and made up the bed as Billy-Ray lit the stove and sorted the groceries. Billy-Ray finished his chores before Lucca and he stood in the doorway of the bedroom, watching her thin, wiry form as she forced a pillow into its linen case.

"What's your problem, Billy-Ray?"

"Huh?"

"I have the feeling you're in a hurry to be doing something."

"I'd like to walk along the beach, before it gets dark. I just... I just want to walk."

Lucca straightened and looked at the young, handsome man, standing in a wooden doorway, his hands working, bunching and releasing. She knew he was too polite to press the point, and too fired up to sit out on the porch and wait for her. He looked hungry for something, loose almost. And a long, long way from home. "Let's go." Lucca dropped the pillow and walked past Billy-Ray, picked up a bottle of wine, a corkscrew and two glasses, put them in a bag, which she slung over her shoulder. "C'mon, let's go."

The two of them walked silently along the spit, clambered down a rocky path and began to tramp the hard, damp-packed sand, which crunched satisfyingly. Billy-Ray took off his boots and socks and walked barefoot, turning every now and then to watch his shallow prints fill with brine and then fade. After a half-hour Lucca stopped, unhitched the bag from her shoulders and sat in the dunes, held the bottle and corkscrew out to Billy-Ray, who took them and stared at the corkscrew as if it were an unwanted weapon. He had never used one.

"Here, give it me." Lucca, a cigarette hanging loosely from her lips, her eyes screwed up against the smoke, wielded the corkscrew, drove it snug into the cork, handed the bottle back to Billy-Ray. "Just pull on the damn thing."

He pulled and heard the sound of air phutting.

"Here, fill 'em up." Lucca held out the glasses.

Billy-Ray thought of the gnarled Portuguese corks his father yanked from his bottles of firewater. Thought of miraculous wafers, thought of a tall blonde woman firing into the air. He looked at the blood of Christ he held in his hands and he wondered. Billy-Ray had never drunk wine other than on his knees. He fell to his knees by Lucca and glugged the wine into the glasses. He turned and sat, looking out over the restless water, gunmetal grey, its surface skittering, catching sky-light. Next to him, Lucca buttoned her jacket and wrapped her arms round her tiny waist.

"So, Billy-Ray, I guess this where you get to tell me about your family and why you left them." Lucca groped for the ever-present packet of cigarettes and busied herself with her party-trick.

Billy-Ray drank the wine, a poor Californian from a failing vineyard – swallowed it down in a draught, like a rabid man, like a drunk, like a *vampire* – and frowned. "No."

"OK. Then this is where you tell me about your childhood sweetheart and how you miss her."

"No." Billy-Ray poured himself another glass.

"Right – so this must be where you tell me about how misunderstood you feel."

Billy-Ray turned his cold eyes on Lucca. "I don't."

Lucca shrugged. "OK." Drew deeply on her cigarette and burning specks of paper flew in the breeze.

The two of them sat on the damp sand watching the light in the sky change, drinking, Lucca waiting for him to say something, to ask her something about her life. But Billy-Ray just drank the wine and stared at the horizon as Lucca remembered the selfishness of the young, their preoccupation with their lives and how they might be lived.

"Blue earth," Billy-Ray said suddenly, and smiled.

"What?"

"Blue earth – that's what the sea is like – blue earth."

Lucca frowned, held her hair back from her face with her hand. The breeze had picked up. "Didn't you say you came from there? Blue Earth something?"

"Blue Earth County, Minnesota."

"Look, can we go back? It's getting cold and I'm hungry as hell. You can come and stare at your blue earth all day tomorrow if that's what you want to do." Lucca gathered together the empty glasses and bottle, stood and shouldered the bag. Billy-Ray lurched to his feet, staggered a little. "Hey – you OK?"

Billy-Ray winced, rubbed his thigh. "Yah."

"You're limping."

"I have a problem with my leg – if I sit too long or it gets cold. I'm fine. It will go."

Billy-Ray cooked the steaks over a small fire he built in a sand hollow beyond the porch as Lucca drank more wine and made potato salad. When the food was finished Billy-Ray banked up the fire and the two of them huddled by it as the damp rolled in across thousands of miles of blue earth, precipitating itself at their feet. Lucca drank brandy, chain-smoked, moved to lean against the bulk of the young man. Billy-Ray drank vodka, listened to the salt water dragging pebbles, grinding them down, heard brine percolating through sand.

Lucca downed the last of her drink, tossed the butt of her cigarette into the fire, watching it flare green, before moving forward, kneeling in front of Billy-Ray, between him and the heat. She looked feral, her eyes narrowed, predatory. She took his face in her small hands, felt the beard against her palm, felt the bones beneath her own. As she pulled him towards her, Billy-Ray spilt his vodka, soaking his trousers, dropping the glass, and he reached for Lucca's bird waist, tugging at the blouse tucked there. Still Lucca held his face, kissed him, running her tongue around his lips, pushing at him as he tore cotton and his hands moved to her small, almost limp breasts, moving them against her ribs. Embers scattered around them as Billy-Ray kicked out, wanting to have more purchase, and a log tumbled. Something was gathering at the base of

Billy-Ray's spine and he wanted to concentrate on that. As if a gyroscope was spinning there, growing hotter.

Lucca drew away, still holding his face, holding it tight. Leaning over him, her short, dark hair blowing across her face, a face that looked somehow heavier, vascular, expectant almost, she asked, "Do you want to go to bed?"

Billy-Ray, breathing heavily, nodded.

the treatment

from a novel **by mo hayder**

When it was all over, DI Jack Caffery, South London Area Major Investigation Team (AMIT), would admit that, of the all the things he witnessed in Brixton that cloudy July evening, it was the crows that jarred him the most.

They were there when he came out of the Peaches' house – twenty or more of them standing in their hooded way on the lawn of the neighbouring garden, oblivious of the police tape, the onlookers, the technicians. Some had their mouths open. Others appeared to be panting. All of them faced him directly – as if they knew what had happened in the house. As if they were having a sly laugh about the way he'd reacted to the scene.

Later he would accept that the crows' behaviour was a biological tic, that they couldn't see into his thoughts, couldn't have known what had happened to the Peach family, but even so the sight of them made the back of his neck tingle. He paused at the top of the garden path to strip his overalls and hand them to a Scientific Support Unit forensics officer, pulled on the shoes he'd left outside the police tape, and waded out into the birds. They took to the air, rattling their petrolly feathers.

Brockwell Park – a huge, thrown-together isosceles of forest and grass with its apex at Herne Hill station – rambles for over a mile along the boundary of two very different parts of South London. On its western perimeter: the badlands of Brixton – where some mornings council workers have to drop sand on the streets to soak up the blood – and, to the east: Dulwich – with its flower-drenched almshouses and John Soane skylights. Donegal Crescent lay snug up against Brockwell Park – anchored at one foot by a boarded-up pub, at the other by a Gujarati-owned corner shop. It was part of a quiet little council estate, rows of Fifties terraced houses bare to the sky, no trees in the front gardens, windows and doors painted chocolate brown. The houses looked on to a horseshoe-shaped piece of balding grass where kids skidded their bikes in the evening. Caffery could imagine the Peaches must have felt relatively safe here.

Back in his shirtsleeves, grateful for the fresh air outside, he rolled a cigarette and crossed to the group of officers next to the Scientific Support Command Unit van. They fell silent as he approached and he knew what they were thinking. He was only in his mid-thirties – not a senior-rank war-horse – but most officers in South London knew who he was. *One of the Met's Young Turks,* the Police Review had called him, he knew he was respected in the force and he always found it a bit freaky. *If they knew half of it –*

"Well?" He lit the cigarette and looked at a sealed plastic evidence bag a junior forensics officer was holding. "What've you got?"

"We found it just inside the park, sir, about twenty yards from the back of the Peaches'."

Caffery took the bag and turned it over carefully. A Nike 'Air Server' trainer, a child's shoe – slightly smaller than his hand. "Who found it?"

"The dogs, sir."

"And?"

"They lost the trail. At first they had it – they had it good, really good." A sergeant in the blue shirt of the dog handlers' unit stood on tiptoe and pointed over the roofs to where the park rose in the distance, blotting out the sky with its dark woods. "They took us around the path that scoots over the west of the park – but after about half a mile they just drew a blank." He looked dubiously at the evening sky. "And we've lost the light now."

"Right. We need to speak to Air Support." Caffery passed the trainer back to the forensics officer. "It should be in an air-drying bag."

"I'm sorry?"

"There's blood on it. Didn't you see?"

The SSCU's dragonlights powered up, flooding the Peaches house, spilling light on to the trees in the park beyond. In the front garden forensic officers in blue rubberised suits swept the lawn with dustpans and, outside the police tape, shock-faced neighbours stood in knots, smoking and whispering, breaking off to huddle around any plain-clothed AMIT detective who came near, full of questions. The press was there too. Losing patience.

Caffery stood next to the Command Unit van and stared up at the house. It was a two-storey terraced house – pebble dashed, a satellite dish on the roof, aluminium framed windows and a small patch of damp above the front door. There were matching scalloped nets in each window, and beyond them the curtains had been drawn tight.

He had only seen the Peach family, or what was left of it, in the aftermath, but he felt as if he knew them. Or, rather, he knew their archetype. The parents – Alek and Carmel – weren't going to be easy victims for the team to sympathise with: both drinkers, both unemployed, Carmel Peach had sworn at the paramedics as they moved her into the ambulance. Their only son, nine-year-old Rory, Caffery hadn't seen. By the time he'd arrived the divisional officers had already pulled the house apart trying to find the child – in the cupboards, the attic, even behind the bath panelling. There was a thin trace of blood on the skirting-board in the kitchen and the glass in the back door was broken. Caffery had taken a Territorial Support Group officer with him to search a boarded-up property two doors down, crawling through a hole in the back door on their bellies, flashlights in their teeth like an adolescent's SAS fantasy. All they found were the usual homeless nesting arrangements. There was no other sign of life. No Rory Peach. The raw facts were bad enough and for Caffery they could have been custom built to echo his own past. *Don't let it be a problem, Jack, don't let it turn into a headfuck.*

"Jack?" DCI Danniella Souness said, suddenly at his side.

"Ye alright son?"

He looked round. "Danni. God, I'm glad you're here."

"What's with the face? You've a gob on you like a dog's arse."

"Thanks, Danni." He rubbed his face and stretched his arms above his head. "I've been on standby since midnight."

"And what's the SP on this?" She gestured at the house. "A wain gone missing, am I right? Rory?"

"Yes. We're going to blow some fuses on this – he's only nine years old."

Souness blew air out of her nose and shook her head. She was solid – just five foot four, but she weighed twelve stone in her man's suit and boots. With her cropped hair and fair, Caledonian skin she looked more like a juvenile dressed for his first court appearance than a forty-year-old Chief Inspector. She took her job very seriously. "Right, the assessment team been?"

"We don't know we've got a death yet. No dead body, no assessment team."

"Aye, the lazy wee bastards."

"Local factory's taken the house apart and can't find him. I've had dogs and the Territorials in the park, Air Support should be on their way."

"Why do ye think he's in the park?"

"These houses all back on to it." He pointed towards the woods that rose beyond the roofs. "We've got a witness saw *something* heading off into the trees from number thirty. Back door's unlocked, there's a hole in the fence, and the lads found a shoe just inside the park – "

"Okay – okay – I'm convinced." Souness folded her arms and tipped back on her heels, looking around at the technicians: the photographers; the divisional CID officers. On the doorstep of number thirty a camera operator was checking his battery belt, lowering the heavy Betacam into a case. "Looks like a shagging film set."

"The unit wants to work through the night."

"What's with the ambulance? The one that almost ran me off the road?"

"Ah yes – that was Mum. She and hubby have both been trundled off to Kings. She'll make it but he hasn't got a hope. Where he was hit – "Caffery held his palm against the back of his head " – fucked him up some. Danni – " He checked over his shoulder then bent a little nearer to her, lowering his voice. "Danni. There're a few things we're going to have to keep from the press, a few things we don't want popping up in the tabloids."

"What things?"

"It isn't a custody kidnap. He's their child – no exes involved."

"A tiger then?"

"Not a tiger either." Tiger kidnaps meant ransom demands and the Peaches were not in an extortionist's financial league. "And anyway when you look at what else went on you'll know it's not bog-standard."

"Eh?"

Caffery looked around at the journalists – at the neighbours. "Let's go in the van, eh?" He put his hand on Souness's back. "I don't want an audience."

"Come on then." She hefted herself inside the SSCU's van and Caffery followed, reaching up to grip the roof rim and swinging himself inside. Spades, cutting equipment and tread plates hung from the walls, a samples refrigerator hummed gently in the corner. He closed the door and hooked a stool over with his foot and handed it to her. She sat down and he sat opposite, feet apart, elbows on his knees, looking at her carefully.

"What?"

"We've got something screwy."

"What?"

"Whoever it was stayed with them first."

Souness frowned, tilting her chin down as if she wasn't sure whether he was joking or not. *"Stayed with them?"*

"That's right. Just – hung around. For almost three days. They were tied up in there – handcuffed – no food or water. DS Quinn thinks another twelve hours and one or another of them'd be dead." He raised his eyebrows. "Worst thing's the smell."

Souness rolled her eyes. "Oh, lovely."

"Then there's the bullshit scrawled all over the wall – "

"Oh, Christ." Souness sat back a little, rubbing her stubbly head with the palm of her hand. "Is it sounding like a Maudesly jobbie?"

He nodded. "Yeah – but he won't be far – the park is sealed now; we'll have him before long."

He stood to leave the van. "Jack?" Souness stopped him. "Something else is worrying ye."

He paused for a minute, looking at the floor, his hand on the back of his neck. It was as if she'd leaned over and peered keen-eyed through a window in his head. They liked each other, he and Souness: neither was quite sure why, but they had both fallen comfortably into this partnership. Still there were some things he didn't choose to tell her.

"No Danni," he murmured eventually, re-knotting his tie, not wanting to hear how much she guessed of his preoccupations. "Come on – let's have a shufty at the park, shall we?"

Outside night had come to Donegal Crescent. The moon was low and red in the sky.

From the back of Donegal Crescent, Brockwell Park appeared to ramble away for miles into the distance, filling the skyline. Its upper slopes were mostly bald, only a few shabby, hairless trees across the backbone and at the highest point a clutch of exotic evergreens, but on the west slope an area about the size of four football pitches was thick with trees: bamboo and silver birch, beech and Spanish chestnut, they huddled around four stinking ponds, sucking up the dampness in the soil. There was the density of a jungle among those trees – in the summer the ponds seemed to be steaming.

At 8.30pm that night, only minutes before the park was sealed off by the police, one solitary man was not far from those ponds, shuffling amongst the trees, an intent expression on his face. Roland Klare's was a lonely, almost hermitic existence – with odd tempers and periods of lethargy – and sometimes, when the mood was on him, he was a collector. A human relative of the carrion beetle, to Klare nothing was disposable or beyond redemption. He knew the park well and often wandered around here looking through the bins, checking under park benches. People left him alone. He had long, rather womanly hair, and a smell about him that no one liked.

Now he stood, with his hands in his pockets, and stared at what was between his feet. It was a camera. A Pentax camera. Old and battered. He picked it up and looked at it carefully, holding it close to his face because the light was fading fast. Roland Klare had five other cameras back at his flat, among the items scavenged from skips and dumpsters. He even had bits and pieces of film-developing equipment. Now he quickly put the Pentax in his pocket and shuffled his feet around in the leaves for a bit, checking the ground. There'd been a summer cloudburst that morning, but the sun had been out all afternoon and even the undersides of the long grass were dry against his shoes. Two feet away lay a pair of pink rubber gloves, large ones, which he slipped in his pocket with the camera. After a while he continued on his way through the fading light. The rubber gloves, he decided when he got them under a streetlight, were not worth keeping. Too worn. So he dropped them in a skip on the Railton Road. But a camera. A camera was not to be discarded lightly.

It was a quiet evening for India 99, the twin-engined Squirrel helicopter out of Lippits Hill air base. The sun had gone down and the heat and low cloud cover made the Air Support crew headachy: they got the unit's twelve fixed tasks completed as quickly as possible – Heathrow, the Dome, Canary Wharf, several power stations including Battersea – and were ready to switch to self-tasking when the controller came through on the Tactical Commander's headset. "Yeah India nine nine from India Lima."

The Tactical Commander pulled the mouthpiece nearer. "Go ahead, India Lima."

"Where are you?"

"We're in, uh, where?" He leaned forward a little and looked down at the lit-up city. "Wandsworth."

"Good. India nine eight's got an active, but they've reached endurance, grid ref: TQ3427445."

The Commander checked the map. "Is that Brockwell Park?"

"Rog. It's a missing child, ground units have got it contained, but look lads, the DI's being straight with us, says you're a tick in the box. He can't promise the child's in the park – just a hunch – so there's no obligation."

The Commander pulled away his mouthpiece, checked his watch and looked into the front of the cockpit. The Air Observer and the pilot had heard the request and were holding their thumbs up for him to see. Good. He noted the time and the Computer Aided Dispatch number on the assignment log and pulled his mouthpiece back in place.

"Yeah, go on then India Lima. It's quiet tonight – we'll have a look. Who are we speaking to?"

"An, um, an Inspector Caffery. AMIT – "

"The murder squad, you mean?"

"That's the one."

northern lights

a short story **by julie hayman**

All the children in Norway ski. I told him. They ski before they walk, and snow is like seaside sand to them. He wouldn't listen. He'd smile his big, white, Yankee smile, bundle Herga up in layers of clothing she didn't need. Let her breathe, I said, let the air get to her. No, he said, She'll get frostbite, she's not yet two. In Norway, I said getting angry, in Norway children aren't smothered and cosseted like in your pampered country. Here, they learn to respect the elements, to work with them, adapt to them. She won't grow strong if you keep her too close, I said. Listen to the folktales about ice men and snow palaces and seal people and the need for bravery and cunning in this harsh, beautiful landscape, and you'll see. Ja, ja, mama, he said, not even listening. Not even listening, but calling me mama.

Mama. Not his mama. Not mama to a warm, womanish man who dresses his daughter like a doll. When my Sigrid was small, she was always in the snow, I made her sleep out in it sometimes on a reindeer pelt under a canvas tent that I put up for her, that I weighed down with blocks of snow and ice to keep it standing, that I insisted she endure. That's the way to survive in this land. Survive and thrive. But when Sigrid cried from the cold and her fingers and toes swelled and her nose was blue and her eyes slushy, then I was not strong. I let her come in, took her into my bed and wrapped her fat in eiderdown, let her sleep warm. I should have been stronger, should have taught her how to respect ice.

Now my Sigrid sleeps always under snow, her face smashed, her limbs mangled by his hot-weather automobile. Not designed for ice, you see. But Herga survived, the snow likes Herga, the land likes Herga.

He was glad enough of me with Sigrid gone, glad enough to listen to my talk then. Glad enough to have a mama to mix the baby's milk and mop her stains while he sobbed and choked in the corner of the kitchen for days on end as if no one in the world had ever died before. As if he didn't know about snow, didn't know what it could do. As if he thought life could just go on forever as he wanted. It's the way of things, Bob, I said, using his foreign name, Things die. Especially soft things, I added under my breath. He nodded and sobbed, melting away like a river in spring thaw.

I spoke gently at first, wiping his watery face with the corner of my apron while I stirred the fish-head soup on the stove with my other hand. He sat on the stool and rocked; sniffed and snotted and rocked like a baby, his face as red as the fire. It's just the way of things, I told him, and gave him aquavit to drink to float him to sleep, oatcakes to eat to keep him alive.

Long days went by, and still he wept. It's the way of things, Bob, I said less gently, Things die and we must adapt. You're lucky to still have Herga. Herga won't come to harm here in Norway, she's special. Sigrid is gone, but you still have Herga.

He looked at me as if I were the advocate for death, his eyes overflowing. Unmanly. He made me ashamed. It's the way of things, I told him sharply, Now eat your broth. I will help you take care of Herga. She's special. Nothing will harm Herga. Nothing will harm he here in Norway.

In time, he stopped crying and went back to his work. Foreign correspondent. Writing, writing all the time, articles for newspapers, magazines, for journals. He was paid more than anyone else I ever kn and he sat on his money like a dragon on a hoard. I didn't mind. What need did I have of money? I had Herga, and I had enough coins to buy herrings and pickles and salt and sourdough from the market; let him keep his money, let him write his words and keep his money.

He wrote in the kitchen, the only room warm enough for him. He had his space by the fire, the space usually reserved for invalids. His writing left him little time for interfering between me and Herga but, occasionally, he would get tired of typing and look up and notice things, and that's when it would all go wrong. Put more clothes on Herga, he would say, She'll catch her death of cold; or Take that dirty bread out of her hand, it'll give her stomach ache; or, once when I was making pies, Stop her playing with those bloody fish-guts, it's revolting, she'll catch God knows what. If I was tired, I would do as he said, but if I was more myself I would say, Don't you have more writing to do, Bob, Don't you have more words to write? And he would look at me with my grey plaits and my frown and he would think of Sigrid and his face would close down. Then he would turn back to his typewriter and throw himself into another torrent of words.

Bob was easy for me to handle. I thought he was easy to handle, with his writing and his useless, money-making articles. He had ambitions, he told me, ambitions to write a book. A history book, about Norway. I think it was a history. He wanted me to tell him what I knew. I told him I knew nothing. He smiled his false white smile, asked me to tell him the history of my family. I shook my head. Why not? he asked, Why not, mama? No use writing history, I said. It's all here. Tapping my head. And here. Touching my breast. And here. Pointing at Herga. No use writing it, no use at all.

But Bob could be persistent when he wanted to be, and he drip-drip-dripped his request on my head. So I gave in and told him about my mama and grandmama who had lived farther north, near Kvaløya, where one had to be sharp about blizzards and trolls. I told him they taught me how to appease weather-sprites by spilling oats on the doorstep, how to dispel bad luck with rhymes and salt. I told him my mama could smell a storm coming a day before it reached us, and that the northern lights spoke to her. Secrets. They told her who her husband would be, I said. Told her Rune on the whaling ship, and Rune it was. Told her other things, too, I said. Told her not to smother her children, I added cunningly.

Bob wrote down all I told him, reading it back to himself silently. Fascinating, he said, Folklore, yes, fairy tales: stories made up to explain things people didn't understand, to pretend mastery over their environment. He looked up at me with his lavender-water eyes, and a crevasse of misunderstanding stretched between us from north to south.

Herga I kept safe. While Bob wrote, Herga was out in the snow playing herself pink. I brought her in when I saw him pack up his typewriter or when the cold began to nip her cheeks yellow. Each day I'd leave her out a little longer, to get used to the snow, make friends with it. Sometimes she'd bang on the kitchen door with her little fat fist, Mama, mama, let me in, I'm cold. Bob never noticed so long as he was writing. One minute, little one, I'd whisper through the latch, one minute Herga. Let her grow cold, I'd think. Let her grow hard. Let her grow cunning. This time I would be strong.

We lived together like this for almost a year, Herga getting hardy and tough. She's not big enough, Bob complained, She's lacking nutrients. She's lacking nothing, I told him, She's small and sturdy like an alpine plant, that's the way to be in this land, that is how to survive in snow. I told him this, but Bob wasn't happy. He took Herga on the train all the way down to Trondheim to an expensive doctor who weighed her like a prime catch and measured her and gave her vitamins and injections and told Bob she was eating the wrong foods, she had the wrong diet. Bob came home from Trondheim with Herga and sat huddled over the fire all night, rubbing his red hands, not writing, watching me as closely as if he were a goatherd and I a hungry wolf come to snatch his kid away.

The next day, Bob said that when he was in Trondheim he'd spoken to the doctor about me. The doctor came from a local family – perhaps I knew of them? – and he wanted to come and visit, to see if he could be of help. Can he catch fish? I asked. Can he dig livestock out of snowdrifts and drag them home to be cut into joints for the winter? Can he weatherproof a roof? He's a doctor, mama, Bob said, pleadingly. Then I have no use for him, I replied. And Herga has no use for him.

Not long after, Bob told me he was leaving Norway. Going back to where it was hot and dusty and the towns had Spanish names of angels and devils. I didn't mind, didn't care. He could do as he pleased. What do you think? he asked, What do you think about that, mama?   I shrugged. Good decision probably, I said, You'll have new writing to do, I expect, lots of hot words. Good riddance, I thought, Snow doesn't like you. Norway can do without your writing, without the white of your smile.

Bob looked relieved. He let a small hush of air out through his mouth as if he had been holding it long in his chest, as if it had been trapped and feared it could never escape. You must come and visit us, he said. What? I asked. You must come and visit us. Us? Me and Herga. In America. You must come and visit, mama. It was then that ice replaced my blood, and winter came to stay. I saw that his cool cunning was too smart for mine. He had money. He had money to go all the way down to Trondheim and halfway round the world if he wished, for as long as he wanted. With Herga. Forever. You must visit us, he said, you must come for a visit. Visit that hot place, I replied. No. I am a creature of ice and snow. And I was.

He completed his plans quickly. Made his phone calls, booked his tickets, packed his bags. I sat on the wooden stool in the hot kitchen, sweating ice. Watching Herga play with an ice-cube on the floor, her full-moon face, her sleek, slippery skin, her funny little feet so like flippers. It was then that I saw the truth of mama's stories. The northern lights spoke to me, and I heard them. They told me what I must do to keep Herga safe.

I dressed Herga up warm in her red quilted coat, just as Bob liked. Put the woollen mittens on her chubby fingers, pushed her hair under the blue bobble hat, tied her scarf round the outside of her coat to keep the hood up. Herga laughed and swung her legs to and fro on the stool while I put her kamik on. We sang an alphabet song together; Herga singing it right, me getting the letters jumbled and the tune wrong. Then I took her out in the snow, strapped to my back like a pile of sticks. She didn't weigh much. Herga and I skied over the landscape of Norway which is like no other landscape in the world. A harsh place. A beautiful place. A place where history is not written in books.

We skied, Herga and I, and the weight of her on my back settled like snow. Her baby chatter, her plump fingers losing their gloves and reaching under my collar for the warmth of my neck. There, in the cold, in the snow, with the hush of centuries all around us. Herga was never a hot weather child, she would never get her tongue tied by Spanish. You belong to Norway, Herga, I said. You belong to me. And to Sigrid.

Herga giggled, rested her cheek on the back of my neck, sighed. All the little baby sounds. A trail of dribble dropped from her lower lip onto my spine, froze as it flowed down my back, a miniature glacier. I skied as I had not done for many a year, like a young woman, like a woman whose joints are oiled.

We reached the coast where the seals come in their season. The air was biting where the wind blew in. I took Herga gently down off my back, took off my ski to stumble over the shingle to where the waves suck and pluck at the shore. Cold as it was, I waded into the water to give her a good send-off, a good start. Herga was reluctant to leave, and that is always a good sign. Bye-bye baby Herga, I said, helping her to her first dive in the waves. She went to live with the seal people, for one must always adapt. And it is said that those with relatives among the seal people never go hungry for fish.

six poems

by jennifer hunt

written in chalk

Beneath this swaying field of flax,
blue spaces deep, a sea-bed swarms
with coiled creatures; tiny ammonites,
cochlea echoing with remembered surf,
snails curling round pebbles,
imprinted with the cicatrice
of fallen petals.

Below the keel of plough,
fossil fish spawn in salt-white sponge,
swim through ancient coral,
brittle as bone.

Close layers lie undisturbed –
memory, written in chalk.

When the moon brims over Knowle Hill
a tide still turns beneath the earth.

Moths move in shoals
through scented waves.

the path

As you grew older your scar stayed the same
curving over the back of your hand –
bright and new as a sickle moon.

jennifer hunt

Sometimes you'd draw back your sleeve,
trace with a finger tip its burnished line
lying like a silver hair over blue-roped veins,

and we would talk about the summer
when grass grew beyond the blade of mower;
how you got Grandpa's hook from the shed,

took it to the swathes of meadow grass.
How you stooped elbow-deep among the stems
of *sheep's fescue and brome*, pollen smoking,

as you scythed through the wild garden,
carving a path, pale and shining
as the one you made that day across your hand.

a feather falling

Your old sheepskin gloves are lying in the stable
this morning, holding the shape of your hands
curving upwards, cupped but empty.

Two years since you wore them, yet
still moulded inside like last summer's nest –
downy with past warmth. Abandoned now.

Slipping my fingers in, I touch familiar contours
inside out. Big knuckles, the thumb worn thin,
my hand small in yours, safe. I keep them on –

scoop corn, feed the hens, gather eggs,
stiff fingers unbending, curving round
brown smooth shells – a feather falling.

I take off your gloves –
a faint forgotten scent
clings to my hands and is gone.

fossil

There is rain in this fossil –
caged water,
seeded with quartz,
wishbones pressed flat
with the weight of millennia.

An egg of stone
sinking in my palm,
printed with a radial mark
as though a bird had walked
carelessly through blue clay
under a shining sky,

just once.

And left the lightness of its passing
heavy in my hand.

pebbles

She's drawing pebbles in the bathroom.
The light is cold and from the north,
washing round the calmness of stones
on the window sill – a space between tides.
Reflections, pale in coloured pencil
grow slowly in the stillness of white paper.

Grey shades the early morning,
sleepless veils of sand,
salt-water rawness,
the tick of a tap dripping,
slough of pencil point
like surf across the page.

Her phone switched off, she doesn't hear
his sound waves crashing, eroding the silence
she's made in the centre of each paper stone.

jennifer hunt

september

This evening
picking beans after a thunder shower
shed blossoms cling like drab insects
to my fingers.
Late sun, yellow as pumpkin flowers.

Now, with my colander,
by the open kitchen door,
the sun makes a square on the red lino.
Outside, white hens peck at shreds of light.

Soon bats will draw down the dark,
but I'll leave the door open,
breathe in the honeysuckle air
while moths circle the lampshade
dizzy from touching the moon.

the duchess

from a novel **by paula hutchings**

He traced the smooth curve of her cheek. His supple fingers played with her ermine collar. He could almost smell the warmth of her in the chestnut fur that circled about her neck. With long, elegant strokes he caressed the black satin gown hanging from her shoulders like ravens' wings. A faint blush remained smarting on the paleness of her skin. When he studied her hands, he sensed the nervousness in her fingertips as she twisted her wedding ring. But not once did she remove her eyes from his face.

He was so engrossed, he barely noticed the lady-in-waiting as she moved about the room with an easy grace, occasionally glancing at her mistress. He had forgotten Sir Philip Hoby, who sat in a high-backed chair in the corner of the room, trying to look relaxed in his own company. Even the aunt who paced back and forth, straining to look over his shoulder, did not disturb his concentration. She was the sole object of his gaze.

He had just three hours to capture her likeness. His task was both simple and complex. He was under instructions to produce a portrait of Christina, Duchess of Milan. For Henry the Eighth, King of England, had caught rumours of her beauty whispering like perfume through his court. Not a moment was to be lost. The King's bed had been cold for too long. Without a moment's reflection the King's artist, Holbein, and his special envoy, Sir Philip Hoby, were dispatched to Brussels in search of a fourth wife.

paula hutchings

A fine cloud of chalk hung above his easel, dust motes dancing in the stream of sun that poured through the windows of the grand chamber. His portrait would determine her fate. If Henry was pleased with it, there was little doubt that he would make a proposal of marriage. She was niece to Charles V, the most powerful man in Europe and would receive a handsome dowry. She was also young, just sixteen years of age. And Henry was an impatient man.

His reputation was the gossip of all the courts in Europe. He had already divorced an aging wife, married his mistress, beheaded her and then married her lady-in-waiting. Holbein wondered what fate would befall the Duchess at his hands.

It took some time for him to notice her smile. She was biting her lip, and two dimples squeezed her fleshy cheeks. He preferred his subjects not to smile. Such was the nature of the Court, a smile could stand in the way of the truth. It could deceive. Holbein did not like any emotion to intrude on his portraits, any sense that the sitter was imposing her personality on the viewer.

He must have looked at the Duchess a little harshly, but still she continued to smile. She was amused. He stopped drawing for a moment and stood back from his sketch. On this occasion, if he did not paint her smile he would not reflect her true nature. And so he began to draw the outline of her upturned lips. As he sketched, he could not help but smile himself, unusual since he did not often allow himself to experience delight.

Perhaps his smile aroused some suspicion, for her aunt, the Regent Maria of Hungary, asked, "Are you going to paint the Duchess, in such a direct way? Might an averted glance better capture her modesty?"

"His Majesty the King has given very specific instructions," Holbein stuttered and immediately felt a sense of shame at his complicity.

"I am sure that he has," said the aunt, her thin lips unsmiling.

"Indeed," added Sir Philip Hoby, who had risen from his chair to stretch his legs and look at the portrait. "He asked for the likeness to be as explicit as possible." He coughed. "Understandable, as I am sure you can appreciate, given he could not view the Duchess for himself."

Holbein winced at Sir Philip's lack of diplomacy. It was not the first time he had witnessed such arrogance in this Englishman. He watched as the aunt's anger rose and shook her bird-like frame until finally she spat out the words, "We do not make a habit of parading our daughters around like horses in a sale. You are lucky to be allowed to paint the Duchess at all."

Her words silenced Sir Philip who looked down at his feet. He was a tall man who took too much confidence from his height. The length of his limbs always exaggerated his mannerisms and confirmed many foreign envoys' views of the English.

The Duchess smiled again but too quickly for anyone else to see. Holbein bit his tongue and continued to sketch. She continued to look deeply into his eyes and he found himself blushing. He fumbled inside the wooden box containing his chalks. Although he had sketched many beautiful women in his life, he had never been affected like this. Up until now, sketching a woman had always led to a sense of disappointment. When he had painted his wife, he realised with each brush stroke, that he did not love her. And in painting his mistress he came to understand that he was in love with the idea of her and not the woman herself.

Sir Philip was tugging at his sleeve, rousing him from his reflections. Holbein had not noticed him standing behind him, examining the portrait. Sir Philip's words carried in the grand chamber, "Try not to make her face appear so brown. It implies she has been too much out of doors."

Holbein bristled. He was not the only person to have heard these words.

The aunt stood within three feet of Sir Philip and despite her diminutive stature, seemed twice his size, as she hissed, "How dare you talk that way about the Duchess of Milan? What do you Englishmen know about gentleness?"

There was an awkward silence. Sir Philip trembled and coughed as he took out a handkerchief to wipe the corners of his mouth. Holbein laid down his chalks.

For the first time that afternoon, the Duchess spoke. "I am feeling fatigued and I am quite sure Master Holbein is finding it difficult to concentrate on his work. Perhaps it would be easier if everyone retired to the other room, whilst he finishes what he has been sent to do."

The aunt glared at the Duchess.

"Sophia can attend on me," Christina said, looking at her aunt in such a gentle way that she soon led Sir Philip from the room with a promise of refreshments.

The Duchess waited until the door closed. Then, much to Holbein's surprise, she began to giggle. Her laughter seemed to begin in her toes, gathering in strength as she let her whole body succumb to it. She rolled her head back, delighting in her mirth. One could not help but be affected by it. Holbein experienced a lightness of heart he had not allowed himself to feel since he was a child. Her maid Sophia also laughed. He noticed the fondness they shared in the way that the Duchess touched her maid on her cheek. Taken aback by such familiarity, he was also moved by it.

"Is this not fine entertainment indeed, Sophia?" The Duchess clasped her maid's hand, her shoulders still twitching as giggles continued to bubble to the surface.

Holbein heard his own quiet laughter but, remembering the nature of his task, soon felt it die in his chest. Noticing the anxious expression on his face, the Duchess made an effort to regain her composure. She let go of Sophia's hand, stretched her arms above her head and walked around the room. As she looked out of the window at the gardens below, the sunlight caught a strand of auburn hair that had escaped her black cap. She stood for some time, her eyes closed and her chin raised, enjoying the warmth of the spring sun on her face.

Holbein became aware that Sophia was looking at him and smiling as she regarded him watching her mistress. In spite of himself, his admiration for the Duchess was blazing on his face. He looked down quickly and began rearranging his chalks shade by shade.

The Duchess turned back towards him and mistook his actions as a sign that he was impatient to continue with his work. She walked back to her position in front of his easel, "Now, let us continue with this, shall we not? But only on the condition, Master Holbein, that you allow me to ask questions while you sketch."

He nodded simply and started to draw her face.

"I envy you your art, Sir. It must be the finest thing to be able to draw so well."

He smiled a little. It was a torture too. Sometimes it was easier not to examine things too closely. For often, when he held things up to the light, he saw not their beauty, but their imperfections.

But as he observed the Duchess speaking, he noticed the way her lips seemed to kiss the words that came from her mouth. She caught his gaze and looked down. "I am recently bereaved," she said quietly.

He stopped drawing for a moment. Her whole face had changed from light to shadow. There was such tenderness in the way she described her loss. She found it easy to describe her feelings and seemed at once both older and younger than himself. He wanted to touch her face and erase the sadness that had settled there.

"The Duke was a kind man. My match made a good alliance with Spain. I was thirteen when we married. He was like a father to me."

He recalled the jokes that had been made at the English court. How her liveliness of spirit had led to her husband's early grave. He too had joined in the laughter. Now he had met her, he felt nothing but shame.

She remained silent for a while and then added, "When he died, I had to prise his fingers from my hand."

He was surprised how much she was telling him. She had a soft voice but it was not weak. Her confidential tone drew him in and made him listen closely to her words. Often he looked for the truth in the way people said things rather than in the words they spoke. Spending too long in the time of courtiers, he had grown to mistrust words. Dishonesty was an art the English took a delight in perfecting. It had left him cynical and detached from a language that was not his own.

"What is your opinion, Sir, of King Henry?"

The directness of her question caught him off guard. What should he say to her? That he is a tyrant, but despite his power, in need of love. Should he tell her that he finds him charming but childish? That as he grows in size so he does in lust.

He was not used to being asked for his opinion. Instead, he contented himself with seeking to represent the truth in his portraits.

He found a certain solace in it. Remembering the drawings he had completed for Henry's portrait, he offered her his sketchbook.

She turned the pages slowly. In silence, she pored over his sketches. He began to wish he had chosen better examples of his work. After a while, she looked up from the pages with a faint look of fear and murmured quietly, as if to herself, "Alas, he is more ugly than I could have imagined, both in appearance and in character."

Holbein remained silent. Even this was evidence of treason. His dearest friend Sir Thomas More had been executed for it.

"Thank you for letting me see these," she said, handing him back his sketchbook. "My mother was shown a picture of my father before she consented to marry him. She said she could tell he would always love her but would never be faithful." She paused and added, "Here I see a man who will never love me or be faithful." Her voice became a whisper. "Still, 'tis as my uncle wishes."

The sky had turned pink and the colours in the room grew warm as they stretched out in the afternoon sunshine. It was then he was struck by her height; she was remarkably tall for a woman. Her figure cast a long shadow on the green velvet drape behind her. She seemed to him an angel stepping out of the darkness moving towards an unknown fate with a determined air.

Feigning a serious expression, she said, "There is only one thing for it, Master Holbein. You must make me very ugly indeed. Accentuate all my imperfections. On this occasion, I will not object."

He smiled at her playfulness but felt anxious. If only it were that simple. A Dutch artist had recently painted her portrait to present to King Henry but it did not capture her true beauty. The ambassador grew concerned that it did not, in fact, capture the Duchess's beauty and sent a group of horsemen to retrieve the portrait before it reached the port. The politicians were as much in favour of this alliance as Henry himself.

The Duchess sighed and turned to her maid, "Sophia, I think Master Holbein is ignoring me. He hopes that by not answering me I will fall silent and let him finish his sketch."

Sophia looked at him and smiled.

"Yet alas, I fear you will flatter me, Sir. Is that not so?"

He raised his head but could not meet her eyes. She worried that her playfulness had hurt him and added quickly, "But I am lucky to be drawn by such a fine artist."

The blood rose again in his cheeks. He added the final lines to his sketch from memory, not looking up at her lest she should see the feeling in his face.

Moments later the door swung open. Her aunt entered the room followed swiftly by Sir Philip.

"I hope you have completed your task."

She looked at the completed drawing and smiled. "You have captured my niece's beauty very well and I am sure the King will be keen to make a match."

"Has he painted me with two necks?" the Duchess asked.

"Two necks, what do you mean, my child?" her aunt enquired, surprised.

"Well, if I had two necks, the King is bound to have one of them," she said laughing.

Her aunt gave her an angry glance.

Sir Philip, compelled to defend his monarch against attack added, "The King is kind to those that love him well."

"The Duchess will make a loyal and loving companion for the King," her aunt said, making her way to the door. She made a point of not offering Sir Philip her hand. He bowed slightly and followed her from the room, his shoulders hunched.

The Duchess seemed to hang back. She quickly glanced at the sketch, then, touching Holbein lightly on the shoulder whispered, "Do what you will, Master Holbein. But I am relying on you to be my friend."

She smiled again, a little sadly this time. He could sense she was trying to conceal her fear by the way her hands shook. Before he had a chance to reply, she had left the room.

Back in the privacy of her chamber, the Duchess removed her cap and sat in front of a mirror as Sophia loosened her hair. She found a comfort in the rhythm of the brush as it gently tugged at her scalp. It reminded her of how her mother brushed her hair as a child. She wished she was with her now.

"You seemed tired, my Lady."

She noticed Sophia's concerned expression reflected in the mirror.

"I confess, I am anxious. To leave my home and to live with a man such as he... "

The Duchess noticed her maid's hands shaking as she put the brush into her lap and started to pull out the auburn strands of hair. Would she be allowed to take Sophia with her to England? She would be alone and in a foreign land. And with a man who had already treated her aunt, Catherine of Aragon, so treacherously.

She stared at her reflection, searching for outward signs of her own fear. Her anxieties receded a little as she recalled the way Holbein had looked at her. She tried to see herself through a stranger's eyes and wondered whether he had found her countenance pleasing. Remembering the steady intensity of his gaze, she felt a desire for him she could not explain, even though he was older in years than herself. Yet she doubted he would be able to help her.

Crawling into her bed, she found the heaviness of the furs comforted her. Snuffing out the candles, she watched the smoke's spiral dance in the moonlight that shone through the curtains. She fell asleep thinking of him, remembering how his hands shook when he gave her his drawings. And how she made him smile, this man who seemed to smile so little.

three poems

by elizabeth kay

metrophobia

A fear of poetry runs deep within
the class. The students blanch at words like ode;
trip over feet, feel sure they'll never win;
whatever is a bloody antipode?
It's like an exercise in writing code.
Sestinas come and go, the weeks progress;
the metre's inching forward, stress is less
pronounced. Some hone and polish, some refrain;
some learn the rules, apply them – others guess,
go blank, get tanka-ed up, and try again.

inside the powder

Room, at last. You're in, through the wedged-
open door, gritting your teeth, minding the pees
and queues. And then, suddenly, they don't matter –
not any more. It's one of those Ladies' moments.

The snake of people inside is as out of order
as the plumbing, curled in on itself like intestines.
You start by talking floor area, cubicles, urinals,
male architects. You could be any vintage,
from geezer bird to hot flush to blue rinse.

As you wait, the temperature rises. Now
you're privy to period pains, polyps, Prozac,
uncooperative partners, ungrateful progeny,
quashed ambitions, quick abortions, quiet affairs –
but no hot air, no soft soap, no flannel –

you're dishing out your own dirt, relieving yourselves
of skeletons you won't be revealing outside.

The teenager with the tattoo is in the club,
and the cleaner has a closet lover – Scotch
as the tight blue stocking, also part of the outfit
with her seamless stories and her piquant quips.
"Could we call this a wee problem?" she queries.
You laugh, wince, and cross your fingers.
There's a sweet and sour ache in your abdomen
that flips open the floodgates of confession.
The pensioner with the pale porcelain skin
takes a shine to the chippie China doll, (no flies on her)
whose hair smells of fish-fat and jasmine shampoo.
Both are waste products of queasy love affairs,
men who quit. Engaged: then unexpectedly vacant.

The facing mirrors cry with exhaled breaths,
and the repeating fractals of female forms
get even smaller, parodying your past.
You will never meet these women again –
but Here, Now, on one thing you're all agreed:
the world is designed for a man's convenience.

mmm

The machine-gun melody of magpies makes mincemeat of
    Monday morning.
Middle-men, morose with miserable marriages, manacled
    by management,
March to the main road, masticating morsels of muesli with
    mealy mouths.
Minds – muddled with mountains, molehills and
    money-money-money – mutiny,
Meditating on missed métiers... Manchester United,
    Millwall, Motherwell...
Make me Maradona, they muse, mean, moody, magnificent; master
    of the match-o.

Melt my middle-aged spread, muscle my midriff, mask my
    moulting masculinity.
Mellow my menopausal missus – or magic me a mistress –
    mahogany skin,
Midnight hair, a Messalina model – no morals or modesty. Make
    me matter more.
Modify my mediocrity, muffle my melancholy. Mend this
    malaise; motivate me.
Manufacture me matches for the merely mundane to make a
    meaningful M-pyre.

sisters

from a novel **by cassandra keen**

*Miriam and Anna, non-lesbian-scene, live together in Islington. They are
intellectually suited, but sex has petered out. Miriam offers to accompany
their married neighbour, Bethan, on a drive to Nice.*

MIRIAM
We had intended to stop in Auxerre.

She had the name of a hotel where *they* had stayed. The first time
that she mentioned him. He had delayed our departure from London
by four days. We had timed it to fit in with his arrival. Held up, he said,
in Rabat.

"Miriam," Bethan asked me, when we got back to the car after our
first lunch in France, "how many kilometres is it from Auxerre to Lyon?
Perhaps we'll stay there, look round... There's the textile museum. Lyon
was the Centre – "

"Well," I said, measuring the distance with my index finger. "It's a
good few inches, given the perambulations," looking slyly at her austere
profile, as I checked with the scale at the top of the page.

"In the front of the map, Miriam, there's a matrix giving the
Distances," she'd sighed and smiled at the same time, looking a little
tired, whereas Anna would have got into a rage. Then I don't tease Anna,
with her twisted, ragged humour. And I wasn't much practical help to
Bethan on the way down. With her, I found that I tended to lose my

concentration. And so what if we got a little lost? That is when travel becomes an adventure.

"Oh, let's Get On!" she said, "We can do it," her vowels flattening, in the *Manchester way*. As they do when she gets upset. Still in the low mood that had possessed her at lunchtime.

When she ordered for both of us.

I found that I didn't like Bethan when she spoke in French. Her face went this way and that and became very intense, the words unnaturally high and hard-edged. She sounded like Anna, all Americans, when they try to reach the top notes, *most* of the impossibly high notes, of 'The Star-Spangled Banner'.

Still, it got better. Once we settled comfortably into our drive through surprisingly large tracts of unspoiled countryside, and she asked me to tell her about Africa. What I like about Bethan is that she is interested, and *so responsive*. It was then that she began to look out for a hotel, instead of driving us lemming-like to Nice, and into the sea, as I had at first feared. Stopped to check with her *Relais and Chateaux Guide.*

That book didn't lie. What it wrote about 'traditional decor' and 'local food specialities' was more or less right. But there wasn't *enough* of the truth. The guide *wasn't honest.*

"I can't stay Here!" she announced as we drove into the hotel forecourt, somewhere south of Lyon.

It was one of those modern Meccano buildings – such is my frame of reference – that trim the French suburbs, next to a garden centre called Jardiland.

"Well, *I can,* Bethan," I told her, and got out of the car. "It is eight o'clock and at least there's a restaurant, or so they said in that guide."

She followed me meekly into the hotel and asked for two separate rooms. "Durr," she repeated for emphasis, or that is how it sounded, pointing first at herself and then at me. We were given our two keys and shown to the lift.

"Oh, I don't know," she hesitated, "I usually take the stairs... Claustrophobia!"

"Those rooms of ours are on the Sixth Floor."

"It's like a great big Womb!" she recoiled, when the cage finally arrived, padded out in dark red velvet. "What, Miriam," she asks me, "if we can't get out!"

Well! Even with Bethan in her current mood...

Her room too was "Horrible!"

"Lily-of-the-Valley... Wild roses... " She identified the specimens on the wallpaper. "Fine," she complained, "but do they have to paper the door panels, the cupboard, the Skirting Board... "

Borrowed style?

"Compensating for the outside?" I suggested.

"And the bathroom, even the ceiling... rows and rows of cameos!"

She had a point.

"It will give me a Headache," she said, "And it's so hot in here!" fiddling with the air-conditioning controls.

"We can swap... " I offered, but she showed no interest in my room which, going by the numbers, was just round the corner.

"It won't make any difference," she said. "This place is into overdrive. At least the food should be good. It's got a Michelin star. It is all too easy nowadays to get a really bad meal in France."

The dinner was excellent.

Bethan got them to skin, top-and-tail her sea bass, remove all the bones, so that it was neutralised – could have been flakes of the Lyonnaise potato they served up with my steak.

"Why, Bethan," I asked her, "can't it look like a fish?"

"Oh, I quite agree," she said, sounding *got at*, "that a fish can be very pretty, with the pearly skin, but on my plate I prefer to have only the part of it I shall want to eat... I don't need the whole thing. To be reminded of the way that I came by it – the Hooks, the Thwack, the entire Fish Works – gutting, trimming, and the glue... "

She looked as if she might not eat it at all.

"It might be enlightening," she nagged like a discontented wife, and I had the sudden and unsettling notion that she was talking to someone else. "Like visiting an abattoir," she elaborated, "but that doesn't make me feel good about any of it. Do you always eat Raw meat?"

I had insisted on ordering it myself, in English. Helped the girl with her pronunciation, as she repeated the words after me. She had enjoyed that.

"Medium-rare steak? Well, yes, sometimes. Does it bother you?"

"It's just that it smells different… from the fish. It seems odd to eat one thing and have to smell something else, so strong you can hardly taste what's on your own plate. Smell is part of – "

"Have you tried being a vegetarian, even a vegan?"

"Myopic!" Again she addressed her invisible critic. Someone in the far distance, that could have been Nice or even North Africa. Continuing with a subject I wished I had never raised in the first place. "That's what Jonathan calls me," she says, adding, "and he turns that round into my being an Inadequate person. A wife he must find excuses for."

Well…

"I know, Miriam," she said, coming back to me – cutting off a small piece of her brie and putting it absently to my mouth. Hand-feeding me like a bird. Feeding the feelings inside me. "We did rush this first day. Why don't we look round Lyon tomorrow, then take a small Detour over the Alps, via Grenoble?" And she refilled our glasses with the last of the wine.

"Jonathan won't be in Nice until late Friday night. We could aim to be there first thing on Saturday."

Well! Four days to get to the coast, when we had planned only on three, to suit *his* arrival.

Alone in my room, I poured myself a two-finger measure of the Bells I bought at Nicolas. Whisky is cheaper in France because of that hijack they call a duty back in the UK.

Two fingers, exactly, no more and no less. Although that number has no special significance for me. And I thought again about the pair of almost identical photographs on Beth's glass parlour table, without coming to any particular conclusion. Two of my fingers, and they are small – one inch precisely both together – were a useful measure, that's all.

It was what I allowed myself every night. Anna drinks enough for both of us, and I rarely take wine, although I shared a bottle with Beth over dinner.

It had probably gone to her head. Led her to talk of the 'Detour'.

It was unseasonably warm, not even April. I turned off the light and went out on to my small balcony. So small that I was obliged to sit sideways. That way I found myself almost facing Bethan's brightly lit window, only a little off to the left – the curtains still pulled back. I needed to think about that detour.

Bethan is very naïve. "What things had I tired of doing with Anna?" she asked me in the car. Anna and I are non-lesbian-scene. There is no set-up in our lives for her to pick up on. And *she* is straight. *Married* to Jonathan.

She came into full view. Stood in front of the air-conditioning controls she had tried to adjust before dinner. Looked at them quizzically, moving her head from side to side like a dog asking to be taken for a walk. She was holding a small shiny object that caught the light, could have been one of the knives from our dining table.

And she fiddled with the front of the control box... using her improvised screwdriver? Moved her position just a fraction. Hands raised, then lowered.

And she *dismantled the air-conditioning cover.*

I do know a little about these things because of my conversion work on the houses. So I was able to elaborate – on what I couldn't make out exactly – as she pulled at a small spaghetti of wires. Any one of these might have become disconnected. Her hands performed a light stripping movement, as if she was taking off some of the insulation. Not even changing her gadget. A Swiss Army knife, surely, complete with the tiny pair of scissors.

She needed to put that wire back into one of the sockets.

I held my breath, waited for her rectangular stage to be plunged into blackness... Cold tea for breakfast, as it had been in Calais and thereafter. Hot water apparently beyond the capability of the French, even in the best of circumstances...

Or it could be worse, *much* worse!

I went cold all over. It's too late now, Miriam, I said, forgetting to breathe altogether... As she reversed the process with the cover.

Turned on the controls...

When I opened my eyes, I saw Bethan in the golden gate of her window, holding her skirt up to the breeze of the air-conditioning fan. The wide skirt. Long straight legs. She usually kept them covered up.

"The best things are hidden, Miriam," she had said to me, almost three months ago, when we met on the front steps outside the house that was opposite ours.

Now she danced around the tiny room, moving in and out of my field of vision, with the same ease and grace that she had displayed when she disassembled and reassembled the air-conditioning control box.

I have always been drawn to the womanly woman. Anna could have gone either way. And now I am non-scene entirely.

"Miriam," I have often told myself, "it is natural, as a lover of other women, to want the *feminine* woman, the *real* thing, not one of those girl-boys... And you don't have to *act* on your feelings!"

So I hug them close to me, warm and safe as a secret.

BETHAN

If only Miriam and I had been allowed the four, even three, days to spend as we pleased on the drive to Nice. It would surely take us so long if we were to be Permitted to enjoy ourselves on the way. Not have to fit in with someone else's scheme of things. A man's needs. Miriam, I have found, can be so considerate. Has an instinct to please.

I eased the wide teeth of the tortoiseshell comb over my head, downwards from the nape of my neck to the tips of my hair, intent on straightening out the crinkles in the heat of the dryer. As, with Megan's help, I once used to iron my fringe.

A light tap on the door I hadn't troubled to lock. A small charge of energy as Miriam came into the room. My hair crackled through the comb, a red/yellow-green static against the blue strings of sky, as I lifted my head. As the grass, on the way down here – shot with red, even blue, had acquired a lavender haze.

"The drive over the Alps," I began, feeling really bad, knowing that the detour had become very Important to Miriam, "will take us too long."

She looked at me with all of her eyes. The widening pupil, lost iris...

"You dance very well, Bethan," she said, and I looked at her blankly, followed her eyes to the balcony that hung from one of the rooms. At a right angle to my own room, it looked straight on to my window.

"The best things *are* hidden," she smiled at me, "but not *all* the time."

"It was late," I said, "I didn't think – " that she would have been watching me. In the dark. Her light switched off. Predatory.

And I thought. Oh, my God. She. Fancies. Me!

Tried to push the idea away. Afraid that Miriam would be able to read what was going on in my head. So that the thought would be put into words. Have a shape. Become real. Acknowledged. Everything I did after that, coloured by what I knew about Miriam. Entertaining Temptation.

Hers!

"Jonathan arrived in Nice late last night," I told her, building a wall between the words and the ideas that were running amok. "I spoke to him this morning."

"Why won't you remember your mobile, Bethan?" he had complained. "I have been trying to reach you."

Wasn't alarmed. About Miriam exactly. Grew up with a Girl. Felt just a bit Not Quite Myself.

Now she will think that I have changed my mind. Don't want to go with her on the Detour.

"Three days before he said he would be there," disdain crept into Miriam's quiet voice. "That wouldn't have been deliberate, by any chance? We could have left London earlier, if it hadn't been for *him.*"

I hadn't wanted to arrive at the house of strangers ahead of

Jonathan... Had planned the drive to be there shortly after him. He hadn't been happy about my travelling with Miriam.

"Why is she muscling in on our holiday?" he had asked me again this morning.

Miriam wouldn't be intruding on anything if Jonathan had arrived in Nice when he said he would. Then I can't expect him to like all my girlfriends.

"It was never certain, Miriam, when he would arrive – exactly. He doesn't always know – "

"And now you – *and I* – are expected to fit in with him – " Her mouth curled with disbelief. It said that no one tells Miriam what to do.

"It was flexible. I had arranged to phone him in Nice, leave a message – " Sometimes it was difficult to get a connection on Johnny's mobile, in the out-of-the-way places he goes to.

" – change our plans, for the sake of *three days!*"

"It was always possible... It is his holiday as well... You and I only arranged – "

"And now?"

"We can go via Avignon. The centre is interesting. Narrow streets, small squares... The ancient papal palace. Some power split – "

Miriam raised a brow.

"Then there's Aix..."

"You are invited to dinner this evening."

MIRIAM

"We are going to end up in Italy!" I warned Bethan, who'd had the benefit of Jonathan's instructions on how to get to the villa.

She didn't want to change our arrangement. I knew that. I had already sensed that she was afraid of him. Wary, at least, of his *pent-up-ness*. It is the potential violence in men that makes women careful of them, so they attempt to mollify, dance attendance...

When it was perfectly clear to me that *she should leave him.*

She slowed down, pulled up by a featureless pink stucco wall with an unprepossessing peeling blue door. As high maintenance a door as any of the ones in our square. All at once I felt as if I had come full circle with Bethan. The windows too were shuttered against us. Only one opened out, the skeletal shadow of the frame etched into the wood by a bleaching sun. The whole lot washed up high against the coastal road.

"I expect the house faces the other way," she said, "out to sea," her Manchester vowels collapsing again. Pissed-off, no doubt, with the whole long morning drive that *fell into* the afternoon. The last part of our journey spent on the payage.

Even our *hurry-through* of a day had been pleasant enough, until she became anxious about the time. "Jonathan already there – "

"Well, he can curb his impatience for a few hours, can't he," I said, thinking about her left alone in that house week after week.

When we got to the coast, she turned herself off like a switch.

I laughed at her... *fondly*, as we looked at the backside of the house. "The best things are hidden," I said slyly, and watched the colour rise in her cheeks.

No one could see the face of this house, so determinedly in purdah, unless out at sea – an Olympic swimmer, or in a boat.

"I think it's been divided into flats," she told me.

"So, the outside doesn't matter?"

"This is the Coast, Miriam, the villa is in a Unique position." She lectured me like an estate agent and got out of the car.

It was almost impossible for me to move from my seat, on the passenger side, next to the road that appeared to have been used as a racetrack.

The truth is that I am frightened of feeling like this again. Being taken over. My life not my own. Someone else in control. Once I realised this was happening to me with Bethan – last night, and again when I woke up this morning – I felt the old hopeless wave of despair. As if I were being dragged in by a relentless undertow... only to be pounded back onto the rocks. *Driven* this way and that by the force of someone else's feelings. A straight woman's fads and fancies that can be so skittish. Insecurity will lead her to ask, like all the rest, "Do *you* love me?" Not say, "*I love*

cassandra keen

you... " So that, once again, I am obliged to be reactive. Give more and yet more, knowing that I no longer have any choice.

firefighter

a short story **by simon kerr**
for ambrose bierce

Extinction happened quickly.

I opened my eyes – I was in a clearing, in a forest, amongst burned-black tree-skeletons. I held up my hands. They were flesh. I looked down at my arms, my chest, my belly, my cock and balls, my legs, my feet. All flesh, pink fresh flesh. It couldn't have happened. It should not have. I should have been charred, scarred, dead, in the building. I held up my hands once more to check; I was no longer burning.

Milwaukee was where it all started – at a factory-fire call-out. They tried to stop it, my buddies, but water would not put me out. They fired the hose-jet right at me. It knocked me off my feet, way back nearly into darkness, but the fire re-ignited soon after the water was directed away. My two best buddies, Mark and Al, were engulfed as they tried to rescue and resuscitate me. I felt real bad as loyalty burned but I knew I – a firefighter with six years of service – could not stop the flames. I had made a pact with a higher power. I was not one of their own anymore. So I ran away, west along the boulevard as the crew tended their wounded. Cars swerved to avoid me. I heard their drivers screaming. One man got out of his car and tried to wrestle me to the ground, to roll me. My fellow American caught fire like my mirror-image, a human torch, and burned as he hugged me, to death.

An ambulance and a patrol car caught up with me on the Highway heading to the suburb of Waukesha. The cops jumped out and told me to stop, so I did. They tried using their car-fire-extinguishers to put me out. I fell against their car in the mist of retardants, and the heat of me, the sheer heat of me, must have set the petrol tank off. The explosion scattered singed bits of the cops and paramedics, ambulance and car – across the asphalt. But, when I got blown up, I flared bigger and brighter for an instant – an instant in which I glimpsed the global potential of my life. It was a glorious nightmare. This is what the man in white with the sun-glow eyes inside the burning building had showed me would happen. The man I met in the middle of the industrial inferno where I was cut off from my buddies by falling steel and concrete. He prophesied to me that the roof was going to cave in and kill me if I didn't do what he said. So I did what he said. Accepted his terms. I stretched my hand out to touch him. And he set my body alight.

It started to rain and it continued to for the rest of that first day but I was so hot I melted my footprints into the tar on the roads I travelled. They must have tracked me by them for it was not long before I had a horde of followers behind me on the Interstate. The cops. My ex-fellow firefighters. But that night I got away when we hit the open plains. I walked out into the fields. The wind got up. Beneath my feet the prairies caught fire, and flames and dust and smoke hampered my pursuers. Fire and wind. Wind and Fire. Roaring on the earth. I did not mean it to happen that way. I did not know what I was doing. I just knew that I was hungry.

Over the next week, TV network choppers were the only things that could keep up with me as I scorched a path across three states heading for the great wilderness of the Rockies. As I burned people, animals, woods, crop fields, buildings, bridges, they asked me questions through loud-hailers. Whirling up there were police and media people and religious channels and famous astrologers from daytime shows. Are you all right? Why are you doing this? Will you please stop? Stop or we'll shoot! Are you the new Messiah? Are you Christ returned? Are you a destroying angel? Is this the end? Are you a Fire Sign, are you

Aries? In trying to answer I spoke tongues of fire at them and their machines dropped to the ground. Yea, verily, I seared out the eyes of God's Own Country.

When no one was left to watch I entered Farquhar, the once-steel-town, now a town of rotten wood, where my Mom lived and Pops was buried. She didn't recognise me. She shut the door in my face. I blew it open and embraced her anyway, inhaling – being invigorated by – her maternal love. I dug my father up to kiss him one more time, blessed him and cremated his corpse. It too fuelled my trail westward.

The man in white with the sun-glow eyes said that fire was his power, and because he knew that I respected his power, he would make it mine. He told me that these were the End Times. The End Times. He told me to forget myself, become other. He whispered to me the secret of incendiary and then my spirit burst into flames.

The National Guard must have been called out to stop my progress. The military met me on a field in Montana. They ordered me to stop or they would open fire. I could not stop. I tried to tell them that I was fire, with the wind at my back, but instead I showed them – with a giant fireball. Soldiers, guns, tanks, jeeps, and jet fighters high in the sky, melted or exploded. Thus I met and consumed the might of the country...

Then I was elemental in the forests. Free in the mountains. Amongst burning trees, the pillars of my new temple dedicated to the power of me. With the incense of godhood in my nostrils, I looked back down on the black plains and around at the smoking slopes. Everything in sight was either fired or ablaze. But, my appetite was as strong as ever. Where would it end? I asked myself. When everything is gone – heaped on the pyre, I myself answered. And I was suddenly, massively sad. I wept tears, beads of fire, onto the spoiled earth, and stood in the ferocity of my own sorrow.

I was world-weary of being Fire. I told this to the man in white with the sun-glow eyes, in the building, in my memory. He said I had lost faith. I didn't answer. I just lay down in my clearing, my forest of ashes and embers. I held up my hands to pray. They were a black and charred arch. I looked down at my chest. My uniform was melted and blood soaked, under the crushing weight of the roof of the building. I closed my eyes. I was a firefighter once more and I was glad.

Extinction happened quickly. With fire sighing in my ears, I burned out, was spent.

baber's apple

from a novel **by mike martin**

Baber Mittough (which rhymes with 'sabre ditto') lives with his grandmother, Nan, and tends to adopt an appropriate accent when people misspell his name. His imaginary sibling, Beulah, tells the story of the apples from Baber's rather special tree.

Dolores drives with an enthusiasm that belies her sylph-like build. She likes to be close up behind the car in front at all times. Baber worries that her eyesight may be faulty. Going through the experience of incipient blindness with Nan has awoken his senses to this possibility. Snakethin Stephen sits in the back, as sullen as he seems to have grown lately. He says nothing, which at least means the car is a spittle-free zone.

Dolores sprints from temporary traffic light to temporary traffic light. It is as though she hopes to find at each contraflow the single file empty of vehicles travelling in the opposite direction. Baber has given up trying to understand the meanings of the signals. He remembers a time when red meant stop and green meant go, but this is no longer what drivers seem to do.

Dolores is running another gauntlet of somnolent diggers and overturned cones when a lorry appears from behind a mountain of helpless tarmac, travelling towards us. The cab is clean, and boldly painted with strong primary colours – perhaps all of them – and adorned with shiny horns. Suddenly these horns blare and the headlights flash brightly and Baber can see the driver of the lorry grin over his straggly ginger beard and his eyes light up against the background of his Confederate flag. Now he is leaning out of the window and shouting, "Get out of the way, you coon bastard – these roads is for white folks."

Dolores says philosophically, "White beemers are like red rags to bulls with these rednecks," as she yanks on the steering wheel. The car tumbles onto the unmade surface, knocking over more cones and scraping something underneath as it drops down the ledge between the roadworthy and road-unworthy.

She turns up the volume of her CD player, so that the pounding bass sets the dashboard vibrating. Perhaps she wants to drown out the noise of insults. The CD jumps as we bounce back onto the proper road surface. The bass notes trill like a ship's siren.

A mile up the road Dolores takes a hint from a yellow sign announcing 'The Country Apple Fayre' and turns left. We join the back of a queue of cars and spend an hour in an intermittent meander through country lanes overhung with unkempt hedges.

At last we reach a field crowded with cars and minibuses. A phalanx of white vans is parked in the corner of the field farthest from the gate. Beyond an impressively long stone wall, handkerchiefs of white canvas appear against a harsh background of black green trees and cloudless blue sky.

Dolores says, as she locks her car door, "Check you've got your apples."

Baber points to his pockets with their apple-shaped bulges.

The entrance to the apple fair is through an arched gateway in the wall. An officious woman compressed into a dull green tweed suit is taking a £10 note from everybody in return for the stamp of a purple triangle on the backs of their right hands.

Nothing much shows on the back of Dolores' hand.

"Oh, dear!" the tweedy woman says, when she witnesses the ineffectiveness of the stamp. She turns to some unseen assistance and asks, "Do we have another colour, Jeannie? White, perhaps?"

There is no helpful comeback.

The woman peers at Dolores and says, "No worries then. I'm sure I'll recognise you again," though she doesn't sound optimistic.

Stephen's purple triangle is a publishing success. As she stuffs his £10 note into her satchel, the woman says, "That'll keep the babies in feed for another week."

Stephen says, by way of a snappy riposte, "Fuck off." He wanders away.

"Charming, I'm sure," says the tweedy woman, but she is already giving her full attention to the be-Wellingtoned family of six behind us.

I say to Baber, "Do you think they're expecting rain?"

Baber says, "No, Beulah, I don't think so. They've not got an umbrella between them."

In a sunny corner of a large expanse of stone-slabbed courtyard, a crowd jostles around a barrage of trestle tables. Everybody seems eager to capture the attention of one of the three men standing behind the tables.

Dolores steers Baber through the crowd towards one of the men under siege, one who looks as much like an apple as any of the assortment of specimens laid out on a tray on the table in front of him. His ruddy cheeks are blotched, each with a couple of small symmetrical dark stains like wormholes. His hair is brown and stalky. His forearms are as solid as tree trunks and his fingers long and branchy. His nails are grizzled green, and some of them need cleaning.

This man, this composite apple and tree, sees Dolores and he smiles a beaming greeting.

"Hi! Dolly," he shouts above the heads of the crowd that presses towards him.

"Hello, Sam."

"Have you brought him?"

"Yes, I've brought him. And he's brought his apples."

Sam says to the crowd in front of him, "Let this couple through, please."

"But we've been waiting here for ages," one old lady says, in a rebellious sort of way. She looks around for support, but there is an inherent obedience about the people about her. Those towards the back of the throng are happy holding aloft their apples, as if they were showing a new ball to a batsman. Those nearer the table seem to like to scrabble in plastic or paper bags, so that there is a constant rustling. It syncopates with the general hubbub that moves aside to allow Dolores and Baber free passage.

I reckon this might be because Sam has suddenly become animated. "What is it," I can sense them asking, "that is special about this couple of newly arrived people?" If the man behind the tables says that they are to let this couple through, albeit the girl is black and the man is... the man is – can it really be him? Baber Mittough... ?

Eventually Dolores and Baber find themselves standing across the table from Sam. The crowd has closed around behind them and is pressing forward, to see what's going to happen next.

Dolores says, "Sam, this is Baber."

"Hello, Baber," says Sam.

"Hello Sam," says Baber, shaking five of his branches. They feel warm and supple – hardly branch-like at all.

Sam can barely contain himself. "Well, I've eaten one, but I never took the time to look at it."

Then he goes on to answer Baber's puzzled expression. "I was playing cricket, you remember, that sunny day in August, when someone threw me one of your apples rather than the ball."

"Oh, yes. I remember."

"And then I met Dolly and her friend in the pavilion, and Dolly said they'd get you to bring some along today." His eyes shine in anticipation.

Baber reaches his hands into his pockets and fetches out three of his apples – two from one pocket, one from the other. He sets them down on the table. They glint yellow in the sunshine, then one of them seems to darken to orange in the shadow of Sam's predatory right hand. He picks up this apple. He holds it up in front of him and, under Sam's attentive scrutiny, it seems to me, the apple acquires a blush of red. Sam holds it under his nose and sniffs. Baber can imagine its flimsy flavour in his salivating mouth.

Dolores says, "Honeysuckle?"

Sam shakes his head. "No – it isn't sickly like honeysuckle. More like rosebuds. It has the promise of something grand."

I say to Baber, "Tell him, elderflower. We always think their taste reminds us of elderflower, don't we."

"Pomegranate," says Dolores.

"Italian white wine," says Sam.

One of the crowd about us tries to pick one of the other two apples from the table, but Sam quickly snatches it away, and moves them closer to him.

"Mouthwash," says Dolores.

"New books," says Sam.

"Elderflower," says Baber, at last.

Sam looks at Baber. "Yes," he says. "Elderflower. Elderflower it is." He continues to admire the apple he is holding up, though I can tell he would like to give the other two apples equal attention. This is because his left hand has now closed in a claw around them, albeit unwatched by him. He has them to himself.

"What do you think they are, then?" says Dolores.

"Apples," says Baber, before I can stop him. Even I understand that there is more to an apple than simply being called an apple. I have seen them in the supermarket. Some they call Braeburns, others Golden Delicious. However, we never stop beside them long enough for Baber to have absorbed all this into his consciousness. Baber and Nan only ever eat their own apples. They've never had to buy any.

The tray in front of Sam is evidence of immense variety. If these are all apples, then they have an enormous range of shape and size, colour and texture.

"I'm thinking White Transparent," Sam says. Then he looks at the two that he weighs in his left hand. "But they seem too big and they're too heavy." He reluctantly puts them down again and picks up a paring knife. "May I?" He asks Baber.

"Please," says Baber, though I would have asked, "May you what?"

Then Sam cuts a wedge from the apple. "And the flesh is too rich for White Transparent, I think. Bascombe Mystery, perhaps. It's certainly round enough."

He doesn't sound very convinced.

"Or Barnack Beauty."

He sounds even less convinced.

"Or perhaps, Choristor Boy. The flesh is so dense. And very juicy." He runs a finger along the side of the wedge he has cut out. The juice collects against this knobby branch of his and he sucks at it greedily. "Mmm! Very... "

He has lost the word. Baber's apple is always very something. But it is not easy to say very what, exactly. The apple is not sweet, not sour.

"Natural," Sam says. "Very natural." He looks pleased with himself, as though he had invented a new term to describe something that is rather dry to the taste despite its juicyness, rather mild despite its acidity. Indeed, he goes on to say, "Subacidic," and that gives him an idea, "like a Crawley Beauty."

Then, in quick succession we get, "Joybells? Dutch Mignonne? Winter Banana? Guelph?"

It is now obvious to me that Sam is merely guessing. He has no idea what sort of apple ours is. He tries to match them with those on the tray in front of him, but Baber's apples are either too pale or too round or too smooth to look particularly like any single one of them.

Still beaming his bright apple smile, but with a brow that has started to furrow, Sam suddenly lurches along behind the tables to the man nearest him, and interrupts him in mid-sentence (he is saying, "Definitely Spartan," to what looks like a disappointed lady wearing a hat fit for Ascot) with a, "Norman, I need your help," and Sam grabs him by the elbow and steers him towards us.

"What do you think?" He passes Norman the smallest of Baber's apples.

Norman suggests "Wyken Pippin." Then Sam holds up one of the others, and Norman immediately says, "No. Too big."

"How about Gascoyne Scarlett?" says Norman.

"Not enough red," says Sam.

"Exquisite?"

"Not greasy, though, is it."

"Dutch Mignonne?"

"I thought that," says Sam, pleased to have found at least one label, upon the possibilities of which they could agree.

"In which case, it could just as easily be Reinette de Cassel," says Norman.

"Or Forfar Pippin," says Sam.

These alternate possibilities seem to disappoint them.

"When does the tree blossom?" Norman asks Baber.

"April," says Baber, after insufficient consideration.

"And does the fruit keep well?" Sam asks.

"I should think so," says Baber. "After all." And he scrutinises the apples in their hands until he finds the one he is looking for. He points at the smallest of the three.

"That one is last year's crop."

"Is it indeed?" Norman asks, and Sam looks incredulous.

"He's right," says Dolores, who presumably has also sensed their basic unbelief. We've been eating them all through Spring and Summer.

"Lord Burghley?" Norman suggests.

"So it's prolific?" Sam asks.

Baber shrugs his shoulders. How does he expect us to know the answer to that?

"Is it an old tree?"

"I don't really know," says Baber. "But it has been in our back garden for as long as I can remember."

"Does it fruit equally well each year?" asks Norman.

These two experts seem now to have become centred on out-asking each other, rather than trying to work out what sort of an apple we have brought for their inspection.

"I'd like to see it," says Sam. "The tree."

"Now?" says Baber.

I say to Baber, "You've left the house in a very un-Nan like state. I don't think she'd appreciate visitors without a bit more housekeeping on your part first."

"You just keep out of this, Beulah," says Baber.

Sam is gesturing at the crowd about us. "I don't think now would be a good idea. How about I take down your name and address and I come round and see you. Next week, perhaps."

"Next week would be fine," says Baber.

Sam scratches, with a stub of pencil onto an earth-brown stained piece of paper, his attempt at Baber's name. M, I, T, O. Now we are Japanese, I think.

"Ah, so," says Baber. "Vely stlange appres."

"Mutsu," says Norman.

"Noh. Mito," says Baber.

A brief flash of puzzlement invades Norman's stony features. Then he says, "The apple. Is it a Crispin? Formerly called Mutsu?"

Dolores says, "Baber – I might need to call you Crispin Mutsu from now on."

Baber says, "I don't think so, Dorry. I plefer Baber Mittough. Onry because it's my name."

"And it's all your parents ever gave you Baber," I say to him. A name and a patchwork of disjointed memories. There is one, for example, where a scrawny man, a man of long bones and pointy joints, a man he has always taken to be his father, blows billows in long hair that keeps falling across his face whilst he paints the side of a van in a pattern of purple and lime green.

Sam is dismissing the idea that Baber's apple is a Crispin, formerly Mutsu. He has taken his paring knife and cuts one of the apples in half along its equator. He says, "The lenticels are too indistinct." Then he cuts the as yet uncut apple in half in the direction that you or Baber might, and he says, "And the cavity is far too narrow."

"Not Dutch Mignonne after all then," says Norman.

"Monarch?" asks Sam.

"Langley Pippin?" says Norman.

"Kent?"

"Merton Worcester?"

"Houblon?"

Now they really are guessing.

"Wildling Neverblight?"

"Sweet Coppin?"

"Le Bret?"

"Improved Hangdown?"

"Sidestalk Jersey?"

"Court de Wick?"

"Court de Wick. Yes. Court de Wick."

"Congresbury Beauty?"

The fruitful dialogue fades behind Dolores and Baber as they bustle their way out of the crowd.

"That an apple by any name should smell as natural," I say to Baber.

"Sweet Pethyre... "

Dolores says, "I expect they'll be glad to get back to their Bramleys and Lord Lambornes."

"Shoreditch White... "

"At least that'll be something they'll know about," Dolores says. She sounds as though she's lost some confidence in her friend Sam.

The children in Wellingtons are soaking wet. Baber says, "Perhaps they were light to be expecting lain."

I say, "That's enough Japanese."

Dolores says, "I expect they've been bobbing for apples."

In the shade of a snow white canvas awning, we find Snakethin Stephen sampling a plastic tumbler of cider at the cider stall.

"Why did you bring him?" Baber asks.

"In case you brought a friend, too," says Dolores.

She means Sita, of course. But Sita has not yet returned from India where she went with her father two long months ago. About once a week, Sita telephones Baber, who doesn't have a number for her, so he has to wait for her to make contact. The calls, not as frequent as he would like them to be, play to a background of busy city streets, the thrum of motors and blare of car horns and jabber of passing voices. The time delays in their conversations mean they frequently interrupt one another. Sometimes the line crackles and fades. On the whole it is not a medium sympathetic to the easy ripening of a new love affair.

mike martin

"I think thith ith my favouwite," Stephen says, with a distinct hint of alcohol to his lisp. He holds it up so that we can all admire the uric colour of it.

"Yes. Very nice," says Dolores.

"It'th called Sheepth Nothe Number Thwee."

"Don't you start," says Dolores.

I rather think she's had enough of apple names for one afternoon.

under the sea

from a novel **by vivienne mayer**

Normal Proportions *explores the bittersweet relationship between an alcoholic therapist, Alice, and her estranged globe-trotting son, David, separated since childhood after his mother's mental breakdown and imprisonment. As they anticipate a reunion in a week's time, the rising heat of guilt, loss and anger forces them to reassess the last twenty years. In the following extract, David recalls the last day he saw his mother.*

The last day I saw Mum I promised to help dig the Channel Tunnel. It was part of a deal I made with God.

It was a daft promise to make. I was only ten – the Tunnel would be finished long before I was old enough to work on it. But that's the thing when you're a kid; you really think God can do anything. It was daft and it was selfish too. It wasn't like it would have been a proper punishment – I'd been obsessed with the Tunnel for as long as I could remember. Mum watched me sometimes, gluing the newspaper cuttings into a scrapbook with 'CHUNNEL' emblazoned in blue foil across the cover. "There's no knowing how a child's mind works," was all she said. "There's just no knowing." I don't think it ever occurred to her to try to find out.

It was at the stage when everyone was waiting for the Frenchman and the Englishman to meet in the middle of the seabed. Everyone was wondering if the two ends would line up. I was actually hoping they would miss. I was hoping the whole Tunnel would have to be re-started, because then I could go and dig on it when I was sixteen. I had this stupid idea that if I could be the one to meet in the middle with that Frenchman, I would have saved the country from dissolving, from being eaten up by coastal erosion or something. I thought if we got any smaller we might just fold in on ourselves and slide into the line between the Atlantic Ocean and the North Sea. The Tunnel would change all that and I would have done something good, and someone important would shake my hand and say, "David, *you* have fixed everything. *You* have connected us to the world." I had this idea it would make up for the mess I'd made.

Of course I found out the truth later. I realized the Tunnel meeting up wasn't anything to do with the workmen; they just dug where someone else pointed, which ruined it all a bit.

The thing about that last day with Mum is that it took me by surprise. I'd only just got back from my first stay in the care home. "Everything's going to be all right now," Mum kept saying, pushing my hair back from my forehead, over and over, as if it might stay there. I believed her because – well – because I didn't want to think about those six weeks in that care home, or her in that mental hospital. And in my stupid childish head I suppose I thought once something terrible had happened it couldn't happen again.

I can't remember how those six weeks even started. I really can't. I've tried to fill in those last few hours, to pull the before and after together, but the two ends never quite meet. All I know is that at some point I was sitting on a bed looking down at a grey lino floor. I could hear boys' voices echoing down a corridor. "Oi, you," and, "Eh, get OFF!" A thud, an "Urrgh," and then laughter; hesitant, self-conscious laughter, the sort that knows it's really no laughing matter at all.

I watched a man's brown lace-up shoes step across the lino toward the bed I was sitting on. The weight of him sprang me up as he sat down. I scanned the room without moving my head, returning to the same spot on the lino where four tiles met. "You must try to sleep now," he said. I wondered who he was talking to. I even wondered if he was real, I really did. I started to think I was imagining him, and the boys' voices too, and the hard unfamiliar bed, and the child slouched like a dummy on the mattress opposite, his feet like a dead man's; dangling. I thought I might have lost my memory, that I'd forgotten who I was. The man touched my shoulder and the back of my neck shivered. "I'm real," I whispered.

"Oh, you're real all right." And he sounded so ordinary that I knew I couldn't be dreaming. "I'm Andrew, and you're David, right?" I didn't answer.

He paused and took a deep breath. He clasped his thick fingers together.

Then he said, "You know your Mum's in hospital and that's why you're here don't you?"

I wasn't sure if I knew it. "I suppose so. She's ill," I said. I didn't know if I was asking or telling, or how I might know such a fact.

"Sort of," he said. His voice was all doughy and whispery, like he was telling me it was teatime.

He pushed my hair away from my face like Mum did. I pulled away. The boy on the other bed was watching us now, like we were the latest episode of Grange Hill or something.

"What you looking at?" I heard myself say.

The man put his hand on my shoulder again. I let him keep it there this time, seeing as I was having another, more serious thought.

"Will I? – Will I? – "

"Yes, yes," he said. "But not for a few weeks. You'll see her before the court case."

I didn't know what the court case was about then, but I found out later. I pulled away from him again, only this time like I really meant it. The boy opposite was looking up from under a wad of blond hair, like something was about to happen. And that's when I said it, it's the first time I'd ever said it to anyone, and I didn't even know who I was saying it to really.

"FUCK OFF." It went on and on like I couldn't finish the 'O' of the 'off', like you see blokes at football matches when a goal's scored and their whole bodies are screaming, and it's more of a noise than a word. In the end it was like it was coming from somewhere else, like I'd been waiting to say it forever and didn't know it.

When my voice went quiet I realised my body had curled in on itself, my face was bent into my chest and my arms were up over my head, like I was waiting for a bomb to drop. I waited. I didn't know what for, but I was sure there would be a price to pay. And I didn't even care. I wanted to say, "COME ON THEN," because I knew nothing could have made me feel any worse than I did already.

"What's the matter with him?" I heard the other boy ask. And then the weirdest thing happened. The bloke with the doughy voice put his hand on the back of my head like I was a puppy or something. I thought, "What's going to happen now?" I wondered if he was some kind of weirdo, the ones Mum always said to watch for in the park. He just left his hand there without saying a word, like he was doing it for my benefit, the way I did for Mum sometimes when the gin sent her to sleep. Then he said, as casual as you like, "Yep, you're allowed to be angry."

I don't know what it was about the way he said it, but the words kind of crashed into the middle of my chest and made me cave into him. I was breathless, another thick ball of something was rising in my throat, my eyes stinging and then my mouth opening again until, whoosh, as Mum would say, another noise was coming, sort of mangled this time, like the sound I'd imagined Jesus making as he hung up there on that cross above my old bed, his eyes all rolled back into his head.

Except that my eyes were closed as tight as fists, and my mouth was locked wet and open against the man's chest now. As the noise burrowed into his sweater I could hear his heart beat; a steady thump, thump, thump, that seemed to coax something else out of me, something I didn't know I had. "Don't leave me," I said.

The day after I left the care home, Mum waved and smiled as hard as I'd ever seen her do either. She did it until I was halfway down the school corridor, she couldn't have even known I could still see her. The night before we'd had a picnic in her bed and I woke up next to her with crumbs against my stomach and her face on the pillow next to me, all soft and puffy, her hair covering one eye. It was the happiest morning of my life.

I knew I shouldn't have gone to school that day. She wasn't ready. While I stared at the back of a bald-headed teacher, who hypnotised us with his droopy eyes and a voice like a gnarled audiotape, me and Mum's fresh start was turning sour.

That's the thing with being a kid, you don't realise how your whole life can turn in an hour, a day. It's only adults who say, what if? I was living in the here and now, see, absorbed in the activity of the moment, imitating the teacher's way of saying 'chil-dren'. Drawing another picture of the Tunnel. In fact it was one of the best I'd ever done, as soon as I got started on the yellow workmen's hats and the French diggers' moustaches, I knew I was on to something. I surprised myself that day. I had the men digging their tunnels from either side of the page under a big blue sea. The teacher held it up for the whole class to see. "Very top-ic-al," he said. If only Mum was here, I kept thinking. I couldn't wait for her to see it. I don't think she ever did.

But it wasn't really her fault. It's like I said to the house-mother at the care home, "She can't help being the way she is." "Look Miss," I said, "there's something you should know about Mum." She rolled her eyes and said, "Go on then." I told her, it really wasn't Mum's fault at all: the booze, the illness, even the baby – she loved that baby. She just had one of those lives. That's what Mum called it: "One of those lives." She told me once, "Just when I thought everything was turning out normal: Whoosh. I was sweeping up the dust."

"Whoosh," I had repeated. And from then on it was our secret joke. When she sighed at the old Italian photos of her and Dad on the kitchen wall, or rolled her eyes at something on the news, I'd say "Whoosh" and we knew exactly what each other meant. She would smile when I said that, and her face would sort of come undone and reveal itself. It was like she'd remembered who she was for a minute, before her life had become 'one of those lives'. I liked it a lot when she looked at me that way, as though I was worth something after all.

I was watching TV when the social workers arrived. I would never have phoned them if I knew what I know now, that it was the last time I'd see her. "It wasn't your fault," I was told afterwards, by this one, that one, everyone except the one that counted. But it doesn't change the facts: if I'd never made that call it might never have happened, the whole thing might have taken a different course. Bloody might haves.

She was on the sofa, see, when I got back from school, out for the count – another empty bottle of gin pushed under the coffee table. I shook her shoulder and she didn't wake up. I shook her so hard I thought I felt her blouse tear and then I pulled her eyelids apart, but all I could see were the whites, all milky and floaty, with a red rim around them. I opened the balcony doors; it was sunny and the air was still. I didn't know what to do next. I'd always been able to wake her up before. I pulled a bag of frozen peas from the freezer, laid them on a cushion over her stomach and put her hands on the bag of peas, I'm not sure why. I sat on the edge of the sofa just staring at the white skin, tracing her long thin fingers with mine, round and round the curved tips of her nails. Every now and then I tapped the tops of her hands and looked up at her face. Nothing happened, and soon I saw the white half-moons of her nails springing out against a deepening, dusky blue. I dragged the peas up over her neck and face to her forehead. And all the time I was thinking, "If I hadn't gone to school none of this would have happened."

When her face felt as cold as the peas, I went through her handbag to find Natalie's number, one of the social workers. I knew it was in her address book. It was with a whole load of other numbers under 'H' for help.

And I did it. I picked up the phone and I dialled the number and said, "I can't wake Mum up."

Then I said to myself, "Stay calm David, stay calm," like they do in the films. "Natalie will be here soon." And then I was okay for a second and convinced she was going to be all right, and I almost grinned at how scared and stupid I was being. But every time I looked back at her face, my throat felt like someone was squeezing the breath out of it, and I had to close my eyes.

Then something happened. I saw the pearls in her handbag, the ones I'd bought her. They were broken. I just seemed to hold my breath and go still. Then I took them over to the fire, turned on the TV, put the sound down and threaded. I waited and threaded, threaded and waited, waited for Natalie to arrive, for Mum to come alive, and just for time to pass.

On the TV, more men in hard yellow helmets were silently drilling and sweating at the rock face under the Channel. They were still digging when Mum woke up. When I saw her eyes open I had to run over to make sure it was true. I didn't let on, though. I just showed her the re-threaded pearls. She pulled me toward her and rested my head on her shoulder. And all the relief of her being alive seemed to drain out of me and fill up with guilt.

"I phoned Natalie," I said. "I didn't mean to, I – I – I thought you weren't well."

And she just closed her eyes and said, "It doesn't matter." Which must have been a lie. And then she said some things she'd never said before, some really nice, lovely things. The sort of things you'd say if you weren't going to see someone again. And I couldn't work out if it was her icy skin that was sending a chill through me, or her words.

Next thing, it was all happening again – the whole bloody nightmare. Natalie was in the room with another bloke and a couple of ambulance men. One leant over Mum's head at the end of the sofa, and the other from the side, like you see road workers doing; stood around, scratching their heads, deciding. I pushed my way in and sat up by her shoulder. One of the men put his hand on her forehead and I shoved it away. "She's all right now," I said.

But it was no use, the room was coming to life, they were all talking at once, reaching over me. "Come on, now." "Don't worry." "Everything will be taken care of." The ambulance men started to pull Mum off the sofa, Natalie took hold of my arm, "Come away now," she said. The other social worker started shifting the coffee table. All I could think to do was scrabble the mended pearls from the floor and put them in Mum's handbag and zip it up.

The other social worker crouched down and said, "I'll take that, son," and pulled the handbag away from me. "NO," I screamed in his ear. He nearly toppled backwards and he said, I never forget this, he said, "Jesus Christ boy, you're not safe here." I looked at Mum, who was sat up now. Her eyelids lifted, as though they were struggling against a heavy weight. She looked up at me for a second. Not safe. I had to think about that, because I thought I was pretty safe, I mean, it wasn't like anyone was belting me and I said to him, I said, "What are you on about?

She's never laid a finger on me."

He sighed and shook his head like he knew some big truth that I didn't, then Natalie leant over and tried to tuck my shirt into my trousers.

"What you doing?" I said. I was so surprised I was sort of stuck to the spot. I just watched her hands tucking in the cotton, her fingers poking against my stomach.

"There's a lot more to feeling safe than not being belted David," she said. And I don't know why but I thought of Andrew in the home, his soft doughy voice, his big hands and his steady heartbeat. *Yep, you're allowed to be angry.*

Before they closed the car door, Mum broke free from the social worker and reached into the back seat like she was going to pull me out. But she didn't. Instead, her thin arms and fingers wound around me like pipe cleaners, and it's funny, that's how I always think of her, even now – twelve years on: soft and wiry like a pipe cleaner. "Sorry, sorry, sorry," she kept saying. She pulled my face against hers. The two ambulance men stepped back on the pavement with their arms behind their backs, watching. Natalie leaned in behind her and started tugging at her shoulder. It didn't make any difference at first, my face just parted from hers for a second. Air rushed through the gap, and her tears turned cold on my face. As she pulled me back to her I could smell that smell she always had. Smoke, powder and booze. I never told her this, but sometimes, when she was out of the flat for a long time, I'd find one of her gin bottles, unscrew the top and just hold it to my nose to remind me of her. She never knew, I put them back just how she'd left them, label side facing in.

She squeezed me in the back of that car like she was draining a glass of gin; like her life depended on it. I couldn't seem to say anything but I just kept thinking, "It's okay, I'll be back soon and I'll get it right next time, they can't keep me for six weeks again. Things like that don't happen twice."

And I still couldn't speak as the car pulled away. I just looked at Mum, piled on the pavement, crumbling under the sun. I knew, deep down, it was my fault that she couldn't get up. So I made that stupid deal with God. I said, "Just bring me back soon and I'll do anything, anything at all – I'll dig the Channel Tunnel!

animal passions

a short story **by susan mcmillan**

Steven and Persephone had lived happily together for almost ten years. Like most couples, they had been through many sticky situations, but these had only drawn them closer together. When Steven left college and faced the yawning abyss of dull, uneventful employment, Persephone was there to comfort him. When he bought his flat, Persephone made it feel like home. When Steven's father died, she had been his shoulder to cry on; she never nagged if he stayed out late or turned her head away if he woke up bleary and beery. Persephone was everything a man could want from a parrot.

Steven had won her in a drunken bet at college and originally she'd been called Tracy. But after falling temporarily in love with a statue of Persephone after two bottles of ouzo in Greece, he renamed his bird after the goddess. It seemed much more exotic.

"Per-seph-o-ne!" the parrot had screamed when Steven announced her new name, "Persephonepersephonepersephone." She upended herself and looked at Steven coolly, showing off, hanging on with only one delicate toe. Those dark eyes that met his seemed to have an intelligence that he hadn't encountered for some time. When he placed his face close to the cage, the parrot gently touched his nose with her beak and 'harumphed' at him under her breath; 'harumphing' being the only way of describing the guttural, gurgling breaths she made which seemed to indicate pleasure. Persephone was very satisfied with her new man.

"Say Steven, Persephone."

"Say Steven, love Steven," Persephone gurgled coquettishly, fluffing her feathers up.

Steven had been warned that she had a mean streak and he wasn't to let her out of the cage, but on that first day, the day that Persephone had announced love, Steven felt like David Attenborough. He opened the cage door and Persephone awkwardly minced up his arm, sat nibbling his ear. From that day, Persephone and Steven were inseparable. It was unconditional parrot love.

All Persephone needed was water, sunflower seeds and Steven. All Steven needed was the parrot, his Led Zeppelin vinyl collection and the occasional kebab. On Saturday nights, Persephone would screech loudly and enthusiastically along to the music as Steven paraded round the sitting room with his imaginary guitar.

"Ah, Perse," Steven cooed one Saturday, slumping down on the sofa after his usual fantasy-Grammy winning performance, "if only I could find a woman like you."

At the mention of 'other women', a steely glint would appear in Persephone's eyes and she would respond with a perfect impersonation of a lead guitar solo with wah-wah effects. It was as if she knew that this would immediately stop any hot-blooded male of a certain age talking about female competition. But of course she was only a parrot; she couldn't possibly know what she was doing.

It was a Saturday just like any other. Steven went off to football and Persephone watched him from her cage in the window of the sitting room.

"Have a nice day! Have a nice day!" she screamed, and the moment Steven's car had disappeared from sight she lifted the catch of the cage door and hopped out. Flying round and round the room she impersonated every noise she heard: the passing buses and trains, the low-flying jets coming in to land at Wenbury International Airport and next door's cat, whom she had traumatised with weeks of verbal abuse. Persephone particularly liked playing with the answer phone and by pressing the buttons she could get the machine to play and record. She had learnt to mimic the messages and could now impersonate Steven's best friend James perfectly.

"Hi, yeah, Steven, it's James, do you fancy a drink tonight? Ring me. Squark!" Even Steven's mother wasn't safe.

"Steven, darling, please pick up the phone. It's your mother. Are you there, Steven? Let me know you're still alive. When are you going to get a girlfriend? Keep Mummy informed. Love and kisses."

When Steven played back the messages he had no idea it was Persephone leaving them.

Drunk with her own cleverness, Persephone would fly into the kitchen and skid along the shiny Ikea work surfaces, before returning to her cage to watch with envy the birds flying in the garden and to wait for her beloved's return.

"Steven," she crooned to herself, and closing her eyes she waited, sitting demurely in her cage, ticking away with Steven's novelty Simpson's wall clock. "Tick, tick, you're late Steven, tick, tick."

For a parrot who liked routine, Steven's lateness was a little unsettling. On Saturdays, Steven always returned home at the same time, so she began to bob up and down, bingeing on sunflower seeds. Just as she began to peck irritably at her tail feathers, she heard his car scratching the gravel of the drive. Her head bobbed up alert, and she called out of the window to welcome him.

"Steven!Steven!Ste...... !"

Persephone stopped in mid-squark. Steven was not alone.

"Hello Perse, this is Tanya. Say hello to Tanya, Perse." Steven gently probed the parrot's breast feathers with his forefinger, ruffling them so that the white undergarments showed.

The parrot said nothing.

"Does it bite?" Tanya said, nervously staying some way from the cage. Persephone and Tanya eyed each other.

"It's a she, sweetie, and she's very perceptive, so watch what you say."

"Steven and Persephone, Steven and Persephone," the parrot shrieked, turning attention-seeking somersaults, not for one moment taking her eyes off this woman who had flagrantly invaded her territory.

"She's probably in a bit of a sulk because I've bought you home with me," Steven said, bemused, if not a little chuffed by the fact that there appeared to be some degree of rivalry between the two females. "Give her a sunflower seed or something."

Tanya advanced unwillingly to the cage, clucking unconvincingly and un-parrotlike; a painted smile, for Steven's benefit, snaking across her face. Persephone glared from the cage.

"Look, she likes you, Tan," Steven said encouragingly.

As Tanya stepped closer, the parrot seemed to soften, dipping her head so that the woman could reach in with the tip of her claw-like false fingernail and ruffle the bird's feathers.

"That's it Tanya, tickle the nape of her neck, she likes that," Steven laughed.

Tanya had an expression on her face that said she had found something unpleasant on the soles of her fluffy white mules.

"It doesn't have fleas, does it?" she turned enquiringly to Steven and that was Persephone's moment. The parrot turned her head and, looking as if sunflower seeds wouldn't melt in her mouth, sank her beak hard into the woman's finger.

There was much caterwauling and shouting for the next half-hour, interspersed with Persephone screeching with delight.

"Go home Tanya! Go home Tanya!"

She watched Steven administer plasters, TCP and gin and tonic, and as Tanya wiped away the blobs of mascara leaching down her powder-pink cheeks, Persephone, a look of angelic parrot-innocence on her face screeched, "Pretty Persephone!"

That was when Steven shouted at her. He had never done that, not in ten years. And if that was not bad enough, Persephone began to see that her attack had not had the desired effect. Far from driving the competition away, it had brought Steven and this woman closer together.

The placatory effect of the alcohol and the fit of hysterics had broken the ice. Tanya and Steven were now going through all the little signs and signals of the human courtship ritual. Even Persephone could see that.

"I'm afraid your parrot doesn't seem to like me, Steven," Tanya whimpered, preparing a roast chicken she had bought for their dinner. As she stuffed the hapless bird, she stared directly at Persephone. Persephone stared back, watching her deliberate movements with hatred. Tanya pummelled the chicken, twisting and contorting the body to make sure every last cavity was full of sage and onion.

"Oh, she's a great bird, she'll get used to you," Steven mumbled distractedly, as he prepared the salad. It was difficult for him to concentrate on two things at once

"She'll have to, Steven," Tanya purred, placing her greasy hands on his cheeks and kissing him. Behind Steven's back Tanya pulled a face at the parrot. "Otherwise she's cat food."

Within a month, Tanya had moved in permanently; within two the flat had changed beyond recognition. Cuddly toys clambered over Steven's duvet, together with pink accessories and pictures of kittens.

As soon as Steven left the house for work each morning, battle would commence. Whenever Tanya entered the room, Persephone turned violent, spitting sunflower seeds and screeching uncontrollably. She listened in on Tanya's phone calls, and screeched along with them. When Tanya was in the bath, Persephone would impersonate the phone or the doorbell. Tanya would rush, slipping and dripping, to answer, but there was never anyone there. When Tanya had a lie-in Persephone would mimic the burglar alarm. When she dressed up to go out, the parrot would announce, "Fat! Fat! Fat!" at the top of her voice. Persephone enjoyed every minute of it. But Tanya was a formidable opponent. Beneath the veneer of pink fluffiness was a woman who would do anything to get her own way. She had decided that Steven was the man she was going to spend the rest of her life with, and no oversized budgerigar would get in her way. Persephone's cage was moved to the garage.

"It's for the best, darling," Tanya purred when Steven came home, "I was only reading today that parrots can pass on disease, and it's best that it has a room on its own. It will like it in there."

Persephone would watch Steven going to and coming from work

every day, but he had changed. He only ever stopped briefly at her cage to say hello and sometimes – oh, how Persephone pined for these moments – he would place his face close to the bars, as he used to, so that she could gently nibble his lower lip.

"Bye Steven, love Steven," she would whisper to herself in the concrete silence of the garage; she didn't feel like talking much these days. It was not long after that she began plucking out her feathers, one by one.

One evening Steven wandered into the garage and took Persephone gently out of her cage, caressing the little bare patches of skin that showed through her once thick plumage.

"Oh, Perse, it looks like we're both going bald together!" he smiled, half-heartedly.

She sat on his shoulder and hummed a tune. It had been their favourite once, but it brought an air of melancholy to the stark garage so she began her Tommy Cooper impersonation instead. Her tiny heart wasn't in it but somehow she knew that, like a prisoner at visiting time, their time was short. Tanya, hearing low giggles coming from the garage, strode in.

"Here comes trouble," Persephone called, followed by an impersonation of a burglar alarm. That made Steven laugh.

"Steven, haven't you got something better to do?"

"Steven, haven't you got something better to do?" Persephone whined back, in a perfect impersonation of Tanya's nasal voice.

"I've really had enough of that bird, Steven."

Persephone, remembering a few drunken evenings with Steven's friends, and bolstered by this rare moment with her man, shrieked, "Sod off Tanya! Sod off Tanya!"

It made Steven laugh even more as Tanya's face went the colour of her puce leggings.

Out of the cage, Persephone knew she had power. She flew off Steven's shoulder, and with Hitchcockian enthusiasm dived at Tanya's head, driving her from the garage before returning to Steven's shoulder.

"If I didn't know better, Persephone, I'd say you were jealous," Steven laughed, playfully ruffling her wings.

Later Persephone heard raised voices and crockery smashing, but the only words she heard clearly were Steven's.

"Of course I love you more than the parrot."

A few days later, Steven walked sheepishly into the garage, bringing newspaper, food and water. Persephone made the most of this quiet moment with him and bobbed up and down his arm, sitting on his head as he cleaned out the cage and carefully placed the newspaper on the bottom. She sang a few lines from a drinking song Steven had once taught her, but this time it didn't make him laugh.

"I know you won't really understand this Perse, but Tanya can't live in the house with you here. She just doesn't like birds, you see."

Persephone looked at Steven adoringly.

"I'm so sorry, Perse."

"Sorry," Persephone repeated.

"Steven, I need you in the kitchen," a voice called from the distance.

Steven gave Persephone a kiss on her head, looked at her as if it was the last time he would and left.

If Persephone could have read the newsprint lying beneath her feet, she would have seen the 'Pets for sale' column of the local newspaper and, halfway down the column of Labrador puppies, mynah birds and pythons, a prominent boxed advert which said: African Grey Parrot for sale. Clever talker, mimics all sound. Ring 97456. That evening, all she could hear from inside the house was the phone ringing.

The following morning, after Steven had left for work, Tanya put her head round the door into the garage.

"Bye, bye, parrot," she sneered, and, forgetting to close the door that led from the garage to the house, she left, whistling. Watching the open door with some interest, Persephone waited, listening. As soon as it was quiet she let herself out of her cage. As she flew round the house, she remembered her wonderful life with Steven. Before Tanya, life had been good; before Tanya, Persephone had been happy; before Tanya, Persephone had never doubted that she and Steven would be together for ever. She didn't fly as well as she used to, so she came to rest on the telephone table by the hall mirror. She examined her reflection closely.

"Pretty Persephone?" she enquired weakly.

"Pretty Persephone," the reflection mumbled in synchrony, tufts of shredded feathers sprouting from naked skin. She gazed at this image that wasn't her, thinking parrot thoughts.

The phone rang, snapping her from her contemplation. The answering machine clicked on.

"Hello, I'm ringing about the advert for the parrot." Beep. Persephone hopped onto the machine, hitting the play button. Last night's messages played again.

"Hi, is the parrot still for sale?" Beep.

"Steven, it's mother. Are you there? You're not selling the parrot are you?" Beep.

"Hello, we talked last night about the parrot – just to say I'll come round to collect it this afternoon." Beep, beep.

Persephone began bobbing up and down, on and off the answer phone buttons. She began repeating lines she had heard from Tanya's phone conversations and from previous answer phone messages before she had been banished to the garage; messages that Tanya had deleted. In a panic she flew off into the bedroom and began throwing clothing around the bed, mostly Tanya's. As she tossed the last item of pink lace onto the floor, she heard a car turning into the drive. Screeching, she darted for her cage and closed the door just as Steven drove into the garage.

"Hello, Perse," he said a little sadly.

"I love you, James," Persephone mewed. But it wasn't Persephone's voice it was Tanya's.

Steven dropped his keys in surprise.

"What did you say, Perse?"

"James, darling, it's Tanya. He's gone, come round now, I'm waiting."

In the silence of the garage you could hear a sunflower seed drop. Steven stared at the parrot, not quite understanding. Then he picked up the cage and strode into the house. Automatically, he played the answer phone as he always did when returning from work. The messages echoed round the hall.

"Tanya, it's James." Beep.

"Tanya you were wonderful." Beep, beep.

"I need you Tanya." Beep, beep, beep.

Steven strode into the bedroom – Tanya's underwear littered the room – and with a great sense of timing, Persephone began to screech at the top of her voice, "Oh, James! OH, James! OH, JAMES!"

Survival instinct is strong in animals.

Steven stood looking a little dazed, the doorbell ringing snapped him back into reality. He opened the door.

"I spoke to your girlfriend last night. I've come to collect the parrot,"

"She's not for sale," Steven snapped, slamming the door.

The doorbell rang again and Steven opened it, still holding the parrot's cage. Tanya breezed in.

"Hello darling, I forgot my keys," and, seeing the parrot, "Hasn't that bird gone yet?"

On cue, Persephone repeated her lines in Tanya's voice. Steven looked accusingly at Tanya. "You're not going to believe a parrot are you?" she laughed.

"I'll help you pack your bags," he said.

"Bags!" shrieked Persephone delightedly

At that, Tanya snatched the parrot cage from Steven's hand and flung it through the front door. As it tumbled, the cage door sprang open and Persephone flew out. She flew up into the infinite space above the trees, screaming with delight. Below she could see Tanya throwing suitcases into the back of a car, and Steven running from the house, running down the street looking at the sky.

"Persephone, Persephone," he cried as she rose up higher than she had ever been, freer than she had ever been, as she flew off into the green of an English summer.

play nation

from a novel **by kate megeary**

Fridays are banana days for us. I can't remember why it started, a joke probably, but it was Kali's idea. It's turned into a weekly routine. It helps to have some kind of routine, an anchor, so you know where you are. Otherwise weeks can go by and you wouldn't even notice. Every Friday, we go up to Second Street Market and buy three bananas each. Then we go back home and see who can invent the best banana recipe. It was easy to start with, but it's difficult to come up with something different every week. I said we should start using another fruit but Kali said that would ruin the challenge and, besides, there weren't any other fruits as versatile as the banana. Sometimes some of the others join in, but mostly they can't be bothered and it's just me and Kali. Like today.

Second Street Market is mental. It's the shouting that gets me. Everyone trying to be louder than everyone else, all at the same time.

"*Twen*-ty *cents* a *pound ba*-nanas." In a singsong voice that goes up and down.

"C'mon ladies, come and look at this. A fiver for the lot. You won't see a better deal this side of Walford. Come on ladies, gather round." From someone who thinks they should be on television.

"Four packs of superglue for a one-er." In a desperate, whiny, wavering kind of way, like he knows he should never have got saddled with the stuff in the first place.

Like anyone's listening. It's not like this in Oliver Twist where the market vendors wait their turn and sing songs to try and sell their stuff: "Who will buy my sweet red roses? "

All the other things that happen at Second Street Market make up for the shouting, though. Today, there's a lady convulsing on the floor in an epileptic fit, or maybe she's got heat stroke. A box of spring onions has spilled onto the floor next to her. Everyone is crowding round to see if she's all right and blocking out her air. Ambulance men are trying to push their way through to help her, but the market is too busy and nobody notices them. People are dithering by rails of clothes, fingering fabric or hanging around fruit stands, squeezing mangoes and squinting suspiciously at oranges. It's impossible to get anywhere quickly. Individuals in the crowd are meandering, stopping suddenly, without warning and causing human traffic jams. I like looking at all the different people. A delicate Muslim lady with a cream headscarf wrapped around her flawless face gobs on the floor. Her spit scrapes the hem of a fancy dress patterned with shapes and colours that seem to shout. It belongs to an African woman whose turban matches her frock.

The sun makes things go rotten quickly. Vegetables and cardboard boxes decay together in the gutter and turn into brown mush. The fish stalls stink. It's too hot for dead fish even though they're covered in ice. The fish have names that belong to other things: bass and plaice and sole. There are big blue crabs with their pincers tied. I thought crabs were supposed to be red. I poke one.

"Is it still alive?"

The fishmonger laughs and picks it up, turning it on its back.

"Yeah, look."

He pours hot coffee from a paper cup over the underbelly of the crab. It waves its legs around like an upturned beetle, but not as fast. We're a long way away from the sea and it's mid-afternoon.

"Come on, Lottie." Kali pulls my arm.

There are Kurdish women in headscarves and long skirts and woollen jackets, loitering. Maybe they're not Kurdish; they look like gypsies. Proper gypsies, I mean. They look dodgy too. I don't know if that's their intention or whether they are doing a bad job of trying to be inconspicuous, but they're selling contraband so it could be either. Their pockets are stuffed with boxes of perfume or watches or something and they clutch bulging carrier bags. Kali stops and talks to one of them. She wants to buy cigarettes, but the woman shakes her head and pulls some salami out of a plastic bag.

"No, no, *cigarettes,*" Kali says, gesturing with two fingers in front of her mouth.

The woman puts the salami back in her bag and shakes her head again. She twists a gold ring off one of her fingers and offers that to Kali instead.

"No cigarettes?"

The woman shakes her head. Kali shrugs and turns away.

I like looking at the things in the market but I never buy anything, except bananas. The toy stalls are the best. They've got these gorillas that sing funky tunes and swing their hips in time to the music, and there are hula girl dolls with grass skirts that do the same. The mobile phone stalls have got holograms that you can stick on the screen of your telephone. Three-dimensional eyes and spiders and things. I don't like looking at the butchers' shops behind the market stalls, though, but I do it anyway. There are buckets filled with pigs' feet and buckets filled with slices of pigs' noses. Pink circles with two holes in them. There are other buckets with thin pink squiggly things in them. Kali says they're pigs' dicks but I don't believe her. They look like tails to me. There are featherless chickens dangling from the front of the shops like decorations. Their necks are long and their skin is covered in little lumps as if they're feeling cold. There are massive carcasses hanging from hooks. Half a cow. I've seen the men unloading them from white vans, hurrying into the butchers' shops with big dead streaky pink things on their backs. It must be hard work, carrying half a cow.

Kali gets bored first, but I don't want to go home yet. I know it's the same every week, but I still like looking.

"You're just stalling for time because you can't think of anything to make."

"No I'm not."

"Are."

"I'm *not.*"

"Let's go home then."

I do know what I'm going to cook. Kali will be surprised. We walk back down Market Road. There's a lady in a wheelchair outside the supermarket.

"'Scuse me," she says. It starts off as a hiss and then the 'cuse' jumps out at you:

"'SssssssssssssCUSE me."

It gets people's attention. They turn round and see a woman in a wheelchair and fall over themselves to help her.

"Have you got any spare change?" she says. They have to give her some money. We don't stop when she says, "'Scuse me, " though. We know what she's going to say and, anyway, we don't have enough money to give to her. We know that she goes and spends all the money that people give her on lottery tickets because we watched her do it once.

We walk past the crack dealers on Acorn Street.

"All right geezer," they say to Kali. They think she looks like a bloke.

"All right darlin'," Kali says. She doesn't care what they think. I told her she shouldn't buy crack from them because then they'll always be hassling her. But she did and they don't. They know she doesn't care what they think. I don't talk to them, though. I don't even smile at them. They scare me.

When we get home, the dogs are barking. They are Kali's dogs and they wait at the door for her and bark when anyone walks past. Kali undoes the padlock and takes the chain off the door. The dogs push it open with their noses and run out into the alley, wagging their tails. Malcolm is bigger but Zippo is cleverer and so she's the one who gets the most attention. I go upstairs and leave Kali to get the dogs back into the house. Rose is in the front room playing Super Mario on the Nintendo.

"Got your 'nanas then Lottie?" she says, as if she' s concerned.

"Yes, thanks." She's being sarcastic. I know she thinks we're stupid, but she's completed Super Mario three times and she's still playing it. She says she wants to get a Playstation. I reckon she needs to get a life.

"You're a twat," she says, staring at the screen.

"No I'm not. And I want to watch TV." She ignores me. "Turn it off,

Rose. I wanna watch TV."

"I'm in the middle of a game." She's always in the middle of a game.

"Why do you have to spend all day playing stupid computer games anyway?"

"Kills time. Why don't you go and split your bananas, or whatever it is you do with them... Shit." She lost a life. I smile. I'm not a twat. It's healthy to eat bananas, especially on a Friday. I switch the aerial on the back of the television.

... crisis worsened in France today as another pack of the so-called terror-dogs were released onto the streets of Paris. Eight separate...

Rose gets up and goes to switch the TV back to Nintendo mode.

"Rose, please, I just wanna watch the news, okay?" She sighs and sits back down.

"Dunno why you bother."

... third time in a month that the unknown extremist group has struck, strapping explosives to the animals and releasing as many as twenty dogs...

"*The Simpsons* is on," says Rose.

"Yeah?" I change channels. Bart is being chased around Springfield by a mob of people wielding green pitchforks. I like *The Simpsons*. Kali comes upstairs. The dogs follow her.

"Aren't you cooking yet? These two are starving, I'm gonna feed them and then... "

"*The Simpsons* is on."

"Oh, right." She sits down in the armchair and watches it with us. I like it when we all do something together.

When it's finished and Kali has fed the dogs, I go into the kitchen. It's filthy. Somebody should clean it up. I get my bananas out of the bag. A Jamaican lady at the market told me to chop up the bananas and fry them in oil and put some coconut milk in and some vegetables and some chicken and some spices. It's not going to be as easy as she made it sound, though. One of the rules of the banana game is that you can only use ingredients that are in the kitchen already. It's like that programme where people bring in their favourite ingredients and the chefs have to make something out of them. They always come up with something nice.

I like pretending I'm on television when I cook. I take some sunflower spread and melt it over a low heat before adding a clove of crushed garlic. I stir gently, taking care not to burn the garlic. It turns golden and I put in the sliced banana and fry it for two minutes. Half a greenish pepper and some mushrooms follow. When they are cooked I add a quarter of a pint of soured cream. It doesn't say soured on the carton but it must be by now. There are a couple of Bounty bars in the fridge. I start to peel the chocolate off one of them using a sharp kitchen knife but then I think that chocolate might add an unusual twist to the recipe, so I just chop them up and sprinkle them in. It's as near to coconut cream as I can get. It smells the same anyway. I add a spoonful of crushed almonds and simmer. It's missing something. There's no chicken. No one ever buys meat. It's too expensive, I guess. I can make up for it with something else, though, but I reckon I'll have to boil it for a bit longer. I stare at the bubbling liquid. It's hypnotic. We did *Macbeth* once at school. Bubble, bubble, toil and trouble. Fire burn and cauldron bubble. Those are the only lines I can remember now. There's a pot of basil growing on the windowsill. I know it's basil because it smells of aniseed. Fresh herbs always make food seem posh so I throw a couple of leaves in. No one has ever made a savoury recipe before. Banana and Marmite sandwiches don't count. I think I'm quite imaginative when it comes to cooking.

I call the others in and they sit round the table. China's just woken up. She's been asleep all day. She's always asleep. Even when she's awake, she doesn't seem to notice it. She says she's got narcolepsy. Rose says she's just a lazy cow. I looked narcolepsy up in the dictionary. It says it's an extreme tendency to fall asleep whenever you're in relaxing surroundings. China can fall asleep with her head in a speaker that's banging out bass to a roomful of people. I don't see how that's relaxing. Anyway, I know why she's always asleep. It's because of the baby. No one else knows and I think even China might have forgotten. Rose has managed to drag herself away from the Nintendo. Kali looks surprised. I knew she would be.

"Smells good, what you got there?"

"Today, I have surpassed myself," I say in a proper voice, "I present to you stir-fried banana with coconut."

Rose doesn't look impressed. She never does. "You watch too much daytime TV; all those cooking programmes've gone to your head," she says.

"Shut up and try some," I tell her. "You might even like it."

She won't admit it even if she does, not that I care. I dish out the food and give everyone a plate. Token's not home from work yet so I keep some back for him. China starts eating, chewing slowly.

"Mmm. Blue triangle... twisted edges... " she says. China can taste shapes.

"What does it *taste* like, China?"

"Umm... All right actually... bit weird... sort of sweet... but... um... not sweet... at the same time... sort of... sticky as well." China speaks slowly too.

Rose is already halfway through her plate so she must like it, but I'm not asking her.

"What do you reckon Kali?" I say. She takes a mouthful then spits it back on to the plate, quite violently, and runs into the bathroom shouting.

"You stupid fucking bitch... what the fuck are you playing at... you fucking idiot." She keeps shouting and shouting and the others stop eating and stare at me as I realise something with mounting horror. Rose doesn't buy meat because she lives on takeaways. China never buys meat because she hardly ever goes out. But Kali doesn't buy meat because she doesn't eat it. Kali only buys food for the dogs. If she did eat meat, I'm sure she would never have noticed that I put dog food in the banana stir-fry instead of chicken.

the happy lover

from a novel **by sarah menage**

"Hither each man's pleasure draws him, young and old alike. Some demand the grass, some the water. Here slow and swift fish are caught with the rod, here the limbs of the weary are refreshed with gentle swimming. Here too the student wanders meditating the arts, and the happy lover walks with his darling."

Millerd's Classic Map of Bristol (1673)

Tim was determined to dawdle. After all, Suzie would be late. She was reliably late – ten minutes, fifteen minutes, even half an hour. You could also rely on her to get there in the end, which meant you had to be patient; you had to stick it out; you couldn't assume she wasn't trying.

It was pissing down and everything was grey – tarmac, pavement, cars, scaffolding, polythene, sky. Grey rain wrapped itself around Tim's brollied cocoon. It slanted into his knees and shins as if to goad them onwards, and he ignored it with a kind of perverse joy, resolutely dawdling past newsagent, restaurant and offices, more offices.

The walls to his right gave way to the forecourt of a petrol station. He'd missed the pub. He turned back to scan the signs. Sure enough, among an assortment of efficient minimalist graphics, a painted anchor was hanging over a stained-glass door. He strolled back and hovered outside for a while. Eventually he shook his brolly and entered, holding the wet thing away from his body as if it might be contagious.

sarah menage

The pub welcomed him with the warm glow of electric light off yellowing, gloss-painted walls. It smelt of ash and stale beer. Tim smiled as he glanced over the scenery. Marvellous. Suzie had chosen the only pub in the street that hadn't sold out to developers – the only one whose snug corners were still adorned with lower-middle-class knick-knacks – a saucer from Margate, an array of miniature fire irons, a gilt-edged plate sporting caricatures of Prince Charles and Lady Di, a corn dolly labelled 'Sidmouth festival 1997', a sheep fashioned out of winkles, and, surrounded by knots and nets, the mandatory framed print of Brunel's floating masterpiece, the *SS Great Britain.*

Tim gave the barman a nod, checked his watch to show that he was meeting someone, and ordered a cup of tea. He never drank at lunchtime. His students – his kids as he liked to call them – might notice if he suddenly became incoherent or enthusiastic. The barman produced a metal teapot, a blast of not-quite boiling water, a little bag of dust, a little sachet of white sugar, a plastic shot of non-dairy milk and a plastic stirrer useless for either stirring or squeezing tea bags. "Thank you," Tim said, kindly.

All the comfy seats were taken, so, after finding a wooden stool and a cushion for Suzie, he settled himself on a backless bench next to the Ladies.

He checked his top pocket. Seeing as he'd stowed the thing there earlier and hadn't been upside down recently, there it still was. It was an envelope – an embarrassingly pink envelope – which contained his excuse for meeting Suzie. His reason for meeting her was simple: he wanted to. His heart raced. The bench rocked forwards, knocking the table, spilling tea. A newspaper was wedged under one of its legs. He shifted it, spilling more tea, and spilled yet more while testing the bench. The tabloid made matters worse, so Tim rescued its warped pages and was soon learning more than enough about the sexploits and addictions of a soap star he'd never heard of.

He recognised Suzie's arrival by the sound effects – a bang, a clatter, an "Oh!", an "Oops!" and a "Jesus!".

A multicoloured brolly lay open on the floor some way from a big fur coat. Inside the coat was Suzie. She looked like a black square, a coppery fluff of hair on top, and underneath, two solid striding calves in red tights and a pair of what she called 'don't fuck me' pumps – hulking thick-heeled affairs in British racing green. "Sorry mate, did I hurt you?" She was touching the elbow of a man in a donkey jacket, who was holding his ear.

"No worries, eh," he said. The phrase was clearly special for Suzie. He must know her. Judging by their smiles and greetings, everyone knew her. She lumbered over to Tim, beaming, and a multitude of faces turned in Tim's direction, nodding with approval.

"Thank God you're here early!" she whispered, shaking her brolly in Tim's face. "I thought I was going to have to wait alone."

"D'you come here often?"

She moved his overcoat and sat down beside him on the bench, so it creaked and Tim rocked forwards. Her coat bristled with drips. She pushed it over her shoulders and left it where it fell, wetting Tim's thigh.

"How's the new job?" he asked.

"Shit."

"And what'll they fire you for this time?"

She shrugged. "Eating the olives, maybe." She wrinkled her nose at his cup and saucer. "I'm getting you a drink. Even you can't celebrate with tea."

As he watched her making for the bar, and the way she pressed herself around it to share some chitchat with the barman, Tim wondered what it was about Suzie that infallibly attracted men. You had to see her move to understand it. It was in the ease with which she blushed, the round suppleness of her gestures, the suddenness of her full-throated appreciation of a joke. There was something about her that made you think of apples and berries. She looked as if she'd take off kit and eat manhood at the drop of a bush hat, and utterly without shame. Energy was what she had – energy and basic good health.

Her good news was about real work. She had a contract. Almost signed. It was going to be all her idea and part of next year's *Art for People* festival.

Though she never flaunted her visual taste, talent or skill, Suzie called herself an artist. Her most recent 'work' was a protest against market research. A group of unemployed actors had paraded up Park Street in coloured bibs printed with the logo *Facthunters*. They'd carried clipboards. These measures entitled them to accost innocent strangers with barrages of absurd personal questions. What's your favourite smell? Who makes you sick? Where do you itch? The public responses had been filmed, later to be montaged and presented at the Arnolfini arts centre in a continuous loop.

It didn't go as planned. The lens attracted all Bristol's other unemployed actors who were only too keen to pass on intimate information and more, which Suzie eventually sold to Infosink Inc., simultaneously proving her point while failing to make it.

She was now tapping into the potential offered by the Internet. Two webcams, for example, would film each other at upyourarse.org and upyourarse.com, except that the names had already been bagged by an interactive porn company. She spent long creative hours thinking of alternative titles – cipher, infinity, parallel, waste – and working on her M. Phil., *Menstrual Blood as Artist's Medium: Nora and Beyond*. Nora was a non-existent female Suzie had invented because menstrual blood was old hat and fully covered. Such was academia; such was the state of knowledge that it was blessedly impossible to add to it. As with the state of art itself, alas.

Tim drained his glass.

"I told you men would lose their allure once you got involved in real work again," he said.

"And being involved in real work helped me pull Neil, so who cares?"

Tim's heart sank. Neil was a new name. He didn't want to know about Neil. He let her insist on buying him another pint and sighed deeply as she sauntered once again to the bar.

He fished the envelope from his breast pocket and laid it on the table, adjusting his position on the bench, trying to relax. His fingers were shaking. His bottom bones ached. He leaned an elbow on the table and put his head in his hand. As she returned, he eased his back against the wall. The bench rocked forwards. "I need your womanly advice." He pushed the envelope along the table with a forefinger as she sat down, rocking him backwards again. "This is from Natasha, one of my third-years," he explained. "My brightest and best. And most depressed. She's invaded my pigeon hole."

Suzie opened the envelope and sniffed the paper. "Mmm! Classy." As she read, expressions of amusement, confusion, disgust and anger flickered across her face. Her emotional variety fascinated Tim. For him the note had induced one feeling alone. Dread.

"Sorry but I don't get all this philosophy bollocks," she said, handing it back. "Still, whatever shakes your moneymaker, I guess."

"It's not bollocks and it certainly doesn't shake my moneymaker."

Tim looked again at the note, squirming at the curlicue designs around its border, the flowers, the birds. He'd recognised the brown ink immediately because the girl had a habit of doodling in it during seminars. Her handwriting was tense and tightly formed, but rounded and full of unusual gaps which unnerved him as they seemed to hint at abnormality of some sort. More alarming was the message. She'd been exploring Jean-Paul Sartre's healthless mind, poor thing. Sartre's arguments had convinced her she must do it or die. "It" involved Tim, he supposed. "Die", he hoped, did not. On one side of A4, death featured seven times.

"Perhaps I ought to suggest Prozac," said Tim. "Especially now the nights are closing in."

"What's 'facticity' for fuck's sake?" Suzie asked, tipping back her lager.

Tim was always happy to inform her. "The things you can't change – like the weather, for example. Or where you were born."

Suzie pondered. "So. Blokes. Your family, your talent, your personality, your feelings, your wishes, needs, loves, desires. Your history, your destiny. Most of it, I reckon."

"And that sort of attitude is called 'bad faith'." He angled himself round to point out the relevant quote and felt her leaning into him. "Sartre thought it was one of humanity's most prevalent lies – to deny free will, to deny that you have a choice and you can act on it."

Suzie nodded. Her hair tickled his cheek. She smelt of nectarines.

"So act on it. Why not? Don't you fancy her?"

Tim smiled, and they exchanged a quick glance. "Of course not."

"Why 'Of course'?"

"She's half my age. She's a child."

"She's an adult. She's fair game. She's got knockers and stuff hasn't she?"

Tim blushed under Suzie's scrutiny. He closed his eyes and tried to picture the girl, but Natasha's flimsy image faded into Suzie's vibrant one. She was thin, was all he could think. Physically thin, spiritually heavy. "I'll admit she's rather sweet, but, no." He shook his head. "It would be quite wrong in every way."

Suzie sighed. "Jesus. I wish I got treated as well as you treat women."

He pressed his lips together tight, resting his mouth in his hand; then, when he realised he wasn't breathing properly, put his chin on his knuckles. "I know what I must do, but how to do it for the best, there's the thing. What's the least painful way to let someone down? I thought you'd know."

Suzie puckered her brow. She played rather fetchingly with her mouth while she thought.

"So that she won't go off and die," Tim added. He noticed he was tapping the letter and Suzie stilled his hand gently with hers, forcing him to look at her, sideways. He loved her green eyes. In their clear gaze he sensed a touch of old sorrow that intrigued him and made him want to comfort her. At the same time they challenged him, especially in that position. He noticed a fleck of black make-up in her eyelashes. Left over from the previous night, perhaps. He put his head back in his hand.

"Considering all the options, my womanly advice, and you're not going to like this, but you know it makes sense."

"Yes?"

She whispered it. "Tell her to fuck off."

Tim groaned, and she grinned.

"She wants you because you're nice. You've got to be nasty." She stood up, shaking her head and tutting indulgently as she looked him up and down, like a ward sister assessing a patient. "It could be love, couldn't it? Why not? At least she's on your wavelength with all that philosophy bollocks." She brushed his cheek with a kiss and bundled up her belongings. Tim wanted to stand for her departure, but disappointment stuck him to the bench.

"Look at you. You're so upset, so sweet! Just ignore her, to begin with. I'm sure you can manage that."

He watched her bustle away, accompanied by a chorus of goodbyes and see you laters. The barman shouted "Wey hey!" as the door swung shut.

Tim's own attraction to Suzie was more blue-blooded than red, he liked to think. It wasn't her bodily substance he adored, but her transparency. Her soul was naked, she hid nothing – she told him all. And he would trust her with his own secrets when the time came, simply because she wouldn't be remotely interested in passing them on. Right from their first – no – from their second meeting, they'd been comrades.

It was ludicrous, really, the idea that he could ever go out with someone who said "fuck" more often than "but".

When he got home that evening he washed and changed before discovering the blinking light and playing his messages. There was one from Suzie saying she'd lost her fucking brolly and had he got it. One from Natasha, wondering whether he agreed that Hume's bundle theory of the self was equivalent to existential angst and wasn't humanity essentially schizophrenic in any case? It pained him, this acted thirst for knowledge. She thought he didn't realise how she felt, like a child who thinks you can't see her because her own eyes are closed.

The last was a message from Lou he wished he'd heard sooner, saying, "Hello Daddy." She seemed younger and more vulnerable as a disembodied voice. Her clear breakable tones went straight to his guilt centres, bound as they were to his love centres. And God he did love her, his brown-eyed girl, dark, tousled, cute-nosed, smiley-cheeked and bonny as buttons. Sometimes thinking of Lou reminded him of loving Vivienne. Mother and daughter, they were like clones. She said, "It's Lou by the way," before hanging up, as if she could possibly be anyone else.

He phoned her. Vivienne answered.

"She's at a friend's house." Crisp.

"Which friend?"

"Miles. You don't know him." Harsh.

"When is she back?"

"She's staying the night." Curt.

Tim sighed loudly and gritted his teeth. He felt pressure rising in his temples. "If she needs babysitting, why can't I babysit?"

"We've been through all this before."

"Well, I still don't understand. I wish you'd asked me first."

"She wanted to stay with Miles."

Tim sighed again, quietly this time. He realised it was absurd for a grown man to feel rejected by an eight-year-old. "I can babysit more or less any night of the week you know."

Vivienne's response was well rehearsed and badly performed in an irritating sing-song tone which deserved to be strangled. "We can't afford to give her false expectations. If you're here in the evening, what's it going to look like? She might start to think you're coming back. She might have hopes."

"Hopes! God forbid."

"She's okay, Tim. She probably needs you less than you need her."

If he didn't know Vivienne he'd think she was hurting him deliberately. But he knew her inside out, upside down and the wrong way round. Her cruelty was inadvertent and part of her charm. One day she might know how deeply she'd wounded him and suffer a torment of regret, which she'd do as she did everything, intensely. He wouldn't want that; she'd make everyone feel bad.

"How are things?" he asked.

"You know how things are."

"I mean for you. Are you okay? What have you been up to?"

"Same as usual. I'll tell her you called."

He'd done nothing to deserve this except 'love her in the wrong way'. Loving in the wrong way was a Viviennism – part of Vivienne's personal lexicon of love and hate – a vocabulary with a philosophy all its own and an internal logic you couldn't argue against unless you wanted to look at someone's back all night. Guilt centres and love centres were Viviennisms.

He had an excuse to call Suzie but she was out. He left a message telling her she hadn't left her brolly in the pub.

A phrase from a song he'd heard somewhere was nudging his mind. "What a wicked thing to do... " He couldn't remember the tune or how it went on. He didn't feel like reading or watching television. What was on anyway? Nothing but gardening, cooking and DIY – as if television life and real life had swapped places. Already you could watch people asleep, washing their teeth, shitting. You could watch people watching television. Lucky one's own life was full of drama and adventure, otherwise how could a poor soul escape from hell? How could one purge?

He decided to have a hot bath, being just about strong enough to face a close encounter with his own skin. He looked old in the bathroom mirror. Old, baggy-eyed, furrow-browed, lugubrious. He ran a finger down the line of his jaw, jutting out his chin to minimise any hint of jowl. Not bad. He still had a full head of hair, too, most of it still dark. He smiled at himself, with his mouth, not his eyes. His eyes remained distant, serious, mysterious perhaps. He lit some candles but even after flicking through *Vogue* he didn't feel like masturbating. He just wanted to talk to someone. It's good to talk.

three poems

by janet menzies

an introduction to geometry

For all the years I let a man
I didn't love love me
Love's symmetry

Now I love a man
Who won't love me.
Sweet trigonometry

That plays the metaphysic
Reducing me
To sine and cosine.

His love for me, I,
At our triangle's apex,
Reflect in perfect isosceles.

But there is no base
For our lovers' tripos
Our equation unworkable.
I am simply
At vanishing point
Where two lines appear to meet:

No true convergence
No equal mixing
No world for sea-discoverers.

janet menzies

One hinge, two stabbing points,
Make dividers to chart
Our cruel navigation.

Lesson one: learn that
Passion's precision
Is eternal.

a novice's guide to sinning

The cripple Crouchback found
That to be Catholic is to sin.
It rather suited him
For every Catholic sinner is forgiven.

But there are some, still, forbidden;
Both sins and men may have degree.
They say that suicide is wrong,
By canon law decreed: will committed
And therefore called 'sin of commission'.

On Mendip hills this means that now
The long dead Cannard and Tucker both,
Driven no doubt by darkness and the day,
Must yet unhallowed lie
And each, conveniently beside the road,
Become a pub.

But fonder priests will gently chide, and seek
The smaller flaw, they call a sin
Of omission; where simple absence cries
Oh Father forgive me for I forgot.

Better then aspire to lesser sin.
Omit to live.
As one who, falling, fails to land, so flies
Another, living, fails to last, so dies.

being not peggy

(Basil Bunting dedicated his long narrative poem, Briggflats, to Peggy)

I was not dead, but died
A little death each time
You quivering, came, crying inside me,
Your tears in my eyes.

A stupid Hecuba, I thought
You cried for me
But what was I to you
That you should weep for me?

You wrote your hate,
Those "lines still-born,"
How you came to blame, deserved by me,
For being not Peggy; I failed

And let you leave my womb
Unmarked (though not by choice).
But still those tears of yours did yet beget
A little snivelling, shrivelling, bastard offspring.

Your misery
Is still alive and well with me:
Each time I die I cry.
Some other lover looking down on me
Will see me weep,

So watching my tears blend
Will wonder and assume
In arrogance of desire
That I should weep for him.

But what's he to Hecuba
That I should weep for him?
...
Weep for him.

a three-dimensional cobweb

from a novel **by morgaine merch lleuad**

Apparently, a mirror never lies. And, apparently, a witch cannot see her reflection in the mirror. Or is it that she must not be caught between two mirrors, because they suck out her soul?

I have only one mirror in my house. It is not big, but old, and speckled and cracked. And I cannot see my reflection in it, not clearly. Perhaps this makes me only partly a witch? I have only one mirror in my house, so I cannot test the hypothesis. I often talk to my reflection. I think most people do. After all, there are many different forms of mirrors: other people, for one.

I live on the littoral, on the threshold between earth and water. Perhaps I am a mermaid, the threshold between woman and fish. And perhaps I should stop these ridiculous musings and answer the front door.

The postman is late this morning. My letterbox is very narrow, and so he has to knock to deliver the large, flat, white envelope. I open the door.

"Morning." He smiles at me.

I smile back, and take the envelope from him. "Thanks."

Off he goes, walking down the uneven path, stepping on the thyme, which grows in the stony cracks, then ducking to avoid the honeysuckle around the arch, in a bizarre limbo dance. He closes the gate carefully behind him, making sure the latch catches fast. Then, whistling – I have a postman who whistles – he swings his leg over the crossbar of his bicycle, which he left leaning drunkenly against the hedge, and sways off. Or at least I imagine he does all this, as I can't see him – I keep my hedges high.

My half-smoked roll-up has gone out so, clutching the envelope to my chest, I crouch down to look at the path before I go back inside. Two varieties of thyme, one tiny and dark as wine bottles, one variegated, lemon and lime. They seem to have taken over the stones overnight. I am suitably amazed, as usual. If it wasn't so drizzly this morning, the postman's feet might have released the thyme's warm, green scent. I walk my eyes down the path and up to the honeysuckle, a profusion of leaves and tendrils. When it flowers (very soon), the air of arrivals and departures will be sweetened. They'll complain about fighting their way in through the greenery, of course, and will probably miss the effect. But they are never many. I shall have to go out more, just so I can leave and come back, and sniff. Or invite more people round.

Or perhaps not.

Under slight duress, I'd probably admit to being Taud's best friend. She is the most complicated person I know, layered like an onion. Every time you think you've worked her out, just as you get comfortable with her, another part of her is revealed, if she decides to reveal it. Once she's decided you're worth it, she's yours. She rarely does anything by halves; as she says herself, "I don't do medium." And yet... Taud is the most capricious person I know.

My blackbird is on the branch of the elder tree, which reaches across to the upstairs hall window, his usual perch at this time of the day; and he's singing his heart out, just for me. I look up at him and smile. But the drizzle is chilling my feet, and my coffee will be getting cold. As I stand up, I stumble, and the inch of my cigarette falls on to the step. Even I, slattern of the century, cannot leave it there. I clutch the envelope with one hand and flick the roll-up into the sage bush, disturbing a furiously busy spider, breaking one of her threads. I don't suppose for one minute she is actually glaring at me, but I apologise anyway, and she goes back to her murderous preparations. As I step back inside and turn to shut the front door, I look at the gate, and wonder why the postman always closes it so carefully. Is it to keep people out, to keep me safe? Or, to keep me in? I close the door quietly, and go to find my cold coffee.

To quote Taud: "Most of us are like cobwebs: regular, but complicated weavings of our culture, personality, experiences; interconnected threads from all of our existence." We once saw a cobweb, heavy and white with dew, woven with such intricacy that it had become three-dimensional. It looked as though it were freestanding, although it couldn't have been. Taud is a three-dimensional cobweb.

The envelope is still large, still white and still thin, when I finally look at it. I perch on the edge of the chaise in the kitchen, a new, hot mug of coffee within easy reach and a new cigarette clamped between my lips. The envelope is damp, and the smoke from the roll-up is making my eyes water, so it's not easy reading the words. As usual, they – whoever they are – have got my first name wrong. It's "Audley", not "Audrey". (All known deities protect me from pretentious parents.) But I'm used to it. Some people have called me "Aud", but not many, and not for long – I don't like it. I let a couple of very close friends call me "Taud", as I quite like that. Well, I say a couple, but I mean Andrew, really, and perhaps the occasional lover. Very occasional – I don't seem to have much luck. Anyway, mostly, I insist on "Audley", in full. Names are important; people should make an effort. It's only courteous, respectful.

I take a quick drag on the roll-up, lean it in the ashtray and have a swig of coffee. Opening letters is always exciting, if you don't know what they are – all that potential. Even now, the sounds of the gate squeaking open – I never bother to oil it; I like the early warning system – of the postman trying to shove things through the letterbox, of the paper hitting the mat: even now, all these sounds make my heart beat a little faster. I've never outgrown the anticipation. Or the disappointment, for that matter. I'm still not great at dealing with disappointment, even with all the practice I get. And I'm never sure whether it's more disappointing not to get any post, or to get the mundane, uninteresting stuff. Is there a way to measure disappointment? Perhaps I should try, see which is worse: bugger all, or missives from Mundania.

I'd like a sign on the gate: "You are now leaving Mundania. Please have your brain ready." Or maybe even secede from the wretched place, declare devolution, or independence, or something, make up my own laws for my own nation state. Brilliant idea. I drink some more coffee, re-light my fag and look at the envelope's expanse of white. Just the thing for a list of new laws. Putting down the mug and the cigarette, I open it carefully. As I suspected; I've been selected from thousands of random people, all minding their own business, to be the recipient of a wonderful special offer. I don't even bother reading what the offer is. I flip the contents of the envelope onto the floor – I'll put it in the recycling box later – and reach over for the pen I know I put somewhere... ah, and then an old newspaper. I sit back on the chaise and prop the envelope against the newspaper. What's the first law of Taudland? "All shoes to be removed inside the house." I try to write "1" on the envelope, even though I haven't written the title yet. The ink runs and splodges on the dampness, spreading the "1" into a fuzzy worm and a star. It's probably symbolic. I sigh, and re-light my cigarette.

You could describe her as 'paradoxical'. Part of her is so old as to be ancient, but she can be childlike (or even childish) in her responses to the world. She's a great people person when she wants to be, yet she despairs of the human race most of the time. Her mind flits all over the place, and yet she can also be ponderous, stubborn. It's not easy to fit Taud into a box, and people who don't fit in boxes are threatening to others.

I manage to avoid my specky reflection in the mirror, propped up against the banister at the top of the stairs, as I pass it on the way to the sock room (which is also the drying room, the collection-of-wools-and-fabric room, the-pile-of-ironing room, the open-the-door-and-throw-it-in-I'll-sort-it-out-later room and the guest room, depending on my mood, or what I'm looking for – although I usually know where I've put my guests). Anyway, I've decided to settle in the kitchen for a bit, and the quarry tiles are cool underfoot, even with the Aga going, hence the need for socks. I catch sight of myself on the way back down, though. A wispy, ghosty thing hovers on the spotty silvered surface, tall, long legs, slim, distorted, black and red stripes, coffee and honey, smoky, neither solid nor quite fey. I can either see myself from the shoulders down, or from the knees up. The former seems the favoured option – I haven't bothered to put on make-up today, or to brush my hair yet. I step forward. The light is better here, because I'm right in front of the window. But I've disturbed the blackbird, who stops singing and flies off. Funny, he's usually quite tame with me. I look out of the window, to see where he's gone, and notice the paper aeroplane on the front path, and the honeysuckle still moving, slightly.

I pad downstairs in my woolly socks and, opening the front door, go out and pick up the aeroplane. The soft rain has stopped. The honeysuckle moves again, and I can hear stifled giggles and "Shh"s. I walk down to the gate ("She's coming!") and peer round the greenery. But feet are running down the lane, the breathless laughter getting farther away. The aeroplane has writing on it. I open it up. There is a crude drawing of a woman, in black, on what I imagine they mean to be a broomstick, with a squashed cat sitting behind her. She is wearing a pointy black hat. Underneath is the legend: "Awdry Laton is a wich." I dare say they're right, whoever "Awdry Laton" may be. Do I know her? (Does anyone?)

I walk back into the house and close the door firmly behind me, smiling. Hah! They didn't dare use the gate, to actually enter Taudland, hence the aeroplane. It's not until I walk into the kitchen that I realise the path was still awfully wet from the rain. I sigh, take off my socks, throw them in the vague direction of the Aga and resign myself to getting another pair. On my way out and then up, I admire the rain-dark footprints on the kitchen and hall floors. Batty old cow. (Although I'm not old.) No wonder they think I'm a witch, wandering around in the rain in my socks. And the cats won't disabuse them of the idea, either. Perhaps I should grow some warts and develop a cackle.

The wet footprints remind me of the Little Mermaid. Hang on, wasn't I a mermaid earlier? No, I couldn't be the Little Mermaid, I talk too much. New socks – not matching this time, I can't be bothered – and

I'm ready to roll again. More coffee.

While I wait for the kettle to boil, it strikes me how bored the kids must be. It's near the end of the Easter holidays, which is enough to bore anyone half to death, but there's nothing but my house and a dodgy cliffy bit up here. And the darks of the wood, of course, which they usually avoid. But no other reason to come up here. They must have made a special trip – I'm nearly flattered.

Taud has manifested the perfect house for herself. Isn't there some Chinese thing about whether you're a rock, water or tree person? Well, with the old cottage affair, the wood at the end of her lane, the cliff a few yards away, and the sea visible from the upstairs windows and the bottom of the back garden, she's got the best of all three worlds. Typical Taud – she's all of them.

I suppose I should write a list of things to do, although I don't have to do anything urgently right now – I'm a woman of leisure, until school starts again next week. But I get bored easily at the best of times, and I'm going through a restless patch at the moment, and I'd better keep myself busy, in case I start thinking about… yes, well, let's not think about it. So, I'll wander round the gardens and see if anything needs weeding or dead-heading or whatever it is you're supposed to do. (Charlie Dimmock I ain't. I haven't got the boobs, for a start. That's why I grow herbs and wildflowers, mainly… not because of the boobs, but because I'm not desperately green-fingered. Herbs are practically indestructible, and look after themselves. Well, that's one of the reasons.) Amazing, really: I'd have thought my garden would have sulked in the salty air, but I must be just far enough away from the sea for it not to matter. Or there's a spell on the gardens.

This time, I remember my wellies.

In the back garden, Bastet and Greymalkin are skulking under the catnip, surprise, surprise. I know the names are a bit obvious, but if you're going to be lumbered with a stereotype, you might as well conform to it. They look both vaguely shifty and complicitous, so I wonder what small wild creature has met with a short, sharp and crunchy end recently. And what bits I'll find somewhere inconvenient in the house, when they decide to do the hairball thing. Grey uncoils himself and stretches, prior to coming over to greet me. I bend down and stroke him from nose to tail-tip, his back arching. I'm sure this must be involuntary – they even do this in public, and they'd never let on that anything a human can do brings them pleasure. Total, complete and absolute cats. Bast waits until Grey has finished being friendly, then wanders over to join in the fun. The big grey tom moves out of her way – no doubt of the hierarchy here, even if he dwarfs her slight, sleek blackness. And here comes Schroedinger, the last, and biggest, of the triumvirate. He is, quite simply, huge – a shaggy, marmalade monster. And a complete wuss, except if he thinks someone's threatening me. Then he growls, and the hairs go up on the back of everyone's neck, including mine. If only they knew. There's a famous experiment, for which he is named – skip this if you already know – with a cat in a box, together with a vial of poison, and a radioactive source. If the radioactive source emits a thingon of radioactivity, then the poison is released and the cat dies. The whole point of the experiment is uncertainty – you can't tell whether or not the thingon has been emitted, the poison has been released and the cat is dead, because the box is closed; you have to open the box to see if the cat's alive or dead. So, in effect, if the box is still closed, the cat exists in a state of aliveness and deadness at the same time... something like that. Anyway, the point of this rambling being that, if it were Schro in the box, he wouldn't know himself if he was alive or dead. You'd probably have to tell him. Poor old Schro: the cat without a brain.

Bast and Grey are bored with me by now, and wander off. Schro follows me as I start my research trip round the garden, getting under my feet, anxious in case an ant should leap out at him, or something. I stop and lean down to scratch behind his ears and make appropriate reassuring noises. He replies by chirruping – a cat that chirrups? By this time, the winds have chased off the dismal greyness, and the sea haze promises lazy heat. Yes, working in the garden today – a chance to commune with nature, sort out the garden, and get brown. I'll try and persuade Schro to fall asleep somewhere, so I can continue my perambulations unencumbered.

I walk back to the house, Schro attached to my left heel, and into the kitchen. Obviously, a complete waste of time getting the Aga going at the crack of stupid o'clock this morning, given the promise of summer outside. Naturally, Bast has appropriated the spot right in front of the Aga, Grey being relegated to a respectful distance away. But both have acquired a piece of paper to sit on: Bast, the ex-aeroplane (shame, I was going to put it up on the fridge, having no kids of my own to produce appalling artwork), whilst Grey is curled up on the still-damp envelope. They've obviously dragged their respective seats from wherever I'd dropped them. Schro mews pathetically, and I anthropomorphise madly, seeing Bast's eyes lift to the heavens in despair. But she does shift over a little, granting Schro half-an-inch of paper to put the tip of a paw on. What a trio – two with too much intelligence and all of them with too much personality.

I go into the front room to see what the time is. Nearly ten, already. Time to get to work. Although, perhaps just one more coffee-and-fag break. After all, it's my holiday. As I leave, I glance, casually, at the phone. It's not ringing. I didn't think it would be. But I never give up hope. Optimism? Denial? Or refusing to let go?

Taud has a very strict moral code. The fact that it bears only passing resemblance to anyone else's – and that resemblance only due to a vague sense of propriety when she's in public (and sober) – is beside the point. Taud is a law unto herself, whichever self she happens to be at that moment. She can enter a room several feet before she actually does, if you know what I mean. But that's only one of the layers. Remember, appearances can be deceptive. Remember Schroedinger. And mirrors often reflect what we think is there.

three poems

by paul meyer

a vision of akhmatova

The night is cold and the stars don't blink as much as vibrate
As the great poet looks out a tiny window from one of those
Meat-gray Soviet equipment planes. The plane lifts away
From her beloved city of Peter, and from the Germans,
Who threaten everything, everything.

The co-pilot turns, sizes up the crowd of refugees:
Dozens of them sit freezing in the vast space of the cargo hold.
How could this co-pilot know that the clump of paper
     the dark-haired woman wrings in her hands
Is the great Seventh Symphony, by Shostakovich?
He thinks she might be some kind of schoolteacher,
Or seamstress, and imagines himself spending the night with her
When they land in Tashkent, have each dined on rich food,
And shared a bottle of sweet wine.

The plane hits an air pocket;
And the co pilot returns to his duties,
Missing altogether the brief smile on the woman's face
As she figures yet again how to put all those awful years
Into a just few small words.

creation myth

First there was The Mall
And then The New Mall.
After that The Riverside Center
And then The New Riverside Center.

paul meyer

Along came The Oaks
And blew everybody's mind.

Now the big thing is The Outlet
Which is at least twenty miles up the road.
It gives people a sense of how shall I say
Exclusivity that The Outlet is so how shall I say
Distant, like the time
Before time, like the time
Even before The Mall.

ghosts

The ghost that seeps from a battery.

The ghost of Marcus Garvey and the ghosts of his enemies.

The ghost that rests behind that half-moon of your fingernails.

The ghost of the 20th Century, falling backwards into the ether.

The ghost of Caspar, the Friendly Ghost.

The ghost of Carmen Miranda, singing 'Mama Eu Quero'.

The ghost of your favorite shirt, which is gone, gone, gone, gone, gone!

The ghost posing as our president.

The ghost of you, my friend.

The ghost camper at the ghost campground, out on the old
    GhostHighway on the outskirts of Ghostumberland.

The ghost of wilderness, which is everywhere, everywhere.

The ghosts of your family pets, come back from heaven for one
    last big 'ol kiss.

The ghost that steals your buttons, breaks your laces.

The ghost of Chance.

The ghost of yesterday: Mnemosyne, Memory, mother of all
poetry and art!

The ghost of all those unsalvaged ships, stuck on the ocean floor and
posing for the cameras on The Ghost Channel.

The ghost of winter, haunting a forest in springtime.

My ghost, which bids you adieu, farewell, adios, until we meet again...

the van

a short story **by peter o'connor**

Claire Jones took my virginity. It was at a quarter past six on August the ninth, 1975, in the back of her father's 1958 Morris Minor van.

The van, a split-screen MK-II, sat on the drive outside the Jones's council house perched on four splintering wooden blocks. The engine had long been removed, along with the bonnet and all the wings. The headlights were smashed and the windscreen had been recycled as part of a cold frame for Dan Drew's tomato crop. The shell of the van sat blind and unmoving on its wooden pedestals for five long years of my life. The council finally towed it away, after Mr Jones killed himself. But even today, twenty odd years later, the dark patch of mixed fluids that dripped from beneath its body can still be seen on the drive of No 68 Moore View. It's much duller now, worn by the passage of time and numerous attempts by new residents to scrub it clean. But it stubbornly resists all attempts to erase it. And, even if it did finally disappear, I would still see its ghost on the drive of No 68 Moore View.

The spring day Mr Jones and his friend Bob Coles towed the van onto the estate, Claire, Julie, Steve and I were playing out at the huge pile of earth that loomed behind our houses. This spot, which ran along our joined back fences, became our regular playground when the local playing fields and half of John Francis's farm were scraped clean of all life. The council planned to build another two hundred and fifty houses out there. The New Town would have more shops, a purpose-built play area and the man from Tesco's said there would be more jobs. Men from all over the country turned up. They stayed in caravans and portable huts on the site and spoke in foreign accents. For three months our estate shook and rumbled with their monstrous yellow machines; they started their loud growlings at six in the morning and went on under floodlights till well into the dark night. Those bright yellow monsters gaily ripped the rocks and soil out of the ground and playfully flung it till it piled high into the air. The weather-worn heap took on the same rounded look as the earth a grave is dug into; our playing field turned into an empty grave.

The trees that had grown there since Mr Francis's great-grandfather had been a young boy were uprooted and piled like a huge game of pick-up-sticks in the far corner of the site. For a while, sap ran from the huge gashes the jaws of the machines had inflicted on the trees, and still their leaves expectantly opened. But finally the trees must have realised they were dead and over the summer months the leaves shrivelled and the carcasses turned stone grey as their roots became dry and brittle. When the last remaining piece of colourful foliage had been tossed onto the vast pyre, the men casually set it ablaze. The fire crackled and roared for six days and nights; even our drawn curtains couldn't keep the glare from our bedrooms; and the flames sent strange shadows dancing across our ceilings. In the mornings, the fire sent huge clouds of black smoke up into the air, staining black all the back walls of our row, and speckling the washing across the whole village. We could put our cheeks against the back walls of our houses and feel the heat radiating from them. Weeks later the charred grey ash still gave off a faint dying warmth; and if you dug deep enough, red embers would sweep into the air.

But the houses never arrived. Tesco had had a downturn. The council ran out of money. The machines and men went home oblivious to the carnage they left behind. That winter, the foundations and trenches filled with oily, red water. The field became an expanse of sticky, clinging mud, which every child carried home on ruined clothes and shoes. Our parents complained to the council, but it wasn't until six-year-old Charlie Francis was sucked into one of the mud-filled pits and had to be rescued by the fire brigade that the excavations were filled with rubble. A high barbed-wire fence and red signs warning of the danger were erected to keep us out. But the huge pile of earth was outside that high perimeter fence, and it became ours. We had nowhere else to play, and no matter what threats our parents devised we still went there. It was from the highest point of this pile that Claire spotted her dad and Bob dragging the van into our road. By the time we got there most of the local kids from the estate were helping them push it up the slight incline of the drive of No 68. Little did we know that we were helping to erect a local landmark.

"What you going to do with that, Mr Jones?" I asked, as I licked the ice-cream, our reward for helping with the pushing.

"I'm going to restore it, Peter. Make it as good as new. Yes, it'll soon be back on the road. We'll be able to take you and the girls out on trips. Fancy a trip to the seaside this summer, ay?"

"Yeah, that would be great. A man came and took our car away."

"I know."

"Can Mrs Jones come?" Claire asked.

"Maybe... if she's well enough."

For two weeks Bob and Mr Jones were out on that drive from six in the morning till eight at night banging and swearing and laughing. They replaced all the wooden frames around the back windows with abandoned wood they had collected from a building site. They put on a new roof rack Bob's brother made in his garage, and replaced two of the wings with ones Mr Jones had got from a scrapyard. On those mornings, on my way to school, I would ride past on my bike and ask them how it was going. Mr Jones would turn to me, cap on backwards, oil smeared on his cheek, and say, "It's going fine thank you, Peter. Soon have her back on the road, won't we, Bob?" Bob would raise his head from under the bonnet and call, "Ay, nearly there now. She'll soon be running like a clock." Bob and Mr Jones had worked at the local abattoir until it had closed down six months before. "Forty years of my life I spent working there, for what? No pension, a bad chest and an aching back, that's for what," Mr Jones could often be heard saying in the doctor's surgery as he waited for his wife's prescription to be filled. The abattoir had been the only real employer in the area. When it shut, one hundred and twenty men were laid off. Our family was lucky; we didn't have a dad, so the closure didn't affect us. You could tell the ones who had been laid off though: all their gardens were freshly dug, all their houses were freshly painted, and all their cars were freshly cleaned.

"What you going to do with it when it's finished, Mr Jones?" I asked one Sunday morning as he rubbed a green wax onto its body.

"We're going to sell it, Pete. Try to make some money." He tilted his head upwards and raised his hand. Mrs Jones was standing shrouded at the bedroom window. She coughed into her hand and disappeared.

Then we had a month of drenching rain, and Bob Coles drowned on a mackerel-fishing trip off Plymouth Sound. The van sat untouched for six months. During that time somebody stole the bonnet and broke the rear side window. Mr Jones taped up the damaged window, and put a tarpaulin across the space where the bonnet had been, holding it in place with two old tyres. He put up a sign next to it that said, "Please don't touch." It sat, crouched and hibernating, under its blanket covering all that winter.

On the odd occasions I saw Mr Jones after that, usually coming back from the doctor's surgery, I would ask him the same question, and he would give the same reply: "Fine, Pete, soon have it finished, yeh, soon have it on the road. Not long now. You'll be the first to go for a ride in it."

Mr Jones's cough became worse and he stayed indoors all the next winter, the doctor having to go to see him now. But as soon as the weather warmed up I would see him standing on his drive in his blue slippers, mug of tea steaming in his hand, staring at his Morris van. Sometimes I helped him clean it, and afterwards he would apply small patches of rust treatment to its many scabs. One year he filled a hole in the front wing, smoothing the pink paste down with a large bread knife. It looked like sugared icing on a cake. He then taped a plastic bag over the repair. "To keep the water out," he explained. "Don't want it rusting away, do we?" But every year another part would be gone. It was like watching one of the cattle at the abattoir being stripped to the bone.

Mr Jones's wife died the summer he brush-painted the remaining skeleton, and sold the engine to Alan Clark. I didn't see him touch it after that, except to put an old mattress in the back, and two old brown suitcases on the roof rack.

It was later that year the van began to earn its reputation. It became known as Jones's Jump. On warm summer evenings a steady stream of adolescents could be seen making their way to No 68 Moore View. It became the favourite meeting place, and groups of teenagers would smoke and hang around the van's rusting double doors. It had all started with Julie Jones, Claire's older sister. Julie, like Claire, was a big girl, and as such people thought she was ugly. At thirteen, all fat people were ugly to my friends and I. Her flesh seemed to fall down her arms and legs ending at swollen ankles and chubby fingers that used to pinch and tickle me raw when she could catch me. Well, Julie got a reputation as an easy lay. I don't know if the stories were true, but she became pregnant and left school and the area soon afterwards, and – as reputations tend to do – hers passed to her sister, who seemed to pick it up with relish. But Claire was a little wiser than Julie. She saw an opportunity and grasped it with both hands. If you knew the right people and could raise the £3 she would accommodate you. She accommodated me on that August day in 1975 after Crackerjack. I was fourteen, she was sixteen. From start to finish the whole fumbling, frantic, clumsy and sticky process took no more than four minutes and sixteen seconds. I know this time span to be correct because Steve, who was after me, had his stopwatch ticking away outside the van. Claire didn't charge me, as I don't think I fulfilled all the criteria for full fee-paying coitus, and I think in a way she actually quite liked me. The experience, far from exciting my sexual appetite, put me off sex and women for the next two years. Claire was taken away from Mr Jones and school soon after that and sent to a home up country somewhere. I never saw her again. I think I might have seen Julie. She's slimmer now and she's dyed her hair. She was pushing a pram through a crowded high street, her arm wrapped round a young man's waist. But I wasn't sure enough to approach her. And if I had been, what would I have said?

According to the local paper a social worker found Mr Jones. He had been dead for a week. A whole week and nobody noticed. I keep thinking

peter o'connor

I should have missed him, noticed that both suitcases were gone from the roof rack. But the van was just a wreck. Nobody paid it much attention by then. The paper said he had drunk a bottle of whisky and taken a vial of sleeping pills and had just curled up and gone to sleep in the back of his 1958 Morris Minor van.

three poems

by helen partridge

the woman who lost her tongue

Because she had grown tired of conversations
in which she always lost more than she learned
she decided to cut down on her consonants,
thinking to give less of herself away.

First she left out the labials, their too-intimate touch
like sucking kisses. At once she seemed to dance
rather than talk. Her hands made inscrutable gestures.
Men were attracted by her sudden grace.

The sibilants went next. Now she could skate
for days without argument, her blades not lifted
once from the ice, as if the lack of friction
were simply giftedness, or a brand new season.

The fricatives were easy, like a dress
shrugged off in moonlight. No more slough and scurf
of clothes on skin. It was hard to be sarcastic
or smart without them. She found herself adored.
Free of all the articulate abrasions
she opened herself to a sky like a blown shell,
and men flocked down with unread messages,
cirrus frost in their hair, their seals unbroken.

It was obvious then that everything had to go.
The surgeon swabbed her down. Glottals and dentals
curled into his sink. She was coming through
clearer and clearer the more he cut away.

helen partridge

These days she speaks to no one, though she breathes
the words of a hundred lovers, intimate as air.
The men free-fall through her in passing blurs.
None of that rough barging towards sense
that always used to miss. Sometimes a sigh grows
or a moan. All vowels. She has nothing left to bruise.

the mapmaker's mistake

I can see how you cooked this one up
with your visions of God in the year dot, poring
over His plans for the world. What a fit
with your own busy scratching and staring,
your yardstick, your precious bloody map.

A deliberate mistake. So that was your talisman.
In case it should come to His notice
that you had set yourselves up in the practice
of recording Creation. The perfected view
reserved for His angels or a flying machine

you haven't invented yet. You were letting your ink
get big ideas, mapmaker, summoning birds
to nest in your boundary lines, your paper fields
blooming with poppies and green barley.
So you slipped that stitch. And wasn't it just my luck

to be in the wrong place, actually sweeping the yard –
my sound, snug yard – when your river tripped across.
I had to watch my best hen bundled off,
her squawks bubbling in her crop, my good beans drowned
while your useless fish gaped on the naked mud.

Now every rain rolls stones across my sill.
The green weed thickens on my well-set flags.
The goats have broken out, scared by things lost
in other places that turn up in their stall:
hats and needles. Once a haystack, whole.

No callers, not even the priest, not since his prayer
for the health of my new beans and my second best hen
came bouncing back from the closed lid of the sky.
The neighbours remember a house, but not its name.
They scare themselves with rumours of a tear

in the fabric of fields, where a child might disappear
without a sign. Without even being missed.
Think, mapmaker, how someone could play the goat,
unnoticed here, out of the eye of God.
You talk of mistakes and I'm tempted, I confess.

beuhas

from *a cornish bestiary*

Plural as caravans or concubines
they muster by night
in hammocks of worn grass
slung between pylons
on nettles and shockwire.

In the flimsiest nighties
they tune their dawn engines
for a browsing spell.
A brew of stems and sap
hoisted through plumbing
as intricate as an orchestra,
while their high heels put on costumes
of cello-players' shoulders
and tug-o-war thighs.

There is a time for mooching down
to the tubular lips
of mechanical calves
and the barrelling milklorry.
There is a time to be conducted
through muddy passages
by intelligent hands.

helen partridge

But this is not their score.
Dusk finds them practising
sturdy local scales,
sketching with splashy turds
and sudden chasing moods
the all-important cadence of a field.

benedict's creed

from a novel **by john pemberton**

Brother Acius was the first to arrive in the chapter house for the meeting. He was laden down with books for the day's readings. A grey mist hung low in the room at the level of the stone seating ledge. Moisture glistened on the newly built walls. He shivered as he crossed the room and unloaded the books on the bookstand.

He drew *Benedict's Creed* to the front. The book, a set of rules by which the ancient saint prescribed the monks should live, was always the first to be read. But he did not open the book at the leather strip marking today's reading. Instead, he allowed himself to turn its parchment pages. His fingers rubbed their rough edges, then stroked the uneven contours of the surface. He stopped at his favourite illustration. His eyes feasted on the intensity of the red, blue and green ink, and the radiance of the gold lacquer. He savoured the sharpness of the outlines and the delicacy of the decoration. It reminded him of the Lord's capacity to inspire man's deeds, and strengthened his devotion.

Acius sensed movement in the room. He looked up to see the abbot entering, bowed his head in respect, saying, "Good morning, Father."

The abbot nodded. In his monk's habit, his slight frame seemed out of proportion to his large belly. As he crossed the floor, he swayed from side to side with each step. His eyes, staring out from his round shining head, took in the book Acius was studying. They fixed themselves on Acius independent of his swaying. Acius hastily turned the pages back to the leather strip, and took his place on the stone seating around the walls. The other monks began to file in.

The abbot opened the meeting by intoning from *Benedict's Creed* the rule for the day:

> As often as anything important is to be done in the monastery, the abbot shall call the whole community together and himself explain what the business is. After hearing the advice of the brothers, let him ponder it and follow what he judges the wiser course. The brothers, for their part, are to express their opinions with all humility, and not presume to defend their own views obstinately. The decision is rather the abbot's to make so that when he has determined what is more prudent, all may obey. Nevertheless, just as it is proper for disciples to obey their master, so it is becoming for the master on his part to settle everything with foresight and fairness.

Then there was a short prayer, followed by the confessions of monks who had broken the rules. Today, it only included one monk being late for a church service and another talking during a meal. For both offences, the abbot dispensed a day of fasting as punishment.

At the end of the meeting, when it was time for announcements and discussion, the abbot said, "I will be leaving in a few days on a mission for the king. I have just received the summons."

"Ah," said the prior. "I'll be glad to take charge as usual while you are away, and we'll pray that your journey is without mishap."

The abbot's relentless eyes inspected the faces of several monks and stopped at Acius. He announced, "I will take away with me the book of Saint Benedict's rules we have here."

The monks looked at each other, their expressions ranging from surprise to horror. Acius' mind was in turmoil. On royal missions gifts were made to those visited. But surely not this book? There was silence for several moments. The cellarer broke it. "Father, it's a treasure of the abbey, given that we fashioned it here."

"We must not covet possessions," said the abbot dryly.

Brother Geoffrey, one of the monks who had worked on the manuscript, spoke out, "It contains rules for monks. It is only of interest to someone who is a monk."

The abbot stared at the speaker, yet said nothing.

Acius tried to overcome his shock at the abbot's announcement. He pictured the monks bent over their desks day after day copying the text, and Brother Thomas painting the illustrations with his minute brushes until he was almost blind and his hands were locked with cramps. It was so unfair. Acius finally found the words, "Father, the book is a symbol of our worship of the Lord. It will be sorely missed. Could you not take one of the other books in the library?"

The abbot shifted his stare to Acius, but still made no reply.

The silence was interrupted by Geoffrey, "You are right, Brother Acius, we have two excellent bibles, and the writings of Saint Aelred of Rievaulx Abbey."

Another monk said, "The writings of Saint Aelred are not approved by all."

"Then there are the works of our revered father Saint Bernard," replied Geoffrey.

The debate continued about which book might be most suitable for the abbot, with no one daring to address him directly. He looked increasingly annoyed. Eventually, he stood up and said, "No, it is this illustrated book that will accompany me," and swept out of the room.

The monks sprang up and congregated around the prior. His shoulders were hunched and he looked harassed. "Father Prior," one said, "why is the abbot doing this?"

"I didn't know of it until he announced it here. His mission for the king may be to visit the Pope in Rome; he has gone before. Perhaps the king has asked him to take a gift to the Pope or a churchman he is visiting. I've known this happen."

"Is it right that he take it?" asked Geoffrey.

"Well," the prior took a deep breath, "it's in his power, I suspect, and he'll have the backing of the king's request, if I am right."

"This is not like our other books. We created it here," said Acius.

"Look, I don't want him to take it, but the abbot is in command of the monastery. As his second in charge I can only seek to dissuade him."

"Can we not gain the backing of someone outside the monastery?" Acius continued.

"Yes… we could send a message to the abbot of our mother abbey Citeaux. Though, of course, it will take a long time to get there."

Acius' frustration exploded. "That is not going to stop the abbot."

"No, it is not, Brother Acius. But have you any other suggestion?"

"I have to admit I don't; but will you talk to the abbot?"

"I can, but perhaps it would do more good if you did. You're in charge of the library. You worked with Brother Thomas to produce that book, and you obviously feel passionately about it."

Part of Acius knew the prior was sidestepping the task, but part of him wanted to seize the opportunity. "Yes, certainly I will."

Brother Acius went to find Durand, the master mason. He had arrived at Beaulieu Abbey as one among a number of masons five years ago, when work on the abbey church was begun, and had gradually emerged as their leader. Acius worked with him on aspects of the construction for which Acius was responsible as choirmaster and librarian, and had grown to appreciate his different insight into the world. Acius had sought him out before. He was barely literate but he seemed to understand what made men act as they did.

As Acius walked through the grounds, he saw the part-built walls of the long nave of the church. He could hear the insistent tap of the mason's chisels. The walls rose to irregular heights depending where each mason had reached, or how long the stone had lasted. Acius found Durand in the stonemason's lodge. He was on his own, studying a plan he had inscribed in clay for the layout of the nave.

Acius voiced his concern directly, "Have you heard, the abbot is going on another of his missions for the king, and wants to take with him the illustrated manuscript we created here?"

"No, I hadn't." Durand looked up, his hair and the folds of his weathered face coated with stone dust. "I know the high regard you have for that book. What does he want with it?"

"The prior thinks he wants it as a gift to the Pope or some other dignitary, as happens on such missions." Acius sighed. "But why *that* book? All those years creating it. We were so lucky to have Brother Thomas with us. He was our inspiration. Since he died, we can never do it again."

"Didn't he come from Winchester?" Durand asked.

"Yes, he worked for years on copies of the Bible they produced. He grew old doing it. He wasn't a monk; he was a professional artist. When the money ran out to pay him, he wanted to devote his remaining years to creating something he believed in. He admired the Cistercian order and came to join us here."

"And what made him create that book?"

"*Benedict's Creed*, he called it. He saw the importance of the rules we live by and wanted to create a copy people would be inspired to read, to use in the service of the Lord."

"He didn't do all the work, did he?"

"No. Several of us copied the text, in a style he taught us. We left the space for the illustrations, and he filled them in. They are of the finest design and the richest colour. That was his skill. And he included whole pages of illustration, which is seldom done. He told me once the book was the fulfilment of his life."

"I wonder why the abbot picked that book," said Durand.

Acius sat down next to him. "I've been thinking about that," he said. "He asked that the book be brought to his house yesterday, so I took it. He has a visitor staying with him, who must be joining him on his mission. He kept the book all day. I had to collect it in the evening to replace it in the library bookcase."

"So, he showed the book to this visitor, to see if it was suitable to take?"

"Yes, maybe."

After some thought, Durand said, "I've appreciated its beauty when I've had a chance to look on it. I'm pleased I have, now it's going."

"I hope it won't be going."

"No, it shouldn't. I have doubts about this abbot of yours."

"Why? He is devoted to the monastery."

"Well, so he may be, but he lives in his own house, not with you, he has good food at his table, he entertains knights and nobles or they entertain him."

"Yes, he does... but these things enable him to raise the funds for us to build the monastery."

"I think you give him too much credit. And now he's taking your book."

"I don't want him to, but how can I persuade him against it?"

"You're in charge of the books; you must find a way. It's your duty."

"Yes, you're right," said Acius.

When time provided, Acius went to the library bookcase and drew up a list of the more impressive books. He included several that were illustrated, in case this was what had attracted the attention of the abbot, although he knew none had the beauty achieved by Brother Thomas.

He took the list to the abbot in his house. It had been the king's hunting lodge before the abbey was started and was luxuriously appointed. It was constructed of timber, not stone as used in the monastery, and its extensive kitchen was in a separate building outside. As he passed it, the smell of cooking made Acius salivate. But since he had taken his first vows, he had taught himself to ignore the body's response. He liked his monk's abstinence well enough, and did not envy the plentiful dishes that must emerge from the kitchen. In any case, he thought he could smell meat – a food the rules forbade.

He entered the living room of the house and was hit by a draft of heat from the fire glowing in the hearth. Now warmth was something that any monk would covet, given that the monastery had no heat except in the warming room, and that was only to be used for a short time before bed.

The abbot's dog growled from the corner of the room. It had a heavy, round body with short, bowed legs, and beneath its flat nose saliva dripped from a slack mouth. The abbot was sitting in front of the fire on a high-backed leather chair. As Acius crossed the room, the dog kept its eye on him. He was glad it was attached to the wall by a chain.

When the abbot looked up, Acius began the speech he had rehearsed. "Father Abbot, my responsibility for the church services and the books make it my task to speak to you about the book you want to take. The view I express is that of the other senior monks. We ask that you do not take this book; it means so much to the monastery. I've drawn up a list of other books of note in the library that you could take." He held out the list.

The abbot ignored it, and focused his gaze on Acius. "Brother Acius," he began, "the matter is already decided. Your reputation is not enhanced by seeking to keep the book."

The unfairness of it filled Acius' mind. He could not stop himself saying, "Brother Thomas created the book for our monastery."

The abbot narrowed his eyes and spat out the words, "You should be careful of your impertinence. I am charged by the king to go on this mission, and I am obliged to take the book. There is nothing further to be said."

One day later, the abbot was gone, and the book with him.

don't breathe a word

a short story **by joanna pocock**

Graham didn't want to lie, but he'd prepared for it just the same. He'd memorised the year 1952, the birth date that would make him eighteen, although he knew he looked no more than half that. There wasn't so much as a scrap of peach fuzz sprouting from his top lip, despite the daily checks with a magnifying mirror he had stolen years back from his older sister. A quiet thrill would excite him every morning as he examined his pores bulging like fish eyes. Today, as he walked up the steps to the place he'd been watching for the past three months, he thought about his skin, and the strange life it held inside it, and how he was about to start changing all that.

Knocking at the door, its paint peeling in dry black scabs, Graham held the scrap of paper tightly, feeling it soften in his hot hand. He hoped with all his might that the man would be in, but there was no answer. He peered up close to one of the panes of glass, also painted black from the inside, and all he got was a shadowy reflection of himself. Then he squinted through the keyhole where he made out a large sofa, like a psychiatrist's couch, in the middle of a room. Framed pictures covered the walls, not just of women, but of motorcycles and cartoon characters. None of the new ones, though - no Hercules or anything: just Mickey Mouse and Minnie and an Elmer Fudd holding a shotgun. He knocked again, and still no answer. Graham finally kicked the outer screen door until it rattled like two garbage can lids. The man opened the front door with one hand while the other held a cigarette tightly between thumb and forefinger. Keeping the screen door closed between them he eyed Graham from top to bottom. Graham wished he'd had clothes more suited to the place. Maybe something with a Supertramp logo on the front. But the best he could do was his Montreal Canadian T-shirt. At least the man was smaller and less frightening up close.

"We're not open yet," came out with a cough.

Graham marvelled at the grey beard growing in one straight line from just under his bottom lip.

"I know, but I want to book an appointment."

"For who? Your older brother?"

"No, I don't have an older brother... " As he said those words, Cynthia's face came to him and made him want to be sick. "It's for me."

The man laughed. He shoved his hands down deep into his pockets and said, "I'm sorry young man, but you have to be eighteen to come here."

He was just about to shut the door when Graham pushed past him. He'd forgotten the rehearsals he'd had with himself where he made up stories of growing disorders and hormonal imbalances, and worst of all he'd forgotten his made-up birth date of 1952. All of his solitary practice was useless once the man shouted out at him to scram.

"Get lost, outta here!" he hollered, but Graham was already inside, dipping into his pockets. He threw the stolen bills onto the black leather sofa in the middle of the room, hoping they would let him have his way.

"Please. Please. You have to. I need to... " Tears crept up his throat and, before he started to cry, the man picked up each note one by one, eight fifties, and counted them. "Four hundred dollars." He stroked his thin beard and looked hard at Graham. "So what's this all about? Where did you get this?"

Graham calmed himself, and the next bit came out with a naturalness that surprised him.

"On my twelfth birthday," he said, adding two years on for good measure, "my grandparents gave me my own bank account. Instead of putting all the money into it I saved some aside."

"Hmmm." The man sat down on the sofa and asked Graham what he had in his hand. Graham held out the piece of paper with the name of his sister written in big letters. CYNTHIA. He tried to copy some lettering he'd seen on the gravestone at the funeral. Chunky, black letters with curly bits.

"I see. Your girlfriend is it?"

"Not exactly." Graham was hoping not to have to explain anything. Once he started talking he couldn't stop, like the time his teacher took him aside after school. He described the accident and how they'd swapped places and if they hadn't she'd be the one still alive not him. It was worse once the paper had printed his dad's picture. Those who hadn't got all the gossip first-hand spent the next few months whispering behind Graham and his dad's back. He clenched his fists until his nails dug into his palms and said under his breath 'pleasepleaseplease' without moving his lips, while the man re-lit his roll-up and squinted at the piece of paper.

"So where do you want it?"

Graham felt his palms relax. He lifted up his T-shirt and, twisting from his waist, pointed to a spot high up his back. "There."

The man stayed seated, and reaching up let his fingers run along the dip between Graham's shoulder blades. Graham couldn't believe that the hands touching him were those belonging to the name on the sign he passed every morning on the school bus: 'Hal's Body Art'. In small letters painted under the name it read 'Ontario's only Custom Tattoo Parlour. Adults only please'.

"How big?"

"Bigger than I've done it. I want it huge. I want it so that no one will forget it if they see it."

"Gosh, you must really like her."

Graham kept silent.

"Right my boy. Lie on your stomach." Graham watched him pocket the $400. After rummaging around in a room off to one side, he came back with a needle attached to a long tube of rubber, some cotton wool and bottles of transparent liquid, like the ones Cynthia had on her dressing-table where he got the mirror. He set himself up next to

Graham, but before getting started he leaned over. Graham was forced to stare into the man's watery grey eyes that looked like two dirty puddles.

"Now listen young man, we have a deal okay? I do your tattoo, and you keep your mouth shut. Right?" Graham nodded. "If anyone finds out, I'll lose what's left of my license and get into loads of shit. And I don't need more shit. You got it?"

Graham nodded again.

"I want to hear you say it. Tell me you won't breathe a word – to anyone."

Graham replied, "I promise I won't breathe a word."

"And what if your mum sees it while you're in the bath or something. What will you say then?"

"She's dead."

"You'd say that?"

"No, I mean you don't need to worry about that. She's dead."

"And your dad?"

"He's still alive."

"No, I mean what if your dad sees you. I dunno at the beach or something. What will you say?"

"Nothing." Then Graham lied. "He wouldn't mind anyway, he's got loads of tattoos."

"I hope you're telling the truth." Then Hal added: "Not that it really matters. In another couple of weeks all this will probably be gone." He waved his hand through the dusty air. "Gone," he repeated.

Graham didn't know what to say, so he kept still and let the man get on with swabbing his back. The liquid was cool and smelled like the gloves his dentist wore to delve into his mouth, all chemically and clean. Then Hal began tracing the letters with a pencil. It was cold, and Graham tried to imagine how the tattoo would look from the feeling of lead against his skin. While the man concentrated, Graham rolled his eyes upwards to look at the pictures covering the walls. He had seen similar pictures in the magazines his dad kept under the bed. Some of the pictures were signed. One stood out in particular of a woman in a bright red bikini lying across a big black bike. Graham could just make out the handwriting, which was all loose and loopy: "To Hal, Revv that motor big time! Luv Cindi. " He thought it was weird that she almost had his sister's name.

"Now I don't want you to look. Keep that head down." Hal cleared his throat as he spoke and pushed down hard on the back of Graham's head.

Graham heard him get up, and then a click. He lifted his head just enough to see him plug in the long red rubber tube. Then Graham felt the hand again. "I said don't look. Believe me it's easier for both of us." Graham obediently hid his face in his forearms.

Hal turned the drill on and over the whirring said, "This'll hurt a bit. I want you to try and block out the noise. Just concentrate on how it feels and you'll see it's like a hard tickle or a pinprick."

As the man spoke Graham felt what seemed to be a breeze on his skin from the needle machine. Then suddenly he felt it. It was worse than he expected. It wasn't a tickle at all but more of a scratch. It was like when he used to wrestle with Cynthia on the carpet in the living room and he'd get burns on his knees or his elbows, always on the tip of the really bony bits.

Thinking of his sister helped him put up with the pain. Out of sheer stubbornness he wouldn't let himself cry. He stayed as still as he could for as long as possible and let Hal scratch the skin on his back. Once he felt the machine reach the middle, he adjusted his head and noticed his left arm had fallen asleep. It was tingling as much as his skin under the burrowing needle. He didn't dare say anything in case Hal got angry or lost his concentration and then Graham would be left with 'CY' or 'CYNTH' on his back instead of the whole word. He wondered if that ever happened. If there were people wandering around with half-finished tattoos on their bodies.

After what seemed a very, very long time, Graham drifted off into thinking about Cynthia and about what they'd be doing right now if she were at home. Probably eating cookies. She never stopped baking. Their mum used to say that they would all turn into buckets of lard if she didn't stop with the chocolate chip cookies. But Graham and his father never complained. When the pain deepened, Graham experimented with breathing at different speeds, to see if it helped. When it didn't, he focused on the close-up leather of the sofa, trying to make out patterns. Just as he thought he could see the shape of a rocket, Hal stood up and stretched his arms out wide. He turned the machine off and Graham heard him say with a sigh, "There."

Graham began to roll over and the man shouted, "Stay where you are. Don't move!" Graham froze, and then Hal said, "No need for alarm. I just want to tell you a few things before you do anything. And we'll let that scab do its thing for a while." He left the room for a few minutes and returned with some pieces of paper. "You can read can't you?"

Graham nodded.

"Good I want you to read these and then get rid of them in case anyone finds them." He handed Graham some muddy photocopies. The top copy had a large title in bold letters 'Keeping your tattoo clean'. Another one was headed 'Keeping your tattoo bright'. The last one was called 'What happens if you change your mind – removing your tattoo'. Graham folded them up and stuck them down his back pocket.

"Right, I guess you'll want to see it then," Hal said as if reading Graham's mind.

"Yeah." Graham wanted to sound cool, but the excitement was too much and his voice cracked and went all high. The man picked up a mirror and held it up facing a full-length one on the wall.

"C'mon over then." Graham got up and stood between the two mirrors. He was amazed at what he saw. It was bigger and blacker, and more amazing than he had imagined, and the bubbles of drying blood only made it more impressive. Where Graham had drawn tiny, almost fearful, squiggles on his piece of paper, Hal had drawn impressive flourishes, as if he'd plucked each letter from a different alphabet. The tail of the 'y' coiled back around the 'C' and the cross of the 't' snaked around the dot of the 'i'. He had taken Graham's marks and made them into something beautiful. Graham thought of Cynthia looking down at this very moment smiling, but all he was able to force out of his mouth was "Wow".

"Happy customer?"

"Yup." Graham wanted to stand and gaze at his back for ever, but the man was getting edgy.

"C'mon, it's getting late, I've got people coming 'round." He handed Graham his T-shirt. "Now read those papers when you get home and don't forget to throw them out where no one will find them." He tossed a bandage wrapped in cellophane at Graham. "And if it starts to act up, put this over it. It's medicated."

Graham tucked it into his rucksack. "Thanks," he said, still transfixed by the image of his sister's name on his back.

"And come back and tell me what she thinks of it. This Cynthia of yours."

"I'm sure she'll love it."

"Maybe she'll come and get your name put on her back."

"Maybe."

Graham pulled his T-shirt on, and as the cotton brushed his tattoo, he winced. The man caught Graham's expression and added, "And don't sleep on your back for a few nights. It'll be fine after that. You'll never even know it's there."

Graham didn't want to hear that. He wanted to feel it all the time, from the moment he woke up to the moment he curled up in bed. He wanted the pain to be there for ever. He walked down the steps into the bright sunshine and jumped on his bicycle. As he pedalled, his loose T-shirt brushed against his back, flapping like the sail of a boat. The faster he pedalled, the faster the blood pumped around his body, and the more he felt the black ink seep deeper into him.

yorkshire life

a short story **by gilly reeder**

"I don't see why he can't have it in a bag like everyone else."

Her daughter is leaning against the kitchen worktop. She has just popped round after finishing her shift at the Co-op, before she has to pick the children up from school. Behind her, sunlight is filtering gently through the window. Signs of spring at last. A section of peeling wallpaper looks more noticeable. The yellow paint on the wall-mounted kitchen cupboard seems more faded.

"No, Jean, it's no good. Your father won't have anything except the real thing." She tugs open the frosted Perspex door to the cupboard, stuck with age, and removes a small box of PG Tips leaf tea. Deftly, she opens the paper packet inside, retaining the neat line of the folds. As if doing origami in reverse.

"Come on Mum, I bet he won't even notice. And it'll save you time, not to mention having to take all those blasted leaves down to the compost." Jean picks up the box of Sainsbury's Red Label tea bags that she placed on the worktop when she came in. "We have these at home now. They're really very nice."

Lifting up the kettle before it has fully boiled, she pours some water into the teapot to warm it and, swilling it round, edges her way past Jean to the sink, saying, "But whatever will happen to his raspberry bushes then? You know how much Albert Hardcastle" - she enjoys referring to her husband as if he were a distant acquaintance - "loves those raspberries." After a moment, she tips the water away. "Oh, give it here then. We'll risk it."

With a glance in the direction of the partially open kitchen door, to make sure no one is lurking behind it, she takes a bag and pops it in the pot. After consideration she adds another. Watches the bags bobbing about on the surface of the water, before hurriedly putting on the lid. Opening the door to the pantry, she places the box of tea bags in an old, lidded casserole dish that never gets used.

She takes three cups down from where they are hanging on hooks.

"How is Dad?" Jean turns to look out of the window on to their garden below.

"He hasn't sent away for the Scarborough brochure this year." She prods at the bags in the teapot. "How long should I give it?"

"Oh, so not good. How's he getting on with the new diet?"

"Well, he doesn't seem to mind the Flora. If the doctor says he has to have it then he doesn't bat an eyelid, but if you ask me it's awful stuff. No taste!"

"Hair looks nice, Mum. Just had it done?"

"Yesterday morning. My usual lady wasn't there. This one does the curls a bit tight." She tugs at a clump of hair, thinking what a strange do it is at Mrs Williams's salon. Mrs Williams hasn't decorated the place in decades. Sits behind the reception desk all day, smoking. Her nets have turned the colour of tobacco.

With a quick look at the kitchen clock, she picks up the tray, laden with its usual tea-time paraphernalia: teapot, cups and saucers, side plates, paper serviettes, cutlery, plate of cakes. And easing the kitchen door fully open with a pink slipper, she hurries out across the narrow landing, past the top of the stairs and into the living room.

The sun is filling the tiny arena, dancing off a sea of blue and white stripes. Leaning back into the warmth of the deckchair, she smoothes her hands across her green worsted skirt. Raising a hand to check her hat is still in place, she inclines her head to glance at him. He really is very handsome for a Yorkshire man: smooth skin, despite his slightly craggy features (they breed them tough up here), and hair neatly greased. He seems surprisingly engrossed in the thin-sounding orchestra on the stage in front of them.

She hums along with the tune: 'Take Me Back to the Garden of Love'. It's one she recognises from her childhood, when her mother would play songs at the upright in the drawing room. With nostalgia for her younger days, although she has only just turned twenty-five, she taps out the rhythm lightly on the arm of her chair.

Turning his head slowly, he looks at her. As if, she thinks, he had forgotten she was there.

He smiles and lays a hand over her slender fingers, soothing the nervous dance. Gently he rubs her platinum wedding ring with an adventurous finger, exploring its newness.

Scarborough. Maybe not her first choice of honeymoon destination, but as he said, it is smart at the North End, and, as she reminded herself, whirlwind romances never give you much time to plan. Maybe they will go to more exotic places when they have had time to put a little something away. After all, she took a cruise with father to the Norwegian fjords when mother died and she was just twelve. Then last summer she was in Germany with Cynthia; watched all those ghastly youths doing their exercises and performing silly salutes. It's not as if she doesn't know there's a world out there.

In a minute, she thinks, she will ask him to get her an ice. Above them, the faint sun disappears behind a cloud.

She pours the milk into Albert's cup first. Then adds the tea, hoping it's the same colour as the PG. Not looking at him as a drop spills in the saucer.

Leaving the cup just within his reach on the edge of the table, she retreats to the upright chair with the lattice back. Lifts the dessert fork eagerly to her lips: éclairs, her favourite. She watches him chewing the over-baked pastry of his egg custard tart from the baker's. Not saying a word. Insists he doesn't like anything else. The oak dining table, folded away and pushed back against the wall after lunch, stands between them like a barricade.

"Have you booked your hotel yet, Dad?" Jean asks, from one of the 'comfortable' chairs.

He takes a sip of the tea. Both women stare at him surreptitiously, their eyes lowered, forks poised.

"I don't know if I'll make it this year. Can't manage all those stairs to the promenade."

"I've said he can have a wheelchair if he wants," her mother interrupts, with a mouthful of choux pastry. "But he's too proud!"

"No Scarborough, Dad?" says her daughter, smiling. "No Max Jaffa Orchestra?"

Pushing on the arms of his new armchair with its raised seat so that he can get in and out more easily, he stands slowly. *Racing Post* in hand, he shuffles the short distance across the tiny living room – his grey flannels hanging loosely on him now, his cardigan misshapen and sagging – to switch on the television. It blares out next to Jean's head.

Horses are parading in the paddock, in the rain.

"Ooh, it's that lovely speckled horse again," she calls out, wiping a little cream from around her mouth.

"That's Desert Orchid! How many times do I have to tell you, woman?" He shuffles backwards in his diamond-patterned slippers, eyes fixed on the screen, and falls back into the chair just as the horses begin to proceed to the starting line.

"Come on Jean," she says, irritated. "Your father wants to watch his afternoon racing."

She picks up her chipped cup and heads for the bedroom, which adjoins the living room. Here they can perch on the twin beds, ruffling the pink bedspreads, and have a good old natter. Without being told to 'mind their tongues'. "Any more tea there Albert, before we leave you in peace?"

He nods and holds out his cup and saucer.

She stuffs her hands into her Mackintosh and watches the puddles forming in the sand. Sand that is never quite dry and never quite golden. Lucky they packed the Wellingtons. Beside her, collar turned up, trilby squashed firmly down, he stares into the gloomy sky. Unrepentant.

You take your chance with your two weeks, he says. If it rains, it's just bad luck.

But not every day, she thinks, that's a curse. Besides, it's their first year since the war that things have looked up for them. Shouldn't they be having fun?

She draws her legs together trying to block out the harsh breeze. "Brisk", he'd call it.

In front of them, with the hood of her duffel coat up, little Jean trots by on a donkey, looking terrified.

She waves, and vows, "Somewhere different next year." After all, Scarborough will still be here even if they don't come to witness it. Those cliffs will never crumble. The palm court orchestra will play on.

Two linen napkins in silver napkin rings (a wedding present – from *her* family), twin salt and pepper cellars, the slightly tarnished cutlery, and, in pride of place, the tub of Flora that has usurped the butter dish. He always sets the table. In the same way every day since they were married. Never cuts corners, even now.

She lays two steaming plates of fresh cod and vegetables (it's Friday) down on the picture place mats, both Stubbs, and takes her seat next to him. They stare out of the window at a sea of red-tiled roofs. All is silent, save for the sound of cutlery scraping lightly on china. The double-glazing turned out to be a good investment.

Lunch consists of two courses: a choreographed exchange of dinner plates for bowls of pudding and the jug of cream, all acknowledged by a nod of the head.

After pudding, he peels an apple. She watches as the skin snakes slowly into a tantalising coil, before tumbling onto his plate. He cuts a slice and munches contentedly. He still has his own teeth.

It's not yet time for the lunchtime news on ITN. He raises the delicate fruit knife with its mother-of-pearl handle (that belonged to her aunt), and points to his left, jabs the air.

She lays down her napkin and goes over to the sideboard. Picks up the calendar that arrived in the post this morning, from a magazine that he subscribes to annually, *Yorkshire Life.*

"There's a good photo of Scarborough for November, Mary," he says, smoothing out his napkin.

He's quite communicative today.

She resumes her seat and turns the months over slowly, almost flirtatiously. The images are familiar from calendars over the years: colourful Whitby fishing boats; York Minster rising above the ancient walls, surrounded by a blaze of daffodils; Swaledale in a haunting mauve light, under a rainbow. Another world.

On one wall of their living room hangs a watercolour print, set in a clip frame, of tiny Scalby Parish Church in the snow. She's never considered the sketch particularly accomplished, yet it occupies pride of place above the mantelpiece. The village of Scalby lies just a few miles inland from Scarborough. It's the place where he was christened and where most of his family are buried. A family of eight children raised in a single cottage, very poor. By a mother who was tougher than the lot of them put together. Tough as old boots. She kept all of her teeth, too.

She raises a juicy green olive to her mouth, loves eating with her fingers. The waiter is setting the adjacent table, sweeping old crumbs onto the courtyard floor and putting down a fresh paper cloth. 'So little work,' she thinks. Perfect. She wonders what to eat next from the array of tiny dishes in front of her. A little calamari perhaps. "Aren't you going to try some?" she asks. He scowls and angrily cuts up his Spanish omelette, piling his fork with the soft potato filling and the chips that he ordered to go with it.

Opposite, in the shop window, a mannequin models a scarlet halter-neck dress covered in a riot of huge, white polka dots, ending in a sea of frills below the knee. A black crocheted shawl hangs loosely over her stiffly poised arms. Her ebony hair is piled high into a clip, from which descends an elaborate lace veil. Two neat, coquettish curls escape from around her ears.

How she would love to have that outfit for herself – not sure what occasion it would suit, but just to own it would be fun. Maybe she could put it on to do the cleaning? Soon get the housework done with a little music on the radio. When he's on his shifts up at the plant, things are very different at home.

She reaches down into her handbag and pulls out the castanets she

purchased earlier. Raises her hand into the sunshine and clicks them
together furiously, the noise echoing around the courtyard. The waiter
looks over and smiles, stamps his foot to the rhythm, before making his
way back inside.

She has waited ten years for a moment like this.

"Don't be ridiculous!" He leans across the table and grabs her wrist,
stifling the sound.

The first thing she takes down is the calendar. Stuck on October (York
Races: he'd have loved to see that one, if he hadn't been in the hospital)
with no one to turn it over. Scarborough. Thirty years of annual
pilgrimages to feel the icy spray off the pier and cower behind billowing
windbreaks on the beach. The painted jug on the mantelpiece a lonely
reminder of the only variation in all those years: that single, balmy week
in the Costa Brava. Spain was all the rage then. Next door had started it
with their cuddly donkey. He never liked to be outdone.

In place of his calendar, she puts a small one of delicate
watercolour flowers by Elizabeth Blackadder, which she had up in the
kitchen with the family birthdays marked on it. He was 10 January.
Capricorn. The stubborn old goat. She's drawn a ring around her own
birthday, as much for the family, as for herself. Born Kingston-upon-
Hull, 13 May 1914. *East* Yorkshire they call it now. She much preferred
it when it was Humberside: more distinctive.

'Mary, Mary, quite contrary,' he'd often say under his breath, with a
chuckle.

She raises a hand to her hair, notices it's become a little unruly. She
ought to get the woman round to have it done. But she doesn't really like
the way she styles it. Never stays in for more than five minutes. 'Soft
perm' the woman calls it.

There is the faint sound of a key in the front door as she's tucking
into her lunch. She digs deep into the butter dish, warm from where it's
been sitting on the gas fire to soften, and smoothes a thick helping onto
another piece of soft, French bread. The cut-away crusts lie heaped on
the side of her plate.

"Hello, there!" she calls out cheerfully as she makes out footsteps on the stairs, hears the rustle of a plastic bag. Her daughter lets herself in.

Eventually, the living room door opens. "What is that you've cooked? The kitchen smells to high heaven!"

"Green curry."

"Since… "

"It's a 'boil in the bag'. You should try it. Nice and easy."

She watches as Jean sits down in the chocolate-brown Ercol with the springs that have gone, feeling for the arms. Thinks their daughter looks more and more like Albert as the years go by: inherited his good skin. Never had a crease on him. Unlike her own face, a well-worn map of worries. That's one thing she can say for him, he kept his looks.

"Now, come and sit here," she points with her butter-coated knife to his old chair. "That one's no good."

She leans across the table and picks up a brochure, folded back to show a hotel in the sun; rooms with personal balcony, a colourful buffet bar, lounge, pool and huge ballroom. "Here's where we're staying. Looks nice, eh?"

"But you only joined the class a week ago. Are you quite sure you're up to it?"

"You never lose Ballroom. It's like riding a bike."

"But Ballroom in Torremolinos?"

"Sounds fun, doesn't it?"

She picks up her plate and pushes back the chair to stand. A cushion falls to the floor.

"Mum." Her daughter pauses for a moment. "What's happened to the raspberry bushes?"

"Gone."

"Yes, but who dug them up?

"… Not on your own? Those great things?"

"Much better, don't you think? Lets the light back in."

She carries on across the room, licking a little butter from her fingers. Opening the door, she heads towards the kitchen to see what's for later. She fancies one of those lovely nutty Florentines from the new patisserie. But Jean always ends up buying those dreadful fruit tarts from the supermarket. With the egg custard layer.

As an afterthought she sticks her head back round the door. Sees her daughter still sat in that old chair and staring into the middle distance, looking tired. She was always close to her father.

"Have a look on top of the sideboard," she says, leaning on the door frame. "The Yorkshire calendar. I thought you might like it."

four poems

by sarah rosenfeld

the smell of grass

It's almost August, the end of summer.
The cosmos, pink and fuchsia, have shot up,
Thick beanstalks held up by bamboo.
The ivy creeps across the red brick
And drips silently from the guttering.
Dad will be ripping it off soon
In wads of tangled dark green,
Earwigs uncovered from their leafy tents.

Before I go, I'll check the toaster is unplugged,
Dusty running shoes on spongy carpet,
The sun filters through the panes.
There is no sound but of leaving,
A muddy paw print by the back door,
Dust and dog hair floating through sunbeams
Over the brown corduroy couch,
The thud of the door, trapping the emptiness.

The sun prickles my arms at the gas station.
I feel so old in my blue-striped tank top
And hot pink bikini-made-bra tied at the neck,
The gas tank cap unscrewing,
The click and the gurgle, the soft hum
Of the gas as I pump it.
The dog hangs out the window,
Her smoked meat tongue in a constant pant.

sarah rosenfeld

She knows where we're going.
I drive, the city pulsating, throbbing
Behind a veil of humidity, simmering heat.
I'm in control of everything I touch,
The slippery steering wheel, so smooth.
He's waiting for me inside the apartment
In his least clean pair of jeans, the cat
Eyeing the ferrets, upturned pelts in their cage.

"I'm so thirsty," he says.
"I've got Snapple in the car."
We move outside from the hallway,
Emerging into downtown's dead breeze.
My pupils adjust to the bleached brightness,
Black pinpricks, the hazel shining like leaves.
The dog sees us coming, her tail winding
Round and round like a helicopter blade.
The car rolls through the city streets,
The highway carrying us out from granite and glass
Over the mint copper Champlain bridge.
The St Lawrence winks at us and we sink back.
Cornfields stream by in streaks of green and gold,
Reeling through the countryside in slow wide arcs,
Through open gashes in small hills, solid rock
And milky graffiti: "Yvette et Marc – Je t'aime."

Before each rise in the expanding asphalt,
Mirage puddles waver then vanish.
The exit sign looms, grows, passes overhead.
We veer away from the hush of the speed,
Gears grind downwards. The dog stands
Wobbling on backseat legs, nose twitching
At the long tall grasses by the soft shoulder
And the dusty pommes frites stand.

The dog can run into the road in front,
Fragrant with buttercups and black-eyed Susans.
The bottle of ginger ale and ears of sweet corn,
Handpicked pale green husks, have tumbled
From their paper bag in the trunk. She's barking.
"Come here puppy dog. Come on." A couple

Have wandered down the road, walking sticks poised.
"Stupid dog," he grumbles as the dog barrels past.
He's close behind me with the bags.
I can hear his breath, his running shoes
As he steps cleanly on each misshapen stone
Making up the haphazard path to the door.
Dandelions poke yellow heads through the grass.
From the balcony, we gaze at the view,
Tiny white sails, spinnakers sneaking across the lake,
A motorboat bumping its way towards the States.

"I'm going to low the mawn," and we laugh,
"Mow the lawn... and then I'm going to have
A beer, a Molson Ex just like my dad."
His hand rests on the nape of my neck,
The tie of the bikini presses in hard
Where his hand covers the skin.
"You're a little punk," he says, "A punk,"
And I smile at how his lips press together on the p.

The sun doesn't leave for a long time.
No one reads, the glare on white pages is blinding.
I'm sweating between my breasts in tiny beads.
"Move in closer," and I scrape the chair sideways.
We rest our feet on the lowest slat of the railing,
Throw ice cubes onto the fresh cut grass.
The dog leaps up from the shade of the apple tree,
And crunches them between pointy yellowed teeth.
We're hungry but waiting is more exciting.
Toes squelch through the rough pile carpet
Into the kitchen, warm like roast beef.
There's a fly buzzing, trying to find a way out.
The refrigerator rumbles loudly. I like this,
The sound of feet on smooth slabs of pine,
Climbing the wrought iron spiral staircase,
Pulling as many clothes off as we can.

There's a dead fly on the bed and I swipe it away
Before diving onto the blue pool of quilt, rolling
In the last light streaming through the trees.
I squirm under his heavy body, musky sweat,

sarah rosenfeld

So that he covers me completely and our noise,
It mingles with the smell of grass and cooling air.
We lie flat until the blush seeps in, just enough light
To stumble downstairs half-clothed in the almost darkness.

"They all fell apart and some of them just fell in
And burnt. I might be able to salvage a couple."
He smells like smoke and he's leaning, arms pressed
Against the doorframe where mosquitoes swarm
Around the orange glow of the outside light.
Slices of skinless cucumber fall wet into the bowl.
He wipes his fingers on his jeans, leaves a charcoal smear.
The dog thuds to the floor, eyelids twitching as she watches.

The sound of claws grating against the screen
Lifts our heads from bright yellow mustard,
Relish and ketchup slithering off spoons.
I slide open the door and the dog glides past,
Her nose wiping my leg like a moist towelette.
There's a bag of gooey marshmallows waiting
To be toasted over a camp fire in the woods,
Near the tree house that my uncles built.

A farmhouse blinks from across the lake.
He has brought me a sweatshirt, his own,
The bulky hood pulls against my neck.
I light the citronella candle and the wick,
It flickers. High beams travelling down the road,
Our ears perk at the sound of treads
On the road's loose gravelly surface.
The blackness, the open space, I dread it,

The slight movement of the trees, the unseen
Blades of grass matted with dew.
Fireflies ignite the air like beacons,
Bursting flashbulbs, blotting the inky darkness.
There's a metallic yelp, a wincing cry.
He's running down the balcony stairs, quickly,
Across the lawn in his socks, the wet seeping in.
They gleam like bared teeth in the moonlight.

I haven't turned on the porch lights. Barefoot,
I'm running too, my stomach clenched into a fist
That has punched me inside, reaching upwards
To my throat with its strong fingers and I swallow.
He's holding her, a soft shape hanging from his arms,
In the rancid glare of the car's headlights.
I can't look at her, her head sad and limp,
But at his fingers woven through her fur.

The house lights flood the garden with a false glow,
Rousing the closed heads of peonies
Crawling with tiny black ants. The car whines
Down the drive lined thick with fireweed
And goldenrod I picked as a child.
He turns away to the backseat, wrapping her
In her smelly blanket, carefully, the way he tucks
My hair, loose strands, behind my ear.

She went to the vet once when a porcupine
Pierced her muzzle with glossy quills.
We take the back road past the Penny Candy store.
The tar is new, greasy like liquorice.
We haven't made this trip before, shifting through
The blackest night speckled with stars.
"We're almost there," I whisper, and we drive,
His hand wedged softly under my thigh.

april rain

I want to go
Everywhere with you

The pyramids of Egypt
Sand sifting through toes

The turquoise paradise
I see in your eyes

The smells of India you cook for me
Coriander seeds and curry leaves

sarah rosenfeld

Or even a rainy day
Curtains open wide
The room lit up
In silver streams

Rain coming
But not yet
In the moment
Before it starts to spit

So soft and soundless
You come up behind me
Turn me around to face you
Untwist me like a braid

Long threads that fleck
And flatten on the pane
Until finally a splatter

The tension breaks
A slice of lightning
That opens our eyes

Then silence
While we count the breaths
To the expected roll of thunder

I'd spend the day with you
Never leaving the room
Except to make strawberry tea
So red and tart, our mouths water
We'd read our books
You an old dog-eared copy of Borges
And I *The Remains of the Day*
On separate corners of the bed

The soft green sound
Catching your eye
As I fall back
Into the words

long trail, vt

Down slippery chutes of leaves
Through bloody brambles
Legs pricked in dotted lines
Torn, loose rocks sliding underfoot

Private Property – Keep Out
I stole a blackberry by the pickup
The engine still tinkling
Running to catch up
Tripping up the dust into the air
With the sweet berry
In my red-stained palm

Still chewing the seeds
Single file along the highway
A hot desert mile
But there was never any desert
Just oasis after oasis
Tortilla chips and spicy salsa
Hershey bars and Baby Ruth
Pepperjack cheese and pots
Of Ben and Jerry's ice cream
We licked with plastic spoons
Bending
With each strike to frozen cherries
And the trek back
Past the motorcycle shop
A red gem perched in the hay-bale door
Car mechanic sleeves rolled
Squashed-coke-can soft shoulder
And pogo bull-rushes tall in the ditch

We had to hurry back
Sun sinking cherry-red
The lips of the woods
Where we'd run out
A dark sweet maple mouth
Bellies full of ice cream
The bramble scratches stinging

sarah rosenfeld

a bump in the road

I know we said we wouldn't write
But I can't stop thinking about that time
In the car when you said
"Well I know for me its exclusive"

I couldn't lift my eyes to speak
Only pick the red leather piping
And swish my finger round loose change
In between our bucket seats

I can't remember your middle name
 – it's been so long
Save the day we drove through the country
Arms surfing out through the open window
Green grass blurring into an electric mess
And the dead porcupine in the road

four poems

by julie-ann rowell

corruption

I thought it was a dog,
a slug of guts blackened by sun,
fur on its tail still touchable velvet;
eyeless, lacking a tally of ribs.
Blowflies cruised its stench.
Not your frolicking kind of seal then.

"A Selkie's hide, she's gone to get engaged,"
he says, he's good at myth, offers them smiling
like a man armed on the winning side:
I feel I'm on the wrong end of a barrel.

"I wonder if her family knows," he goes on,
"that's *she's* one of *them*, condemned,
air won't comfort like water does,
it'll be like drinking acid. She'll choke,
she'll hobble barefoot.
But they *are* beautiful, selkies, more seductive
than the big tits on page three.
Not lured by cars and mobile phones.
Trappings."

He guides me to cloudberry sand,
a surfeit of periwinkle shells.
It can be overlooked, any carcass, any rot,
any tall tale. I pretend the sea's high glitter
is all that is on show.

julie-ann rowell

return

I recognise the country now –
tractor spill, liquid cow dung
on the road to the other side of the hill
beside the aventurine estuary.

We drive down skating the edge,
one eye on the depth, on the fishing boat
giving itself a little shake, like a dog after swimming.

There's a ring of new houses close together
like dentures, veal-white verandas,
barbecues and children playing.
I envy their tall, chain-link fence.

The stream still carves the beach in two,
flushing the heavy sand, still uncrossable, daring.
I dared thirty years ago and was carried out to sea,

flung out like a sheet on a windy washing day
freed of its pegs. My scream a gargle, I drank brine,
the water covered my eyes like glycerine
plunging me to incomprehensible depths.

We turn west, turning back on ourselves,
the ocean quite filling up the rear.

cargo

Eight weeks in the belly of a ship turned me
tenderfoot, greenhorn, rookie.
My body bucked, convulsed.
I dreamt of crows pinned against a sky,
broken hills, then crashing through the ice,
engulfed by water, I cried for my lost Star of David
on the sea bed – old starfish withered
and for my mother's scarified face.

Delirious on deck, we saw 'Columbus's Tomb'.
Clothes salt-stiff, they piled us on a ferry boat,
thousands blinking, calves out of the winter shed.
We snarled at a baby's cries that carried our terror,
nothing in my life could shield me from
harbour water reflecting a gunmetal sky,
cloud veined like muscle;
the Ellis Island crossing made me sicker.

I crept under an iron awning, rain closing my eyes,
to the Luggage Hall with its smell of sanatorium.
I wouldn't let go of my cloth bag:
grandmother's crystal bowl wrapped in petticoats
jarring my thigh, waiting my turn to register,
mother's dollars curling in my palm, fifty dollars,
and no named place. The wind hightailing
through sculptured railings, chandeliers.

julie-ann rowell

stay in touch

I half-expect a foreign voice
as you describe the New York heat,

how it blasts, cancerous,
the air thick as plum wine

causing a man to drift,
turning thoughts to wiles.

I only want trivial talk tonight
or I'll get no sleep

you pass the transatlantic time
in tales of food –

your soft-shell crab supper
in the restaurant by the Brooklyn Bridge

a giant fairground ride;
the extravagance of the docks' tall ships,

but you didn't say you wished me there
to watch the margarital moon

rise above sea water
the colour of a Cormorant's wings.

You are sipping a vodka martini;
I can taste the salt on the rim,

you've ordered key-lime pie
we could always share a spoon,

and trade a joke or two. I will listen
for how long and how hard you laugh.

maris piper

from a novel **by karen sainsbury**

Maris Piper *is a story of teenage marriage. The narrator is Ryan, a seventeen-year-old boy. This is Ryan and Holly's honeymoon.*

As the ferry turned and drew out into the ocean, the lighthouse on the white cliff winking a solitary goodbye, I felt my insides were on fire. I scanned the horizon, but there was no sense of having been here before. Disappointed, I turned to Holly, who was resembling her namesake, green and prickly, her mouth curved into a frown, "I'm going inside."

She turned and I followed.

We sat and ate chips in the restaurant, the motors thumping beneath us. It was a four-hour crossing. Three hours of this Holly spent in the toilet, or with a plastic coated bag over her face.

The ferry was docking. We knew this because there was a bump as the ferry hit the harbour wall side on, and because the captain announced, "The ferry is now docking." I wasn't sure what I felt as Rosslaire loomed out of the sea, a parade of lorries lining the edge of the industrial landscape. It was flat, I noticed, and not green. The emerald isle was grey in the afternoon drizzle. Behind me Holly was retching into a bag. Beneath me white spray was frothing like toilet paper down the toilet. I could feel my heart beating inside my ribs, banging out the tune to some Irish song I hadn't heard yet. This is really what I had been waiting half my life for. Holly spat a few lumps of sick overboard.

karen sainsbury

We drove off the ferry in silence. Holly peered out of the window.

"Dead scabby or what." Her eyes took in the grey. I felt annoyed, felt that she didn't need to mention that.

We spent the night in Wexford, a small harbour town undergoing a major revamp. The town was a giant dentist, with drilling going through the night. We were starving. It felt weird as we traipsed the streets looking for food. All around us soft Irish voices were laughing and chatting. It was a town of no fish-and-chip shops, so we ate burgers, sitting on high stools next to the counter. There was live music wafting from a pub called Bar Undertaker. We weren't sure if this was the consequence of drinking there or a sideline.

"Do you fancy a drink?" I stopped outside, my first experience of Irish music pulling at me.

"Not in there, looks shite." Holly walked on. I paused for a few seconds before I followed her, the music growing distant as we crossed the road and stepped on to the promenade.

I shut the door behind me and turned the key in the lock. Holly flung herself down on the bed, kicking her shoes off. The room was en suite which consisted of a shower room the height of a piece of plasterboard. Rather than cutting a piece of another bit and going up to the ceiling they had squared it off, making a box inside the room. There was a mark on the door where it had been opened with a crowbar, and the light switch was behind a partition that separated this and the next room.

"Very bloody Irish." Holly sat up and threw her leather jacket on to the floor.

It was our first night together as a married couple. I emptied the change from my pocket as Holly lay naked on the bed with the words 'Guinness, Arth Guinness' emblazoned across her chest from the illuminated sign outside the window. I sat on the bed next to her and touched her nipples. She still looked a bit green round the gills, but she let me kiss her, her mouth dry and tasting slightly of sick. I ran my tongue round her mouth leaving a wet trail for hers to slide down. I really wanted her, felt choked about it. I put my hand on her crotch, my heart pounding as I felt her wetness. I pulled my hand away and sniffed it, breathing in her smell. Then I opened my eyes.

"Fucking hell, you've come on." I jumped up, a red stain glistening off the pub sign.

"I thought I might, was due on today." Holly pulled the sheet round herself defensively. I thought perhaps, as this was her first wedding and quite important, she could have suggested a different day for getting married, but I said nothing and slid in bed beside her. "We can have a nice cuddle instead," I said without much conviction and I felt myself go soft.

"Yeah, that would be nice." Holly spoke without conviction.

I rolled over in bed and opened my eyes. Holly was sitting on the edge of the bed making buttons beep on her mobile.

"It's completely dead." She was dressed already, a tight T-shirt and flared jeans with sequins down the leg. The room was lit by weak Irish sunshine, the Guinness sign had been switched off. My finger was sore from the wedding ring that was pushing into it.

Dadda was born in County Clare, on the west coast, the furthest point possible from the ferry. To me that name had a romance that no one else understood. We hit County Clare thirty-six hours after waking that morning.

"Have we come to the right place?" Holly eyed the telegraph poles, which were standing at ninety degrees. It was the kind of landscape that made your heart sink; flat, nondescript. This was where I was from if anyone asked. It was horrible. We drove in silence till we hit Spanish Point where we parked up to stretch our legs. This was the spot where the Spanish Armada had hit the rocks and lost some boats.

We braced ourselves against the wind and stood huddled together on the beach. The waves were rolling in across the flat beach. Several grey lumps of rock protruded from the water further out. On the grey sand, a thousand tiny jellyfish lay dying, their see-through heads trying to work out at what point they had taken the wrong turning. Further along, a small dog was being literally carried by the wind, its stubby legs an inch off the sand.

"I bet the suicide rate is high around here." Holly spoke into her scarf.

On the grass bank were several tents, pegs straining in the ground. When I went for a piss, the toilets were full of shivering campers, trying to thaw out under the hand drier. I thought of the invaders as I stood back out on the shore with Holly looking round for somewhere that sold chips. Foam spray stained the shoreline as the waves threw themselves at the beach. I imagined the crew standing on the deck chanting, "The rain in Spain stays mainly on the plain," as, one by one, they slit their wrists and jumped overboard.

We drove away in silence, my ears sore from the punching wind. We found a café in the village and ordered chips, our hands red raw with cold. I was alarmed at how many chips we were eating. Every meal consisted of something with chips. I studied Holly as she put some change into a fruit machine. There was no sign on her hips or belly. Her stomach was taut and flat. She didn't have the blue patches or bulging veins that Ma had, or the puckers of cellulite. There was just a slight bulge over the top of her jeans as she bent down to scratch at a midge bite on her leg, but that was quite sexy, as her jeans were skin tight, drawing up her arse into two tight balls that fitted into my palms.

There was a windswept graveyard at Spanish Point. Holly sat in the car as I braved the weather. Fifty or more gravestones littered a small green field next to an ancient looking church. Many of the gravestones had succumbed to the wind, lying face down across graves where the grass had never grown back, leaving parched rectangles in the earth. Holly's face was grim as I dialled Ma's phone number from a phone box in the village.

"Your father was born in Waterford. He's never even set foot in County Clare. Your gran was buried in Waterford; that's where you need to go." I couldn't believe it as I put the phone down. So I wasn't from here after all. The relief was painful.

I studied the map. Holly was shivering in the passenger seat next to me. This was a fucking horrible country. The wind so raw it chafed your lips into blood sores. My hair was sticky with salt, my eyes stinging with the sea spray. All along the coast the beach was stained with froth, bubbling like fairy liquid.

"We could head south." I looked across at Holly. Her face was white, her eyes drawn.

"Whatever."

I felt selfish as I put the car into gear. This was her honeymoon as well as mine. I should have taken her to Spain or somewhere hot. I shouldn't have lied about the air fare.

Killarney hit like dawn after a bad dream. We went from flat fields to mountains in minutes, huge blue peaks, range after range. Even Holly began to perk up, rubbing the sleep from her green eyelids. My heart missed a beat at the coloured house fronts, orange with green paintwork next to purple, next to pink. Killarney was so incredibly alive, physically kicking its front legs into the air. Maybe that was what I was looking for, I thought, as I watched the tourists flocking down every street, every lane.

"God, look at those houses; seriously naff." Holly's face was filled with horror as she watched a man apply another coat of green paint to his walls.

I shivered in my kagoul as the sky suddenly opened its sewer, flushing away buckets of rain like a giant cistern in the sky. Just as suddenly the sun leapt out from behind a cloud, confusing the rain, which paused for a second before tipping down with renewed force. I closed my eyes as the sun popped like a balloon.

We checked into a guesthouse just out of the town centre. The landlady didn't ask our names as she led us up the stairs to our room which overlooked the blue mountains.

"Even the mountains are gaudy." Holly sat down on the bed. It squeaked threateningly.

That night Killarney was heaving. Irish music sprawling out of every pub doorway. The shops were all open late, the streets bright in a town that didn't get dark till past ten. Holly was wearing a short dress that was cut low at the front. She was wearing her thick-soled strappy sandals that made her legs look so sexy. I looked down at her finger in the hand I was holding. She wasn't wearing her wedding ring.

"Where's your ring?" I watched an Irish flag flutter from the big hotel in the main street.

"I took it off. Made me feel a bit old on holiday." Holly scratched at a midge bite.

"Shall we get something to eat? I'm starving."

We ate chips on a doorstep, whilst I thought about the difference between a holiday and a honeymoon.

There was a band playing Irish music down a back street, the bar spilling with people, the ground set with the froth of the black stuff and the occasional shower of rain. We sat on wooden benches and listened. It was dead lively. The beat was really pulling at me. A couple got up to dance, everyone clapping as they jigged; a pissed-up Londoner joined in as well, bumping against tables.

"God, this is dead shit. Lets find a club." Holly was drying out a damp cigarette in the palm of her hand. There was a smudge of make-up on her nose. I didn't answer. My foot was tapping as the band launched into 'The Bells of New York'. I felt a bit choked by the mention of Galway Bay, though I had never been there or heard of it previously. There was a rumble of feet when the song faded out. This big Irish fella who was singing took a swig of beer and shouted, "Now, who's for a rebel song?" There was a mighty cheer that reverberated round the street. I clapped and cheered as well, adrenalin going bang, bang round my heart. The crowd went mad. Everyone stood up to dance. It occurred to me that I didn't know what a rebel song was, or why everyone wanted one. Holly was trying to light her hand-warm fag. Who was rebelling against what? A little bubble popped inside, and I was sitting down awkwardly next to Holly.

"Thought you were going to turn into Patrick Flotley for a minute." Heavy sarcasm. I didn't have the nerve to tell her it was Michael Flatley. I only knew because Ma used to watch him and said he reminded her of Dadda when she first knew him.

Later we slipped into a club with a huge glass front that looked down on the high street. The music was dated, but not so much that Holly wouldn't dance. I slid my arms round her neck and pushed my tongue into her mouth. I could feel her heart beating inside the thin dress, I pressed myself against her. An overwhelming desire to have her was unbearable. I slid my hand down her tiny body, felt the slight swell of her hips that were moving against mine. My hands eased up towards the edge of her tits that were pushed hard against me. Holly's arms were draped round my waist, holding on to the waistband of my jeans, as if to keep her upright. I pushed my pelvis against her, showing her how much I wanted her. I could feel that bulge of sanitary towel, which felt strangely exciting, probably because I hadn't had sex for a least a week. I felt a hand on my shoulder.

"Not in here, son." A huge bouncer with 'Give Blood' emblazoned across his T-shirt nodded towards the wall, where a large poster of the Pope frowned down at us.

It was after three when we arrived back at the guesthouse. We crept up to our room, and both had a gigantic piss down the bog. Holly sat on the edge of the bed and pulled her dress off. She looked like a tiny bird without her high heels on, her legs drawn in at the knees, her lower legs sprawled sidewards. I never realised she was that small, barely five foot. She was still wearing her knickers, but her breasts were pointing toward me, her nipples hard and jaunty. I eased her knickers down. A pot of paint wasn't going to stop me getting what I wanted tonight. She was very wet as I slid inside her. She groaned and pulled me against her. I cupped my hand behind her arse and pulled myself in deep. Then we started to move, gently at first. The bed went into maximum creak mode, heaving like a giant saw as we upped the pace, our lips crushed together, her nipples sticking between my ribs. She was panting hard, letting out louder moans. The bed rocked threateningly as we started humping furiously. The stress of no sexual activity making our hips work together in a fantastic rhythm that would never have ended if a tremendous crack hadn't sent us both plummeting towards the floor where we landed with a crash, freezing like fish fingers lined up in a packet. We counted the sound of feet coming upstairs. There was a jangle of keys in the lock. Mrs Kelly stood framed in the doorway, a pot-plant framed behind her head. We lay together on the tangled sheet, a plank sticking into my arse. Mrs. Kelly had dust in her hair. Christ we really must have been going for it.

Apparently the light had swung so much that the bulb had blown in the lounge downstairs. I had to give her money for a new bulb, as well as a new bed. There was blood on the sheets as well. We were fairly wiped out financially, despite the exchange rate being twenty five per cent in our favour.

slightly september

from a novel **by steve sainsbury**

On each side of the steps there were carved lions, about three feet tall. Beric sat on one and urged it to prowl.

"Get off."

"Ha! Fut. Bloody lion. Move."

"Get off, Beric. Come here."

"Fut."

He jumped off and ran up the steps.

"Careful!"

The door had one of those bells you pull out. I pulled it but couldn't hear anything – assuming the bell was so deep in the house that it was muffled by all that space. After a decent time I tried again. Nothing. I banged on the door. Nothing. I walked round to an unshuttered side window and banged. I jumped back as a face appeared. I walked back to the door. Beric was peering through the letterbox. At last the door opened.

It didn't creak, although I was expecting it to. I also expected bats to wheel round, squeaking inaudibly. Nothing. Not even a moth.

"Oui?" A deeply accented voice came from within. I was ready to turn tail and flee. Beric was already over the threshold. Hansel and Gretel or what? Beric being Gretel of course.

"Monsieur Barbarossa."

A hand reached out of the darkness. It was dripping with gold, rings, bracelets. "Natalya Kerensky."

I shook her hand gently. As I did so, I noticed a finger was missing.

"I must get this fucking light fixed," she said as she emerged into the light, still gripping my hand. "A small thing just ran past me; was it with you?"

"My son. I do apologise."

"No need to, Mr Barbarossa. If he comes to harm then it is his own fucking fault. We have free will. We are not responsible for our cubs once they are weaned from the breast. Please come in."

It was almost completely dark inside. She was still holding my hand, showing me the way. Naturally, the dark would not worry Beric. I listened for him but could hear nothing. At the end of what I assumed to be the hall she pushed open a door.

The room it led into was large and very bright. There was a huge picture window at the far end with a view across Lake Geneva to the mountains beyond. Unfortunately it was dirty, and green moss was growing up from the bottom for about a metre. The walls were covered in paintings and icons, an old-fashioned picture rail making this easy. The furniture was old and dark. There were ornaments everywhere, even on the floor in places.

"Please sit down." She beckoned to a settee, pushing papers over to one side. She then said something in Russian – I assumed. A small grunt came from a room beyond. "Mother says she will join us. And she has your boy with her."

I nearly said, *She conveyed all that information in a single grunt,* but thought better of it. Perhaps Russian has a single grunt-like word that means just that?

Natalya finally let go of my hand as I sat down. I noticed for the first time just how tall she was – well over six feet, or two fucking kilometres as Andy would say. I couldn't work out how old she was; she was dressed strangely, like Laura Ashley meets Rasputin. Her long black hair looked as if she'd only combed it on one side. Her face was startling, things going on all over it. Like an ant farm for features. I felt horribly and stupidly entranced. This was business, for fuck's sake. Her mother grunted again.

"Mother is here," Natalya said as she sat opposite me.

I was expecting a little old lady but, if anything, Mother was taller than Natalya. Her face seemed to have collapsed in on itself somewhat, she was balding and when she spoke I could see she was missing most of her teeth. And, beyond, her tongue seemed black. She held Beric in an arm lock.

"Caught a stealing cub, escaped from zoo I expect." Her use of English was a surprise.

Beric was smiling. "Fut," he laughed. "Fut cub."

"Dirty cub, evil cub."

"The cub, child, is with Mr Barbarossa, Mother."

"Mr Barbarossa?"

"This man. The man who is to buy the place in fucking Versmont. Remember?"

"Remember? Remember? I remember. I am not old. Can he do this? Give you ten."

She fell to the ground and started doing press-ups. Natalya ignored her. Beric ran over to me and sat on my lap.

"Never mind her," said Natalya. "Truth is, I would like to close this sale quickly."

"Me too. Though I must... "

"You do not need to bargain, Mr Barbarossa. We have lived in the west most of our lives. We know how the capitalist system works. My grandfather died for supporting it under Stalin."

"Stalin, the Satan of Shit," puffed her mother. "Nine, ten. And I could do more, but I don't want to. I have nothing to prove."

"Ignore her," said Natalya. "So you see, we could just sign."

"What sort of price are you looking for?"

"What price do you suggest?"

I sat back and smiled.

"Would a drink help?" she asked.

"Dr Pepper!" said Beric.

"Mother, do we have Dr Pepper?"

"Dr Pepper? Dr Pepper? We had to drink rancid water from the Neva strained through underpants during the Siege. Stupid spoilt cubs. I will go and see."

"Can I explore?" Beric asked

"You're just getting a drink. Just wait."

"Fut. Ha!"

Mother's voice came from the kitchen. "We have Fanta, Lilt, Oasis, Coca-Cola... Lucozade, Sprite, Orangina... "

"I am sure there is fucking Dr Pepper somewhere Mother."

"Where? I cannot find it."

"Have you looked behind the samovar?"

"It will not be there."

"Look."

"There was a rat there before."

"There is no rat there now."

The mother yelled something in Russian.

"Cover your fucking ears, Mr Barbarossa," Natalya said. "Her language is disgusting. But I am being rude. Would you like a drink, Mr Barbarossa? Of course you would. You English are always thirsty. Thirsty and looking for loose women, no?"

"Sprite would be fine," I said, trying to ignore the last part of her comment.

"Found it!" yelled the mother.

She came in holding a big two-litre bottle, and handed it to Beric. "Behind the samovar," she said.

"Give the child a glass or something; please Mother, try to remember. And Mr Barbarossa will have Sprite."

"Call me John," I said.

"I never call a man by his first name unless I have had unprotected oral sex in the open air with him," Natalya said. "Mother, hurry. We have a thirsty Englishman, and you know what they say about them."

In my head I was already planning an emergency escape route. If I could I'd take Beric with me, but I'd abandon him if I had to.

* * *

The Sprite, when it arrived, was flat. I noticed that Beric had abandoned his Dr Pepper after just one sip, but was impressed that he hadn't complained. He'd gone off exploring again. Outside, rain began to rattle against the big window, the view closing in.

Natalya loomed over me. "We had great plans for Hooray Henri's; we wanted to make it the premier night spot in Switzerland, but the Commune turned down all our plans. Here." She handed me a large A3 sheet. It was covered in intricate ink drawings. They reminded me of the postcard of Hitler's that I had on the lounge wall at home, of the Schonnbrunn Palace, Vienna.

"You planned all this?"

"Yes. A helipad, sauna and plunge pool, flat-screen televisions on every wall, an outside disco bar area with a balcony projecting above a covered parking area. A bungee pole. But those bastards turned it all down; said it wasn't in keeping, whatever that means."

"I drew up the plans," said the mother, touching her toes. "It took a week to get the ink off my fingers."

"So it is all shit and horror," Natalya continued. "Those prolapses on sticks up in that hellhole of a dump you live in can go fuck donkey. Eight hundred thousand francs, it's yours."

"Eight hundred thousand? Freehold?"

"Of course freehold." She smiled at me. "You want me, it's yours."

"Sorry?"

"It's yours, eight hundred thousand."

"Can I counter offer?"

Her eyes narrowed. "Do pigs shit on the moon?"

"Sorry?"

"No counter offers. The price is eight hundred thousand. I have the survey and deeds here, all the correspondence. Accounts. Valuation. Projections. All this sums shit. I want you to have it. You and your child are nice people. I need an answer now."

Her mother nodded in the background. Then started doing star jumps, her hands almost touching the ceiling as she did so.

I wasn't used to doing business this way, but I wanted to add

Hooray Henri's to my portfolio of Versmont properties. I looked at the papers carefully. They confirmed what I'd already worked out. It was worth what they were asking, to me anyway, but I didn't like being checkmated into not bargaining. Hard stares from exotic tall women, geriatric aerobics filling the room, flat Sprite and a missing Beric were conspiring against me. What the fuck, it's only a few weeks' interest, and I put another piece of the puzzle back in place.

Natalya handed me a pen. I'd just signed "John" when Beric appeared.
"Look Daddy!" He held something aloft.
"Bad boy," said Natalya.
"What is it?" I asked. "Beric, what have you got?"
"Tastes nasty."
Natalya yelled something in Russian. She snatched it from him.
"Dirty boy, bad cub," said the mother.
"Beric, what have you done?"
"Nothing, fut," he said.
"Look," said Natalya, coming over to me. "Look what this child, this cub, has done."
In her hand she held a large pale fish. It was obvious Beric had taken a bite out of it. The fish looked unwell, flapping feebly, mouth opening and closing in rhythmic synergy.
"I'm sorry," I said. "He's normally a vegetarian."
"I've a mind to take a bite out of your child," Natalya said.
"Bad boy, dirty cub,"
Beric hugged me. "Daddy. I only tried to cuddle it."
"Okay, Beric," I said. "See what happens when you wander off. Say sorry to Natalya."
"I'm sorry."
"And to the fish."
"Sorry, fish."
"Can you fix it?" I asked.
"Fix it? Does Arnold Schwarzenegger have pendulous breasts? Have you any idea how much a fish like this costs? It is an ornamental koi carp. Imported from... from... Koiland."

I took my wallet out of my pocket. "Will this cover it?" I handed her a hundred-franc note.

"I wipe my big behind with your money," she said, putting it in her pocket. "This will not even pay for his funeral."

I offered her another hundred francs.

"Keep your money. Come with me please. Mother, look after the child. Gently."

I felt bad about leaving Beric with Mother, but I didn't want to lose the deal. I followed a few steps behind Natalya. She held the fish in her hand. We passed through a maze of corridors and rooms, before reaching a back door.

"Hurry," she said, "this fish is in distress. This way." She opened the back door. Rain hit me in the face as I stepped outside. A huge lawn sloped elegantly down towards the lake. It was neatly trimmed, edged with fir trees. We followed a neat path down the slope at the edge of the lawn. About halfway down there was a group of outbuildings, surrounding a hothouse.

"Through here," she said, walking through an already opened pair of dark green sliding doors. She switched on the light. "I don't know how your child found this place. He must have Lucifer for a guide dog."

"I think you might be right," I said, trying to lighten the mood. *It's only a fucking fish*, I kept thinking.

She placed the injured koi in a separate tank on a bench at the side. It seemed happy to be back in the water, and swam off a little unsteadily, coming to rest in a corner, looking up at us with suspicious beady black eyes.

The building was about fifteen metres long by about ten wide. It was almost totally filled with a huge, dark sided pool. There were no windows, but a few skylights above the pool.

"Come and see," Natalya said, beckoning me to join her. She was standing on a small set of steps, and hanging over the pool. I squeezed alongside her and peered in. The surface was writhing with different colours and then I noticed Natalya was dropping something in the water.

"Would you like to feed them? Here." She handed me something. "Maggots," she said. "A treat."

I dropped the handful of warm wriggly things into the water.

"Watch this," she said. She put her hand just above the water and a huge fish put its head out of the water and ran its body along her hand. "You try."

I did the same, and the same fish ran its body along my hand. "Tame fish you can stroke." I said.

"You see why I was upset when your child tried to eat one?"

"Yes, I do." I was enchanted by the fish. The room had an overpowering atmosphere, the soft sounds of water swilling in the pool, the fish milling around Natalya's hands, the rain clattering on the skylights and the roof, a soft hum from a generator in the corner, the distant sound of cars and a ship's horn on the lake.

"Each day I swim with these fish," said Natalya.

I wasn't sure whether she was joking. "Really?" I asked.

"You know each one is worth about twenty thousand francs?"

"Twenty thousand?"

"More for the bigger ones."

"I'm amazed."

"So will you join me?"

"Join you?"

"In with my fish?"

"Sorry?"

"You can never know fish until you have swum with them. Come on."

"Er."

"In Russia, it is an old tradition. Wait."

She stepped down onto the floor and made her way over to a cabinet. "Vodka?" she called over.

"I'm driving."

She laughed. "Just one, Mr Barbarossa. The water will sober you up."

"Well... "

"I never take no for an answer. Never." She began to pour out two vodkas, in shot glasses. She came back over and handed me one.

"Perestroika," I said, knocking it back in one. This was the real stuff; the surgical spirit meets concentrated hemlock kind.

She smiled up at me after downing hers, and began to undress. "I should warn you that I am tattooed," she laughed.

"I never got round to that," I said, joining her on the floor. Taking off my jumper and shirt, I felt the cold. "They're not tropical fish are they?" I asked, more in desperation than hope.

"They embrace the cold. Heat wilts them."

"Oh. Could I not just watch?" I asked, as she took off her dress.

"You English are such cold fish," she laughed. "Always the voyeur, never the participant. Live a little. Anyway, I will not close the deal unless you join me. It is a very old Russian tradition."

"It is not," I said, slipping off my trousers. "Is it?"

She smiled. "Do you know who this is?" she asked, pointing to her stomach.

I looked at the tattoo, via a sneaky look at her breasts. "Ozzy Osbourne?" I guessed wildly.

"It is Rasputin. A great man. My grandfather knew him."

"Ah, him."

"I must show you this." She pulled her knickers down and her pubic hair formed Rasputin's beard. I couldn't help laughing. "Do you like," she asked.

"I love," I said. "I must get one myself."

"Come on." As she walked past me she whipped my pants off so quickly I could hardly tell what was happening. "You won't need those panties," she said. "Come on. I find it best to just jump in." She climbed to the top of the steps and with a dive and a squeal was in the water.

I walked to the top of the steps and dipped my toe in. The water was freezing. Colder even than the room. I would do this a square inch at a time, get slowly adjusted to it. But before I had a chance to realise what was happening Natalya grabbed my foot and pulled me in. I flapped and hit the water neck first.

"It is very refreshing," she said, as my feet found the bottom. Instantly the fish were all around.

Natalya was swimming butterfly stroke, the fish joining in the frenzied flapping. The sound echoed around the building. The cold was so bad it hurt. I could feel cramp coming on. I started hopping, till I slipped on a fish and went right under. Natalya passed me doing breaststroke, fish in her wake like dolphins following a boat.

"Bet you never thought business could be such fun?"

"This is not fun," I spluttered, regaining my balance, as a big fish looked hungrily at me, before swimming over to Natalya.

Gradually the pain left me, and the fish and Natalya drew me into their world. The sun came out and shafts of light from the skylights played on the surface of the water.

"There is one more Russian tradition we must consummate before you go," she said after what seemed like an hour. She led me from the building, cold, wet and naked, and after ten minutes of ludicrously heightened passion – only tempered by my constant glances around to see if anyone was watching – got to call me John. "Now we sign," she said.

through shadows

from a novel **by susan spencer**

After her father's death in Manchester and an eighteen-month absence from her home in Dorset, Laura returns, determined to succeed in her business as a marketing consultant. There she meets Michael and, in this extract, finally accepts her feelings for him, unaware of how the strange behaviour of his ex-wife Sarah, which increasingly resurrects disturbing memories from Laura's past, might yet affect her future.

"Okay, Laura. I hold my hand up. You were right," said Michael as he sat down next to her. "If tomorrow goes as well as today, I should think we've cracked the business sector anyway."

"Yes. If talking to – what would you say – a few hundred potential customers is any indication," she replied, "I think we can safely say it's been a success?"

Laura slid down the chair and stretched out her legs, easing the heel of each foot, in turn, from the fashionable shoes encasing them. They dangled from the ends of her aching feet and she wiggled her toes inside them, sighing with sheer pleasure and relief. Then she cast a sidelong glance towards Michael, tilting her head to one side and drawing back her lips in a self-satisfied smile.

"Okay," he laughed. "Don't rub it in. It's just that it's usually only the big hotel chains that take stands at Business Travel Exhibitions."

"Yes but, as I said, the Vermeer may not be part of a chain, but it's not small and, besides, it's exclusive. If we don't believe that, then neither will they. And people who've taken the trouble to come along to an exhibition like this are already motivated. They're looking to buy."

Crossing his arms as he leaned back in his chair, Michael smiled at her and gave a slight shake of his head.

"What is it?" she asked.

"I was just thinking I'm in the company of someone who's pretty exclusive herself," he said. She looked up sharply, but the remark was natural enough, not said for effect. "I do believe you're well on your way to making a success of your business."

"Thank you," she said. "That's my intention." Laura let his previous comment go, not wanting to read too much into it, while, at the same time, feeling a spark of pleasure from the undisguised compliment.

She had travelled up to Manchester the day before and stayed with Jenny, an old friend. It was always good to see her. Part of the fun of their evenings in together, which were rare these days, was catching up on their respective lives over a bottle of wine. On this occasion, all the time she was talking, Laura was aware of constantly editing her news, revealing nothing that might portray her relationship with Michael as anything other than a purely professional one – which, of course, was what she told herself it was. Lying in bed later that night she thought again about Michael and realised that lately she had consigned him to the box labelled 'work'. It meant she could avoid having even to think too much about him. It was convenient – and safe.

She arrived at the G-Mex Centre early the following morning and found her way to their stand, which included the package that came as part of the deal: a table, three chairs, power, two spotlights and a bright red carpet. It took her an hour to unload the boot of her car and set up the stand. She'd brought with her a copy of the Official Show Guide, which included a profile written by herself on the Vermeer. Fifteen minutes before the doors of the hall were due to open she wandered up to the café and read it through over a cup of coffee and a croissant, mentally preparing herself for the day ahead.

Michael arrived just after lunch. The stand was located at one end of the hall between a group of travel advisers on one side and a car hire company on the other. There were several groups of people milling around, picking up information sheets and flicking through the glossy hotel brochure, some of them clearly waiting to speak with Laura. She was deep in conversation with two company reps when she looked up and saw him. His expression changed from one of surprise to delight. He moved quickly towards one of the groups.

"Can I help you?" he said, smiling. "I'm Michael Stanton, General Manager of the Vermeer."

The demands of manning the stand – each of them held in conversation with the constant stream of visitors – as well as having to replenish the publicity material, left little time for them to speak to each other during the afternoon. They took their breaks separately, in the quieter moments. Yet, given all that, this was the longest time they had spent in each other's company for at least a month. Preparing for the exhibition had kept Laura very busy in the previous couple of weeks, which had suited her. Now the crowd was dispersing, leaving them alone.

"I've booked us into the Holiday Inn for tonight," Michael said.

"I can stay with Jenny again. It's no problem. Just a twenty-minute drive."

"I won't hear of it," he said decisively. "Driving across the city is out of the question. You look shot at. You need to relax tonight. Besides," he said, affecting a sorrowful expression, "if you're not here, who will I dazzle with my conversation over dinner?"

"Oh, I'm sure you'd soon find someone to take my place," she said, a little ungraciously.

"But I'd rather it were you," he said. She looked across at him, at the slight furrow between his dark brows and the candour in his pale blue eyes.

"In that case, I'll stay," she said, "but I shall expect to be dazzled."

The hotel room was cool after the stuffy atmosphere of the Exhibition Hall. Laura kicked off her shoes and lay on the bed. She thought about Michael, saw again the earnest expression on his face. Soon they would meet up again, have dinner and talk about work. That was where the certainty ended and the realms of possibility began. For so long she had sidestepped whatever was going on between them, and tonight she could no longer avoid the inevitable. Here, on neutral ground, they would be completely alone, just the two of them.

As she slipped off the edge of the world into sleep, she sank into a dream. A familiar face appeared, like a hologram hovering above her – Sarah's face. Moving like a rapid slide show, the expression shifted from blank passivity through cold indifference to a face livid with rage. The images came faster and faster, repeating over and over until, like frames that make up a moving picture, they blended together to form a grotesque mask, the eyes black holes of emptiness.

Laura is seventeen. Lying in bed in her room at home, the curtains drawn against the winter night and surrounded by her own things, it's the one place she feels some kind of normality. It's late, past midnight. Fifteen minutes ago she crept into the house to avoid waking her father. Tom is away and her mother never wakes at night. A few moments ago, as she sat brushing her long hair, she heard Steve's voice again. "You mean so much to me Laura," his eyes tender and shining with love. Feeling warm and cherished she drifts into sleep.

A noise disturbs her, drags her back to consciousness. She stirs, opens her eyes. There is nothing. She sighs, turns over and sees the dark shape of a figure by the side of her bed, silently swaying, leaning over her, holding something. She jolts upright. Her heart hammers in her chest, but she reaches out and switches on the bedside lamp. The knuckles are white on the hand that grips the dressmaking shears. The long steel blades flash in the lamplight.

"One night, when you're asleep, I'm going to come in and cut off all your hair," her mother says, her voice slurring with menace. She is wearing a pale green nightdress made of flimsy nylon; her wasted body hangs inside it. Her eyes stare out vacantly, looking through her daughter. She turns round and shuffles out through the open door.

It is an empty threat, but from that night on Laura is vigilant. Sometimes she stays awake until the dawn light, only then feeling she can lower her guard; always she sleeps with the light on. Steve becomes a memory. Where fear resides, there is little room for tenderness.

The hotel room was still cool, but Laura woke dripping with sweat. She was wrong about herself and Michael. There could never be just the two of them until they faced their own demons. She must tell him – some of it at least. As for him, would he talk to her about Sarah, about himself?

Laura stepped out of the lift and made her way across the foyer into the dimly lit bar. The barman, smartly waistcoated, was holding court, the backlighting of the bar making his white shirt almost iridescent and his sandy hair glisten. He was pouring Michael a beer and, from the wry grin on his face, entertaining him with a joke or an amusing anecdote. Michael's laughter rose up from his belly unrestrained, a deep staccato sound. The barman moved away and Michael turned towards Laura. His eyes swept over her as she approached.

"You look stunning," he said.

"Thank you," she said, smiling at him. She had thrown her black dress in the case at the last minute as a standby. It was the tail end of summer, but still warm, and she had brought at least three other, much lighter, outfits. But the black, plain and simple, won out in the end as she'd guessed it might. She loved the feel of the soft crepe material, which clung – but not too much – and the scooped neckline, which suited the fullness of her figure.

"And you, Michael Stanton," she said, "*you* sound as if you're enjoying yourself. I don't recall ever hearing you laugh like that before."

"Well, the tale *was* hilarious. But you're right. I do feel good. Probably being away from everything, even for just a little while," he said.

"Yes. I understand," she said. "People who can't say No usually have to escape; get right away."

"I see, so now you're accusing me of being a Yes man," he said feigning indignation.

"No, never that," she said, smiling at him. "But there is something I want to talk to you about," she said, her expression serious now.

"Let's go and sit down," he said. He put his hand under her elbow as she stepped down from the stool and they made their way over to their table.

"I have something for you," he said. He reached into the pocket of his jacket, took out a giftwrapped box and pushed it towards her. Before she pulled back the wrapping paper, the scent gave it away. Nestled within the box's black velvet lining was a single white gardenia.

"Michael, it's exquisite. Thank you." She pinned it on to her dress, knowing as she did that only the black could possibly show it to perfection.

"I wanted to remind you of the good things about that evening, the pleasure for me in having you there," he said.

Laura looked into his eyes. "Michael, we have to talk."

"It sounds serious," he said.

"It is," she said. "At least to me it is."

"Can it wait till we get back? Whatever it is I'll tell you anything you want to know, I promise."

Laura wanted to relax and enjoy the evening. Bringing Sarah into the conversation was a recipe for disaster. Whenever they should get round to discussing this whole complex area, it wouldn't be easy, especially as Laura's own reaction to Sarah couldn't be ignored. He was right. Better to leave it for the moment, talk on home ground. At least he'd agreed to it; that was something. She smiled at him.

"Okay. I suppose you're right."

"After we've eaten, we'll go for a stroll down by the canal, find a bar with some music. D'you fancy that?"

"Sounds good," she said.

Deansgate Locks was a typical inner-city conversion; original features from the Age of Industry – in this case the canal and the railway – used as a focal point for leisure and entertainment. At first glance, this combination might appear incongruous, despite the touches of green in the roadside trees and the wooden decking suspended ingeniously from the bridge, with tables dotted all along its length; an alfresco atmosphere above the canal. After all, in its wildest dreams, Manchester could never be Venice. But before long it would be accepted as a natural part of urban culture – stylish, chic and the place to be. The four bars, which overlooked the canal, had been created beneath the massive railway bridge, its four huge arches framing the doors of each of the establishments.

Soulful notes from a jazz trombone drifted out to where Michael and Laura sat at one of the tables. At the base of the arches round spotlights in the decking cast a pale yellow glow upwards over the red bricks of the arch to one side of them, while from across the narrow canal, lights projecting out from the wall illuminated the trees above and the still dark water below. They sat for a few moments in silence. Michael was staring at her across the table.

"I bet you were a sassy little girl – a bit like Rosie?" he said, smiling at her. "She's taken to you in a big way."

Laura smiled. "I know, and I'm fond of her too," she said. "But I'm not sure we're that alike. I think she's much stronger than I was – probably down to you – the closeness you have with her, with them both. I was a strange mixture. Physically, I was a natural tomboy – you know, wanting to throw a ball farther, ride a bike faster, and outrun all the boys – but emotionally I was female, through and through. I think my dad encouraged the tomboy in me, but didn't know how to handle the sensitive side, especially as I grew older. Then they had Tom, a much more straightforward proposition altogether."

"I expect we men aren't good at deciphering more than one thing at once," he said. "It throws us."

"Is this a confession?" She leaned back slightly in her chair, both hands wrapped round her glass, and looked him in the eye. A slow smile spread across his face as he returned her gaze. His blue eyes darkened with intensity.

"I can see how appealing it is, though," he said, ignoring her question. "Softness and strength in one package – the ultimate paradox."

"Mmm, I'm not so sure – maybe appealing at first, but then later, when the reality outweighs the fantasy... "

"You think I'm fantasising?"

"Maybe you're just seeing what you want to see," she said. Michael stared at her for a moment, as if he were grappling with his own questions.

"I'll get another drink while I'm trying to work that one out," he said. "Brandy?" She nodded and watched him as he walked away from her towards the bar, his large frame impressing itself on the space he occupied. She could have picked him out in a crowd anywhere: the size of him, the close-cropped hair, the elongated curve down from the back of his head to his neck, the visible tensing of his body as he took each step. She knew him.

When he returned, her eyes were drawn to his hand, which was cradling her glass; a big hand, strong yet softly padded. This was the feeling she experienced in some way each time she was with him. What was it? Then it came to her. Safety. It was safety. The realisation hit her like lightning; she felt safe, a feeling so unfamiliar for so long she had forgotten what it meant, how it felt – until now.

Her room was on the fifth floor of the hotel. Laura pulled back the curtains from the high window and the moonlight washed over her and flooded the room. Michael, following behind her, clicked on the light.

"Turn it off," she said, her back to him still. He did as she asked, then turned and locked the door before walking across to where she stood looking out into the night. The lights of the city spread out below the window, bright jewels scattered by an invisible hand across a massive black carpet. She could feel his approach and the warmth of him at her back, though he was a step away from her. He stood very still as if waiting for her.

"Touch me, Michael," she whispered. "I want you to touch me." Then his hands were in her hair, his fingers on her scalp, the back of her neck, her shoulders. She was dissolving under his touch.

"Wait," she said, turning to face him. He lowered his head wanting to find her mouth. "No. I want to look at you," she said, her breath contained, pressed tight in her chest. "First, I want to look at you."

She stepped back from him and looked up into his face, his pale eyes reflecting the light from the moon, his lips parted as his breathing quickened. Still there was a space between them. She reached out and unbuttoned his shirt, slipping it off his shoulders, his skin like silk under her hands. Her fingers moved to his waist unhooking his trousers until he stood naked before her, the planes of his body smooth and softly vulnerable in the moonlight. Again she stretched out her hand and, with her fingertips, traced a delicate pattern across the breadth of his chest, over his navel and down to where his torso narrowed and the smoothness disappeared, until finally she stopped and her hand closed round him. She looked into his eyes.

"Laura," he said, as he moved towards her at last and she felt him hard against her.

"Yes," she whispered. "I'm here. I've been waiting – a long time. But I'm here now."

paper snow

from a novel **by sy standon**

Lotte Solomon put pen to paper as it began to rain outside, unaware of the pattering above the flimsy wooden roof of the empty schoolroom. The nib of her pen flashed silver and scratched into the paper, ploughing a dark furrow.

Dear Solomon, I don't know how to start...

Her hand wavered as if writing in the air, trying to compose what she wanted to say. She pushed her pebble glasses back onto the bridge of her nose. Her hand moved to one side.

"That there is a fine nib, Miss Sceptre." The voice came from behind her, belonging to a child standing just to the left and slightly behind in the shadows.

"You should have an easy time writing your letter," said the voice. "I cleaned up the nib real good and I can see the shine from here, Miss Sceptre."

Lotte stopped writing and looked behind her. "I believe you, Sarah. I think you've done a wonderful job." Lotte turned back to the letter.

A drop of water splashed onto the corner of the small school desk, briefly illuminated by the hurricane lamp; it flowered and splattered the paper with tiny dots of water that began to darken as they soaked in.

"You should have no problem writing those letters now. The nib will see to that, it'll stop you throwing any more paper to the floor like you normally do."

Lotte tried to wipe the drops away, but smudged the ink in a long dark smear, obliterating the first line. Another drop of water landed on her hair, which she had coiled up earlier in the morning when the day was clear and fresh, when the wind fondled the frees and swayed them from side to side, shivering them free of their leaves in a shower of gold, red and yellow. A day when she had even let the kids out early to play outside and of course to keep the schoolyard clear; a nice clean schoolyard was the first thing that the governors would walk through to get to the school. And what was a school with an unkempt schoolyard?

Another drop tapped onto the paper, soaking into the smear.

"Miss Sceptre, I think its time to put the pots out."

"I think so too." Said Lotte wearily. All day, even during lessons, she had tried to plan what she wanted to say and finally, now she had the chance, the weather wasn't letting her.

The drops became more rhythmical as Lotte picked up the hurricane lamp, its glow illuminating her sharp features in an orange halo. She had the same Roman nose as her bother Solomon, the same high cheekbones, even the same long rigid jaw, but her eyes softened what could have been an dispassionate face of white angular marble. Her glasses magnified her sky-blue eyes to become lakes of depth and clarity.

"Let's get them put down, or the classroom will wash away."

"I don't think it'll be that bad, Miss Sceptre."

"I was just joking. I somehow think this classroom will be here longer than us." Lotte spoke softly.

Sarah hobbled out of the shadows. Her wiry hair had come loose and fell down one side of her round face. Her top lip was lined with streaks of watery mucus and she drew an arm across her mouth. Shadows thrown from her strapped leg, slinked across the blackboard like coiled serpents.

"Kyle and Hanna made fun of me today." Sarah knocked the blackboard cloth on to the floor and moved her leg with both arms to one side so she could reach down.

"That so, Sarah." Lotte hung the lamp on the hat stand.

"But I ignored them."

"Good for you." She reached behind to pull out a series of jars and buckets.

"I ignored them for a long time, Miss Sceptre."

"Good for you, and good for you for using *ignored* properly." She handed Sarah the smaller pots.

"They said I talked funny."

"Well I don't suppose they've heard that many people from Alabama living in Honnington, or the whole of Vermont for that matter. But it makes you special, Sarah."

"Yes, Miss Sceptre." Sarah looked at Lotte, unsure of what to say.

"Well these pots won't put themselves in place, will they?"

"They won't, Miss Sceptre. Not without us."

Lotte glided around the schoolroom placing the larger containers and buckets where the larger drops fell, while Sarah, her strapped foot bumping and scraping against the bare floorboards, placed the smaller jars on the desks and sideboards.

A gust of wind caught the trees surrounding the schoolyard, making them loll back and forth and showering more leaves into the schoolyard. Lotte sighed; another job for the children in the morning and they seemed to live for this weather.

The white pad of paper stared blankly back at her as she sat back down. This time the letter would come good. She'd know what to write and maybe, just maybe, this would be the letter that got written and got through. This would be the one. She pushed her glasses further back onto the bridge of her nose, lifted her pen and started to write:

My Dear Solomon,

So many days and nights have passed without your company. Your leaving has created a space at the table that can never be filled, no matter who sits there. Miss Swann talks of nothing else and I have to put up with her musings about you all evening. Mr Groadle, however, is a calming influence and talks to me when I am drying the dishes about where you may be. He suggested that I write you this letter. All my hope is that this will be directed, with any luck, to where you may be residing at the moment. I hope that it finds you Solomon, one day.

Mother and Father are as well as can be and I can see in their eyes that they too wonder where you are, how you are doing and wondering if you are still, well, with us. I hope this letter won't stop in its tracks.

Father's hands are getting less and less dexterous, and more and more boots pile up. Mother is even trying to help out. They've even let your room where you kept so many of Nancy-May's things. So now all the rooms, bar the kitchen, have been let. Her things are now in my room, safe and secure.

It's been so long and you never send any word of how you are. There is not a moment that I do not think of you. I bet (to myself – you know Mother's stance on gambling) you must be making lots of money and maybe living in a big house somewhere with a big green lawn, and that you have found yourself a new wife, or someone who is very special to you and maybe even a daughter. I can see you now, walking down your street, people waving to you, a proud man, they will say. A proud...

Lotte stopped writing.

"That nib is writing for you real good now." Sarah said softly.

"You imbued it with your special magic." Lotte looked down and crossed out the last two lines, blocking them with ink.

She sighed and continued.

The bank manager, Mr Sorensein has been asking questions again. It's like a yearly ritual (I think he uses it when he tries to run for Mayor). Each time his article in The Herald *is the same. They brand you as a thief. Can't you come back to at least clear your name before he calls in the marshals to track you down?. Tell me you didn't take the money. Tell me that you made a mistake, or that you have realised what you have done and will return it. Tell me, tell me anything, tell me, just write me, and let me know that you are not the thief they say you are...*

Lotte stopped and looked up. "Damn it," she said, forgetting Sarah, and screwed the paper into a ball. It tapped the floor and rolled under her desk.

"Just one letter; it's all I ask."

The rain on the roof grumbled and the water played a faster tune. One was a perfect C (the steel bucket by the door), which would lower by two whole octaves as the evening wore on, while one of the jam jars at the other end of the room would end up as a perfect A.

"No need to throw that letter away. The nib was writing mighty fine, Miss Sceptre." Sarah was sitting under the hat stand, trying not to look at the dark branches tapping gently against the window.

"I cleaned it so fine that your writing will be just so nice and you won't have to worry about anything because, well, it will kind of do it for you." She rocked her good leg back and forth.

"Sometimes it can be difficult to know what to say." Lotte hunched her shoulders. The new style that supposedly all the women now wore, the 'bob', made the back of her neck susceptible to the cold. If only Mrs Jackson had minded her own business and just trimmed her hair like she'd asked. Now, she'd have to wait months for it to grow back. And with winter coming closer...

"But you said I imbibed the nib." Sarah sniffed, swallowed and rubbed her nose with the sleeve of her dress. The tree tapped again and the hurricane lamp flickered.

"Imbued Sarah, here." She reached into her sleeve. Sarah stopped rocking, lifted herself out of the chair and hobbled over to Lotte who passed her a handkerchief.

"But you said I gave it magic."

"No Sarah, its okay, I only meant it as a little joke."

Lotte looked back down at the pad with the scraps of a hundred unwritten letters.

Dear Solomon,

Please tell me where you are and come back, please just come back, we all miss you so. Go tell Mr Sorensein what you did and...

She tore it out and screwed the paper into a ball. It was hopeless. The letter would never get through. Who in their right mind would stay at a forwarding address after taking money from a bank? Why was she doing this?

Maybe Solomon would write. He'd set things straight. He'd return and live in the house. Mama and Papa would be overjoyed. Her world would be complete again.

Her eyes brimmed. She looked around the schoolroom, Her world, a small wooden building with a globe in one corner next to the blackboard and the hat stand on the other side; chairs and desks in three neat rows. The lighter silhouettes of the desks caught the pale silver glow of the moon through the clouds, presiding over them all.

Lotte looked behind her. On the walls were pictures, patchwork and embroidery. One particular drawing had been framed: a drawing of the sun in yellow crayon above a house with a simple square and a triangle above it. Three figures had been scrawled to one side, one in blue crayon, the other in red and the third in brown, each with a name underneath with big and small letters jostling for position: Solomon, Manny and Lotte. In the lower right-hand corner a meandering signature: Nancy-May.

Lotte stood, tipping her chair over and it clattered to the wooden floor.

Sarah jumped. "No more letter writing?"

"No more letters tonight, Sarah."

Where was he? Solomon had talked often of joining Nancy-May and Manny, just before his disappearance; talked of it as a divine act of release. Divine? How could he be so selfish as to do something like that? How could he?

The wind sighed against the windows and the raindrops played in the background in feeble taps, losing their rhythm.

"Time to lock up now." Lotte fought to compose her voice. "I'll walk you back to the clock tower."

"You sure magic is only in stories?"

"Positive, Sarah. Hurry. Time to go now," she said, fighting back tears.

"The rain has stopped."

five poems

by mary taylor

departure
for les arnold

The room is brightly lit –
streamers twist over the carpet,
over music and the clink of glasses,
over laughter and the cackle of crisps.

He watches and sips martini.
A woman comes up
and leads a man away;
together they sway
in time to the music.

A doorbell rings.
The hostess goes out but few notice.
She returns and beckons to him,
"A limousine has arrived."
He is surprised, "So soon,
but I have hardly spoken... "
"Yes, it is for you,
I have checked."

"Well then... "
He gulps down his wine
and grabs a friend,
"I have to leave."
He waves to another.
"I am ready to go now."
A shout of talk falls abruptly silent.

mary taylor

They walk down the stairs
into the dusk.
In the hallway
moonlight fingers her face.
He kisses her cheek,
"Thank you."
Slowly she climbs the stairs
with one last look back,
"Goodbye."
She quickens her pace
and reaches the landing, the light,
the voices. He is left in silence.

Emerging from the cloakroom,
he removes a greatcoat from the stand
and his hat.
The mirror reflects a man
tired and pale but relaxed.

Outside snow whitens the steps.
Below, under a street lamp,
waits a chauffeur.
Wood and brass slam shut.
"Good evening, sir."
Settling into soft, roomy leather
he glances up at the lighted window.
The car chokes into action
then glides into the night.

In the house
the music is subdued
and one or two are silent.
But the party will continue.

the nunnery, iona

I, Saint Columba
banish women.

Do not lust in your heart.

Nights here are hard, long and dark,
the wind pierces wattle and daub.
We hunger for warmth
and the villagers disturb:
young girls wreathed in orchids
ivy and meadowsweet...

I, Abbot Dominic
believe in the Word.

Solomon had three hundred
concubines.

I did not plunder,
merely did my duty
as I unveiled the nuns.

I, the Abbess
prefer lapdogs.

It is better to marry
than burn with passion.

Maybe, but he abandoned me
and frost blackens desire.

Prayer, we depend on prayer
and he hears us, the perfect lover.

With him, we shall walk strands of light,
bring to birth his image.

Mist descends,
the ruins fall quiet.
Poppies bleed on granite
and petals of starched campion
drift to earth.

mary taylor

pasture of the geese

I have crawled on beaches,
hands sticky with blood and tar

clambered rocks where
the guillemot draggles
oil-slicked wings.
No more angel than a shag,
a junkie tossed to the gulls,
I gobbled up my nightmare
and retched on the dark.

Now, I treasure-trail barefoot,
squat on dunes soft as breasts
where water-flags surge
and lambs shudder the ewe.

Here, in this thin place
I choose to dream.

Milk-blue terns
light
    on water,
like pebbles skim my longing –

for the wild goose
whose wings, alone
can shelter.

The wild goose is a Celtic Christian symbol for the spirit.

the barnakle

Crack of black alder,
        wind barks across marsh
                and a feather sculls

the dark lochan.
        Stamped on mud
                your web-arabesque

melts into grey.
        I am drunk on salt.
                No croodle of doves

bloated milk,
        can hold my hunger.
                Migrant lover, son of thunder

fly the frozen landes –
        with a harsh cry, overwhelm.
                Or come upon me

kneeling in the dust
        and I will cup my hands:
                a beggar for love.

The Barnakle is a barnacle goose.

mary taylor

pomegranate

Nipples hard as stars
cusps sharp around
a sticky dust of anthers.

Tonight, I will let you
gently tear my chiffon veil

reveal the chambers of my heart.
A honeycomb of ivory seed
a casket of ruby crystals.

You will prise them out
one by one
amber, rose, crimson

bittersweet moments on your tongue
gone before you can savour
memory and myth

with each seed
you will almost taste me
yet your thirst is never quenched
for still you do not know me.

taking it with you

a short story **by mimi thebo**

You go into the grave and you come out the other side. I had thought at first to lie there and rest (the funeral had been very difficult), but I heard voices and I got up. 'Got up' is the only way I can think of to say it, but it was more effortless than that, and there wasn't a choice in the matter. There was a small group of people waiting, it seemed, for me.

"Hello, dear," said a woman in a fantastically jewelled turban. "How are you feeling?"

"Fine, thank you," I answered automatically. It was all quite strange. Why should anyone ask a dead woman how she is feeling? A few men attended her, all faultlessly groomed in dark suits.

"Countess," one said to the turban, "I think she's a bit shocky."

"You're quite right, George. Offer her your arm and let's take a turn in the park."

The landscape, if that's what you could call it, had a familiar shape, but was made of volatile vapours that shifted and pitched under my feet. George's arm was most welcome, and I was relieved when the Countess suggested we sit on adjacent benches, which seemed a bit more substantial.

"George Warrington you have met," she said in kind tones.

"Please call me George."

The Countess indicated the other two with an elegant hand. "This is Mr Wellbottom and Mr Clarke."

"Michael," said Mr Wellbottom, smiling.

"Tommy, please," said Mr Clarke.

The four of them looked at me enquiringly and I again made the effort to pull myself together. "Oh, I'm sorry. I'm Mrs Emberly. Elizabeth." I looked at Tommy and softened. "Bets."

"Oh, that's very good, Bets," the Countess said, clapping her hands with glee. "And only three minutes out. Marvellous. You shall fit in splendidly. We don't stand much on ceremony here."

"And," George confided, "we don't much like those that do."

"I'm not really a Countess," the Countess said. "It was just a joke made by Somerset Maugham about Henry James."

Tommy obligingly quoted, "Poor Henry, he's spending eternity wandering round and round a stately park and the fence is just too high for him to peep over and they're having tea just too far away for him to hear what the Countess is saying."

"Of course there's no tea," the Countess corrected. "But I've always wondered how Maugham knew. He couldn't remember when we had him here. He was delightful. And we did avoid Henry."

"Horrible little squirt," Michael concurred.

We relapsed into smiles.

"I didn't really expect... " I trailed off, disconcerted.

"No. No, of course not," George said, soothingly.

"That's a very nice dress you're wearing, dear," the Countess noticed.

"My wedding dress," I explained and felt the first stab at my heart.

Tommy cleared his throat. "Is he... here?" he asked politely.

My hand fluttered to my chest as if there was something there going wrong. Absurd. I lowered it abruptly. "He should be soon," I said. "He's in the last stages of pancreatic cancer. Will I see him again here, do you think?"

Michael looked at George, who cleared his throat hesitantly.

"You had a very simple funeral, didn't you dear?" the Countess interrupted.

"Yes."

She nodded approvingly. "Very good taste, too. Simple pine coffin?"

"Yes," I started to elaborate, but gasped in horror. I had seen three faces at the garden gate. Faces, if you could call them that. They were coated thickly in a luminous white substance in which their eyes and teeth seemed hideously yellow. They stared at me and turned away, leaving me trembling with fright and disgust.

"It's all right, Bets," Tommy hurried to say. "They're just hoping you might be someone they know."

"But their faces!"

"They coat them," the Countess said matter-of-factly, "in a preservative mixture of salt, lime, oh, I forget what all. They," she said, shaking her head sadly, "try to prolong things."

"Prolong things."

"Another thing Somerset was wrong about," Michael said. "It isn't eternity."

"Michael! Do shut up!" George hauled Michael to his feet and dragged him into a corner of the more and more crisply delineated shrubbery.

The Countess sighed. "Are you familiar with the Egyptian concept of immortality?"

I nodded.

"They were spot on, darling. You only last here as long as your body does."

"What happens after that?"

"Well, you see, it's like life and death. Nobody really knows. We call it assimilation, but it's only a name."

I thought again of Jerry's cancer. He couldn't, he just couldn't last much longer. "Simple pine coffin," I said bitterly.

"And very good taste, too," the Countess said. "I was preserved under glass. A silly whim, but I'm here until some booby bangs into me in the family vault."

"We," Tommy said, motioning to Michael and George, "are members of the lead-liners club. There were more of us, but eventually... "

"Eventually," the Countess said, "we all go. The last Pharaoh got so tired of waiting that he pounded his own spirit body into dust about, oh, fifteen years ago now. He couldn't wait for assimilation any longer and he was so bored without anyone to talk to, that he... "

"Oh," I interrupted in dismay, "that sounds awful. Surely you don't feel that way?"

"We have our duties, which reminds me, Michael? George? Two more, four o'clock!"

They crunched down the path. I could now see every bit of gravel, every fallen acorn from the oak tree that sheltered the benches. I only wanted to see Jerry one more time, that was all, just once. We had both been so ill for so long. Oh, the nurses had brought us together now and then, but in the last two years I could only just sense his presence, not speak to him. The morning of my stroke, we had argued over something so trivial I could not recall the cause, although I had thought about it every day of my life and death since. I wanted to say goodbye properly. I wanted him to hold me, kiss me. Then I would go on - on to assimilation or whatever surprise lay in store for me.

The Countess returned. "Not our type. Two Americans, buried in Highbury after an accident. I sent them over to their people."

"How long will I last?"

"Not long." She tossed her fantastic head. "Not long enough to please me, at any rate. Perhaps two, three months? Then, dear, you really must go. I should hate to see you washed in lime, swilling formaldehyde down there, providing entertainment for those who have wasted both life *and* death. It's disgusting."

"Got the Yanks off," Michael said, joining us. "Are you talking about the doctor?"

"Had himself pickled, you know," Tommy put in.

Michael gave him an even stare. "As I was saying," he continued, "runs a ghastly kind of cabaret down there. Those people are so bored, and yet so afraid of assimilation."

"That's because they fear a judgement, I'm sure," the Countess said. "Oh, we'd better explain the boredom to Bets."

"You can't learn anything here," George explained. "You can't memorise anything new. And the cabaret people all watched the same cinema and read the same books."

Michael sniffed. "If they read at all. It's all television and pop songs down there. Poor blighters are desperate for something more substantial."

Tommy nodded eagerly. "At last they see the value of great art, but it's too late for them to have any inside them. I used to publish a small magazine and no one envied me then, but they envy me now. They envy us all, for our memories."

The Countess waved one ring-encrusted hand. "It's the only reason they haven't broken us into firewood, darling. Oh, look, nightfall. Time for me to go back under glass. Do you remember where your coffin is, Bets?"

I nodded, thoughtful.

"Well then, we'll see you tomorrow. Come along, Tommy!"

A day already gone. Oh, Jerry, die soon.

The days in the garden passed quickly enough for us. Soon we were joined by a Classics professor. He too, was lead-lined, and there was general rejoicing by the long-term residents because they now had most of the *Iliad* and some of the *Odyssey* at their disposal. We spent many afternoons on the benches or under the tea tent listening to the professor recite.

I could seldom concentrate. Already I could not walk so far as my friends, and I could not stay up as late. Earlier and earlier in the evening I excused myself to my coffin. I looked for Jerry with a growing sense of urgency.

I began taking solitary walks, which inevitably led down the hill, to the cabaret. The lime pots waited for anyone's use in the middle of town. It wasn't long before I worked up the courage to dash down and seize one for myself.

At first I only painted what was hidden by my dress. In this way, I was still welcome at the Countess's receptions. I'm sure they knew what I was doing, but they also knew my motives and granted me a certain leniency. Of course, I could not keep up this polite fiction for long. As day after day passed and Jerry still did not appear, there was no choice for me. The day came when I painted my face as thickly as if I were rendering a brick wall.

When newcomers arrived, I stood respectfully at a distance, peering to recognise the one corpse I wanted to meet. At a distance, mind, remembering the fright I'd had my first afternoon. Michael would never have to shoo *me* away.

Of course, I drew closer to the cabaret. The formaldehyde they tipped down their throats drew me in. The favourite turns were a philosophy professor and an opera singer. Her throat was six inches deep in lime, but fading nonetheless. I lay in my grave that night and made my decision.

"Well," the doctor said nastily. "I was wondering when I'd have the pleasure of your company." He nodded his head towards the customers visible out his office door. "Gives a whole new meaning to the expression 'beyond the pale' doesn't it?"

I smiled weakly and falsely.

"What've you got worth a pint a day?"

"Poetry, mainly."

He sneered. "Gawd help us. You'll get your ribs kicked in. You'll be assimilated after the first three lines."

My voice shook. "Well, I was thinking Stevie Smith might go down rather well," I tendered. "And perhaps Emily Dickinson, some of it, and I thought A. E. Housman, a bit?"

"You might be on to something there." The doctor reappraised me. "What else you got?"

"Well, I have some Buddhist sutras, as well."

"That's the ticket! They love 'em. Missed out with old Haysoos, you see, want to believe they've got a whole new body waiting for them." The doctor beamed at me. "You can have a pint on the house today and start tomorrow."

"That's very kind." I rose to go. "Um, doctor?" But he knew what I was asking.

"On a pint a day you'll last about three more weeks. I can be more exact, if you wish."

"Please."

"Sit down."

I had not imagined myself capable of generating such pain in my condition. I nearly fainted, or whatever passed for it, on the chair. "Three weeks and four days. You'll go around five o'clock on the fourth day. If you keep painting, and barring any accidents."

I applied lime to the wounded area and limped out to the bar.

My selections were well received, but I did not mingle with the patrons. Although I was lonely and there were those there in whom I yearned to confide, I simply could not risk it. A wrong word in the wrong ear could earn you a chair cracked through your skull and I saw enough scenes of similar horror to convince me that if I wanted to survive to see Jerry, keeping my own counsel and company was safest.

At first I wondered how the customers paid for the doctor's services, but he left his office door open enough to see. I had never been able to understand an appetite for cruelty in life, and seeing it in death was even more confounding and disturbing. Clearly the doctor, unlike his patrons, feared no judgement.

Every afternoon, I wandered up the hill and looked in vain for Jerry.

As the days passed, I was deteriorating. The flesh on the bottoms of my feet was wearing thin, and I did not dare to sit at all for fear of my sharp spine protruding. I felt utterly wretched and was all the more wretched knowing how I hideous I must have appeared. I kept my distance from the Countess and the lead-liners, not wanting to inflict the sight of me on my late friends.

I don't remember envying them as they carried out the duties incumbent on their privilege. They not only greeted new arrivals, but also carried the overly-deteriorated who had refused to re-enter their graves back up the hill. It was a horrifying task, and I wondered how tempted they were to pass on through. I knew Michael's dear wife had not been lead-lined, and that he'd had to see her come and go, leaving without him into the unfathomable dimension of assimilation.

The days passed, and the doctor's prediction was proving accurate. One week. Five days. One day.

The last day, I would have wept if I could as I dragged my bony feet up the hill for the last time. It was two o'clock, and I had but three hours left. I watched the new graves straggle in hopelessly. I was weary. Weary, I thought grimly, to the bone. I dared not even lean against a tree for fear of the bark stripping my back. I reeked of formaldehyde. Flakes of lime compound peeled from my spent body at every movement, as if I had an advanced form of terminal dandruff. Two men climbed out of coffins, assisted by George and Tommy. Neither was Jerry.

It was three o'clock when I began to cry dryly, my fragile ribs heaving without any air. It was the most futile of all my futile exercises and I descended at this point into self-pity. All of my life and death I had always felt some strong force sustaining me, some kind of universal greatness. Now that greatness was gone, and my self-control went with it.

By four o'clock I was intruding just out of Michael's reach, frightening the new arrivals with my repulsive appearance. Woman after woman after man came out of the grave to my ranting curses. At a quarter past four, a grave appeared near mine. I caught my wretched breathless breath and stopped my shaking bones. It opened, and as the lead-liners gathered, he came out, my Jerry.

"Whoa!" I heard him say shakily. "This is a bit of a surprise for an atheist."

The Countess clucked. "Oh, dear," she said. "It's always hardest for your kind."

"Jerry!" I howled from my heart. "Oh, Jerry, darling!"

I had forgotten myself in my delight and was dancing towards him, my arms outstretched. He grimaced and shut his eyes. "Good God!" he said, "What is that hideous thing?"

"I'll tell you later," the Countess said. "Get rid of her, Michael, would you? And bring Mr... "

"Emberly," Jerry said, shielding his eyes from my forlorn form.

"Bring Mr Emberly along."

"Countess," Michael said. "Getting rid of her? It's not on, I'm afraid. It's Bets. This is Bets, Jerry."

"What a perfectly ghastly day it's been." The Countess glared in my direction, but softened as she saw how near I was to the end. "Oh, well, we'd best leave them to it. Come along, gentlemen."

We stood for a few seconds. Jerry was unable to take his hands from his eyes.

"Jerry," I said softly.

"God, no!" he screamed, pressing his hands harder to exclude even the possibility of sight.

"Turn around," I begged him. "Don't look at me, but try to listen."

"I don't know that I can," he said. "This has all been quite a shock. I need some time... "

"Jerry," I broke in. "I understand, truly I do, but I only have ten minutes."

"Ten minutes? This is bloody eternity, isn't it?"

To see him, to hear him, even arguing with me again, was a pleasure so intense that it was worth everything I had gone through.

"Oh, Jerry, I do love you."

"God, don't." His back shivered under his best jacket.

"It's not eternity, Jer," I spoke quickly, trying to remain calm. "You only last here as long as your body does. I've been trying to hang on so as to see you. That's why I'm coated with this stuff and why I smell so foul. It's the formaldehyde. I've been doing a cabaret act to buy it and drinking a pint a day. And I only have – oh, God – five minutes left and I get to spend them with you. I can't help but tell you I love you."

"Bets," Jerry finally said. "I'm sorry. I can't turn 'round. I know it's rotten of me, but I can't."

"It's all right," I said. "I don't mind much."

"Keep talking. It sounds so much like you when you talk."

"The cabaret crowd gets really bored," I babbled. "It's evidently terribly hard to memorise things when you're dead. Do you know what my star turn was? The Heart Sutra! I used it for my encore."

"I've missed you," Jerry said. "I've missed you so much."

"I've missed you, too."

"Keep talking."

"And Stevie Smith. They loved Stevie Smith. *Not Waving But Drowning*, naturally enough, but they also liked *The Cat Who Gallops About Doing Good*. Strange, isn't it?"

"Very strange, my darling."

"The Countess is awfully nice. And I think you'll really get on with George."

"Bets?"

"Yes, darling?"

"You can stop talking now."

A short silence.

"How much time do we have left?"

"Oh, about three minutes." My voice broke on the three.

"Bets, I love you."

I laughed in relief. "Of course you do. And I you. But you are always late, dear."

"I know. But then, you always," his voice broke in a dry sob, "you always wait for me, Bets.'

"Look," I said to his back. "I'll keep waiting in assimilation, too, if I can. I don't mind waiting. I never minded the waiting. It's worth it."

He sobbed away.

"You aren't lead-lined or anything, are you?"

"What?"

"Casket."

"No, they did ours the same."

"Good. Now don't go messing with lime and pickling. Just have a nice time at the garden parties and get back in your grave. If it's at all possible, I'll be waiting."

I saw the back of his head nodding, and watched him gather himself together. "If I keep my eyes closed," he said, "I'm pretty sure I can hold you. Would you like that?"

"I should love it. It's only for a minute or so, but I do pong dreadfully."

Jerry turned around with his eyes shut. "I'll stick it," he said. "Come here."

I went trembling into his arms, but he didn't shrink away from me. "It's okay, love," he whispered into my hair. "You're still you."

And the brave man kissed me on my salt-encrusted lips with his eyes wide open.

nu-touches

a short story **by neil walker**

A deepening low-pressure system was sweeping in from the South Coast when Boadicea came to me with a request for a piece of rope. I suppose most dads would have asked her there and then what she wanted it for, but I retain the utmost confidence in my daughter's judgement. Therefore, without hesitation, I fished out an old piece from the malt house we've tastefully converted into a garage.

It had been used a couple of times – the rope not the garage – once at a campsite when I accidentally reversed the caravan into the River Avon, and again when rescuing a dozen or so of the neighbour's sheep buried under a snowdrift. As such, the rope was coated in a mixture of oil and wool, but was, nevertheless, an example of craftsmanship at its best.

Boadicea wanted the rope squeaky-clean and so asked Mum's permission to put it through the wash. Now I didn't know this, but the conspiracy that is modern science has constructed washing machines with programmes specifically designed for a whole host of miscellaneous items. The list in the manual runs through to such things as shoes, holdalls and doormats, but unfortunately stops short of mentioning rope. We took the risk and it paid off handsomely. The rope came out the most wonderful sugar-brown.

"What next?" I asked enthusiastically.

"Can you tie slipknots, Dad?"

My confidence remained high despite the unusual request and I darted off upstairs to unearth my copy of E. Annie Proulx's *The Shipping News*, which I knew had descriptions and diagrams from *The Ashley Book of Knots* prefacing each chapter. Unfortunately, examples of slipknots were decidedly absent, so I tried the second-hand bookshop in the neighbouring village. The owner suggested, of all things, the *New Oxford Pictorial Dictionary.*

"Look under 'noose'," he said.

Now I wasn't at all sure that slipknots and nooses were exactly the same thing but I took him at his word, and since I had a copy of the self-same dictionary at home, I sprinted back – head down, arms pumping – to deliver the good news to Boadicea.

After locating the chunky publication we turned expectantly to 'noose' and, sure enough, there in a series of three stamp-sized, black-and-white drawings was an illustrated guide on how to tie one. I wondered if the dictionary had, over the years, proved of use to suicidal types in ensuring that everything ran smoothly – one in the eye for Oxford University Press.

The reference was just what Boadicea was after. Her face was transformed into a picture of happiness. I was intrigued.

"Tie it round my neck, Dad, like the dictionary says."

"The dictionary says that?"

"No. I mean the way the dictionary shows."

I have to say this raised the first doubt, but then I remembered Boadicea's Slipknot T-shirt with a masked gentleman holding a noose tied round his neck. Suddenly the request was invested with meaning. A wry smile quickly became a half-stifled spluttering laugh of recognition, the kind of laugh that, if taken the wrong way, can seem patronising. In fact what had dawned on me were the startling similarities between Boadicea's actions and those of my formative years as a pimply punk. Just as I had used symbolic intent by adorning various parts of my body with safety pins, bicycle chains and padlocks, so the noose was now elevated to represent a wholesale rejection of the constraining precepts laid down by society in the guise of its moral codes and ethics – a deceptively clever sub-cultural icon, and one that would send shockwaves shaking the very foundations of those in authority.

"Good for you Boadicea. Carving out your own niche, drawing up your own portrait of societal values betrayed. It's just what we punks succeeded in doing through bondage."

"Bondage?" Her face reddened and she turned her back on me before continuing. "Corey wears a noose all the time." She shrugged her shoulders. "Slipknot are cool."

I assumed Corey was the masked man on her Slipknot T-shirt.

It seemed ironic, given Boadicea's flushed face, that I should find myself exercising extreme caution in avoiding cutting off the blood supply to the head while running the knot up under her chin. I stepped back to admire our handiwork. I had to agree with her. It did look cool. There was even a slight pang of jealousy spasming away inside my gut that I as a teenager hadn't come up with the idea myself. Indeed, the more I looked at my daughter, the greater the significance I was able to attribute to the noose. It wasn't just the outrageous irreverence, there also appeared to be a sexual connotation at play here. The tail end of the rope nestled neatly in the valley between Boadicea's pert, developing breasts, resembling the erect member of a well-hung man. The similarity was underlined somewhat by the bulbous head at the end of the rope where it had been singed in order to seal any loose threads – the thought had me instinctively wincing while reaching down for my genitals.

"Now for the barbed wire." Boadicea smiled as she spoke, her brace glinting with beads of saliva.

"Where does that go?"

"Round the wrists. Has to be authentic."

"No problem," I said. "You remember we helped Farmer Thrasher with his sheep in the snowdrift last winter? He owes us one."

"A sheep?" she quizzed.

"A favour," I explained.

Barbed wire, I thought. Brilliant. Just a strip of cord-like metal with a couple of twists for the finishing touch and *voilà* – such breathtaking simplicity and yet so blatantly barbarian. Again it riled. Why the hell hadn't we thought of it back in '76? Okay, so I was only ten at the time, but still, not even Rotten had contemplated barbed wire, and such a commonplace device enclosing just about every acre of farmland and thus constricting farmyard animals the length and breadth.

As I dwelt on the subject I unearthed an even darker side to this appallingly brutal device. In addition to animal oppression, inherent in its usage was a legacy of underclass oppression which continued to inform the activities of landowners in constructing a no-man's-land to keep the disenfranchised at arm's length. A drawing up of boundaries signifying a 'them and us' situation – the green pastures of the haves and a thin strip of eroded and muddied gravel for the have-nots – the demarcation of a narrow pathway along which the destitute huddled and shuffled while peering enviously at the house on the hill.

The more I thought about barbed wire, the more troubling its impact. Barbed wire has a sordid history. It was born out of violence and, for a fleeting moment, I dreamt up a confusion of ripped-and-torn imagery, a raping and pillaging of army conscripts, a hand separated from the uniformed body and left behind on the wire to point an accusing finger at the generals sat safe-and-sound in occupied mansions just beyond the horizon.

Yes, barbed wire, aptly named with its unerring propensity for spiking and sneering, be it soldier, poacher or burglar. Snagged privates, snagged privation. I found myself wincing and reaching for the genitals once more.

"Corey wears it on both wrists. Has it so that it cuts into the skin." Boadicea talked as we walked to the farm in the pouring rain.

"Isn't that a little dangerous, given that the arteries are so close to the surface?" I retain a hint of fatherly protection. It's my Achilles' heel.

"He looks cool. It's the risk you run these days."

"Hmm. Spurting blood… " I barely whispered the words as I turned them over in my head.

"The more the merrier," she replied cheerfully.

Her words immediately brought to mind Vicious on stage at the Dallas Longhorn Ballroom, blood streaming from his nose after being head-butted by a girl fan, the blood spilling into letters cut deep into his chest. The words "GIMME A FIX" were Sid's favourite salutation to any new face. In the context of rock 'n' roll… no, in the context of life no less... Boadicea was, of course, absolutely right. The more the merrier.

We knocked on Farmer Thrasher's vast farmhouse door and asked him to cut off a couple of pieces of wire from the enormous reel he kept in stock. I joked with him about his seeming readiness to face a peasants' revolt, but it didn't appear to strike him as a subject worthy of ridicule.

On the return journey Boadicea and I talked about the role of popular music in modern society. Despite the torrential downpour, the rain failed to penetrate the Gore-Tex membrane of the waterproofs protecting my Westwood ensemble and moussed spikes. Boadicea on the other hand, in a Marilyn Manson hooded top and lapping canvas trousers, was soaked to the skin. She refused point blank to put her hood up, even though she'd spent the morning colouring her hair with a purple Day-Glo rinse. I wasn't sure whom she was intending to impress, given that the country lane now resembled a turbid river, but she clearly felt that someone important in her life was about to float on by. In the meantime she elaborated on her theory that all forms of music, other than Nu-Metal, were worthless, and added that the howling of wolves and cries of other nocturnal creatures were the equal of anything human beings could muster. There was something miraculous about lips able to speak at length while drinking in Day-Glo raindrops.

By the time we'd finished the discourse we were already back at home and I was employing great surgical precision in wrapping the barbed wire round my daughter's wrists so as to avoid arterial damage. Attila, our eldest, has welding equipment up in the attic and we sought his advice on how best to finish the job.

"A soldering iron," he insisted. "A nice, clean finish without the need to burn flesh."

I'm pleased to report the job was concluded without any major mishaps and I stood back once more to take in the full effect. Aside from the homely quality of the towel wrapped round her head – Mum's intervention – I have to say her shock tactics worked a treat. The only thing that grated a bit was the T-shirt she'd changed into. I felt she'd have been better off with Slipknot emblazoned across her chest rather than the laser-copied photo of Mum and me smiling happily away on a beach in Menorca. It wasn't so much the image that I found disconcerting as the word "OPPRESSORS" printed in cold, black ink underneath.

Of course, Boadicea was simply applying the lessons I had taught her on distrusting authority figures. Still, I thought it harsh in the light of my hands-off approach to rearing – the whiff of fatherly protection excepted. But then this was as much about kids expressing their creative impulses as anything else. Vlad, our youngest, is forever astounding us with his own flights of fancy. Only the other day he asked Mum to sort him out with a woven crown of thorns to complement his stigmata. It has to be said his choice of martyr is a bit suspect and I never tire of reminding him that Sid would stub out cigarettes on the back of his hands as a matter of course. Vlad's lack of interest in punk has, I feel, much to do with immaturity. It's not uncommon in early teens, especially among boys.

By the time the heavy rain relented late evening I was listening to a silky smooth female voice on the radio. Her honeyed tones seemed to soothe the aches and pains of another busy day. In a voice barely above a whisper she spoke of widespread disruption throughout the country, with some parts having received more than twice the average monthly rainfall in just seven hours. The joy of the day seemed unending. What with rebellious kids and a natural disaster thrown in for good measure, I was left wondering whether life got any better than this.

frank and elaine

a short story **by tricia wastvedt**

Frank and Elaine came together by way of an egg flan, a missing copy of
the *Radio Times* and a cello.

When they met, they had two things in common: being twenty and
being at the same university. Frank was seeing a first-year botanist and
Elaine was not seeing anyone. She shared a flat with the botanist and
had heard Frank on many occasions late at night when she would rather
have heard only the thud and gargle of the immersion heater.

She had never seen him nor he her – until the botanist mistakenly
bought an egg flan made with mushrooms to which she was allergic.
The reaction was not serious – an hour of vomiting and eight hours of
sweats – but the botanist wasn't up to the Christmas ball Frank had
asked her to.

"You go, Elaine," she said, knowing that Elaine was no threat and, if
anything, a contrast likely to increase his appreciation. Also, he would
be tethered to a partner of her choosing, leaving her free to concentrate
on being poorly. "It'll do you good and the ticket won't be wasted."

"I suppose," said Elaine. "As long as there's nothing on telly." She
searched for the *Radio Times* and failed. It was under the botanist's
bed and Elaine never did discover what she'd missed. She agreed to go
as a favour.

She didn't have a ball gown and decided that Frank would just have
to lump it. This was fine with the botanist – she didn't offer to lend

Elaine anything, not from meanness but because tall and narrow does not adapt easily to short and wide. She did press Elaine to a diamante handbag and matching earrings at the last minute and was a little unnerved to see how beautifully the earrings sparkled against Elaine's olive complexion.

Frank was handsome, a good sportsman and had been toughened up by his four sisters. Family life in his teens was testing – a pubescent boot camp – you did not show fear, or else you were done for. Breasts, periods and complicated underwear must be met head on. The teenage Frank was spaghetti thin and his jaw unpromising, but he could handle anything as far as the opposite sex was concerned.

By the time he went to university he had filled out and squared up. Girls did not unnerve him. He looked them in the eye whatever they confided or confessed. They interpreted this as maturity and, upon this foundation, Frank built himself the reputation of being considerate, dependable and broad minded, with thighs to match.

He never met a girl who surprised him. He never met a girl who was mysterious. All there was to know he'd found out long, long ago. And, (Elaine could not have known) he wasn't used to lumping it. He had plenty of choice. Frank had assets and was generous. What he required in return was run-of-the-mill perfection, visually at least. Elaine did not know this either and, as such, was unusual material.

The botanist had telephoned Frank to explain – her understudy needed a nice time and did music. He picked up Elaine from the flat on the dot, as was his habit.

When Frank followed Elaine down the path, he tried not to look at her fleshy shoulders or the maternal bustle of her rear, or her sturdy calves that seemed to plummet, ankle-less into large white court shoes. She had not understood the deal and Frank was disorientated, but he would be gentleman enough to see it through.

He opened Elaine's door and she reversed in with surprising grace. Her underwear creaked softly and she smiled up at him: "I'm in. Chocks away." Frank noticed that her long hair was luscious and her dark eyes were very pretty.

The evening was not what he expected. Elaine did not stick to his shoulder and blink at him when he spoke to her. She talked her way through dinner, pulled crackers with her neighbours and told a rather good joke. They moved away from the tables and into a hall where a rock 'n' roll band twanged into key against a backdrop of tinsel. Elaine topped up her glass, scanned the crowd and said, "Don't think I'm going to cramp your style. I'm fine. See you later."

From time to time he caught sight of her with a group of musical friends. They looked dull, but Elaine seemed fine as she said she would be. So he beamed in on a philosopher who turned out to be deliciously flirtatious but had a laugh like a duck, even over the noise of the band. It was almost two o'clock when he thought he'd better find Elaine.

She seemed to have disappeared so he asked around. What followed was nothing compared to romantic fiction, a non-event by the standards of erotic cinema, but it changed Frank's life.

Elaine was playing the cello. She and her friends had gone off all together to an upstairs room, one of the practice rooms, and had been jamming their way through a selection of Vivaldi concerti. They had taken a couple of bottles of vodka with them, some Babychams and a candelabra from the dining table. The room was small and soundproofed. The temperature rose, the boys took off their jackets, unfurled their shirt-tails and let their bow ties dangle. The girls' shawls and little evening cardigans slipped to the floor. As Vivaldi took hold, their shoulder straps slithered and skirts were hitched up to let the air circulate. And so it went on through Beethoven and Bach. Eventually they discarded any clothing that wasn't too complicated to get out of. The candles burned lower and there were some interludes for drinking and familiarisation. People fell asleep at their instruments or in each other's arms.

By the time Frank found them, only Elaine was still playing. The slow, deep chocolatey sound of the cello filled the room. It took a moment for Frank's eyes to adjust to the near darkness. Gradually he saw.

Elaine was sitting, turned slightly away. The candles on the piano at her side caught her profile and sketched her in strokes of liquid light and charcoal shadow. An earring sparkled in her hair. Her eyes were closed and the little flames thumbed gold on her cheek, on the rim of her lips, on her generous shoulder and her hand. So blissful was the look on her face that it took a moment for Frank to register that Elaine was without her dress and also without whatever had creaked beneath it. Her solid thighs straddled the cello, and as she moved, the candlelight caught the lavish curve of a breast and the dot of a nipple, lit for a moment then gone in velvet shadow, velvet shadow down to her belly and down.

Frank, for all his early training, was caught off guard. For the first time in his life he was unprepared. This woman, Elaine, astonished him – a secret illuminated, but still as mysterious as the arcs and coils and serpentine curves of a golden hieroglyph. Frank backed out of the room and returned, dazed as one converted, to the dance floor.

An hour later, Elaine tapped him on the back. The philosopher was hanging on to his lapels, serious now and weepy.

"I'm knackered," Elaine mouthed. "Can we go?"

They walked to the car, Elaine weaving a little but not requiring assistance. When he dropped her off she said, "Don't worry, I didn't see a thing." Frank was still in shock and missed the irony of this.

He married Elaine two years later. It took him that long to learn the difference between vivace and lento, and for her to adjust to the unconventional way in which he liked her to practice the cello.

six poems

by saba zai

beeston

"Artists must be sacrificed to their art. Like bees, they must put their
lives into the sting they give."

Ralph Waldo Emerson
Letters and Social Aims ('Inspiration')

When you lived in Beeston, I wrote in scrawled ink
On the envelope and felt like I was writing "I love you"
Everytime I wrote Beeston.
Something that caught my heart strings,
Something like Bees stinging, the infernal buzz
Of Summer's last, banging and banging against
One sheet of glass, in one spot, trying to get back
Into the sun, trying to feel the wind, as if it were
The last. Beeston, somewhere near the end of the line,
I'm searching for the postal code, sealing the envelope
Standing in a train station, drinking bad coffee,
The tannoy speaks "Beeston" and my lips burn.
As if I am being swarmed, I am stung.

saba zai

in this country, beneath your skin

My grandfather walked across the hills in Kilkenny
at home with the smell of sheep and the burning sun,
wearing the clothes my father told him to,
a knitted beige sleeveless sweater
layered with a brown tweed jacket.

I'm watching him through a small circle
and I can almost hear his breath
as he smiles into the wool of his white beard,
gently bending to pick a long whip of grass,
his teeth expert
in extracting the sweet milk that lies in the roots.

Watching him walk, watching him walk,
I could be camped in the foothills of Mount Kenya,
where the day is always summer
and the night is always winter.
Absorbed in the strangeness,
I gather Africa, into my basket of moss
and fallen stars.

I could be my grandfather,
with his pink and white complexion,
burning in the heat of another post-partition day,
walking through the dust and taking in the land,
trembling with his empty stomach
and the need to pray.

His strong hands awake at night,
busy redrawing the maps of an ancient land,
in the background the sounds of his only son,
who is only a child,
boiling water, cleaning the rice for their daily meal.

Every now and again he will put his pen down
and his aching fingers will dance with the moths,
and his eyes will need to watch the moon
as he makes space for a new border
and his creator.

the father

Skin is strong and you teach me to be brave.
Hair is black and you talk to me about a god that let you down.
Eyes so brown and you make sure no man breaks my heart –
More than you already have.

The skin of my mother tongue lies in your arms.
Those hands that can smash a coconut, naked
And fierce, those nimble fingers that picked the grit
Out of my bleeding wounds; those hands
That held me crying at night, my legs, so full
Of growing pains and pins.

Sometimes I wake up and I can smell your clean
Palmolive, Ponds Cream memory. You loved me
So much. I remember Brighton and the pebbles,
A slight rain, me staying close while you looked
At me: I was the world. I remember that.

When Nani died and Ummi flew to Karachi
I helped as much as any 9 year old could, but
I don't remember what I did to help. I can still
Taste the breakfasts you made, the creamy porridge oats
The fried egg, and the freshly squeezed juice. I smile at the memory
Of you, early morning cooking, in an apron with stripes.

And I can see you sitting under a street lamp
Studying for your scholarship, for your life, and us – your unborn.
Walking for hours, the soles of your shoes falling apart,
You held your head high. Later, in secret, you'd stuff the holes
With pieces of paper and cry in your sleep, aching for love.

Pain is your face at the dinner table when you talk
With broken vowels and tears that fall unnoticed,
Making the chapattis slightly damp, slightly salty.

As you describe her, your baby sister lives on,
Dying of too much sun and not enough care.
This is a pain I can't touch with my hands, but I hold it close
Like a baby sparrow or a broken mouse.

And I am grateful for my siblings, but we cannot give
You back a sister. And we grow up –
These sisters, these daughters, these babies,
We are alive, like tears in your hand,
Needing you to notice that we too are let down.

stranded

In Chittagong my mother
has left a part of herself.

Unclaimed. Almost forgotten.

But when she eats tamarind
she tastes sweet-sour Chittagong.

In Spain, a look skims over
the smooth of my mother's face.

Soaking up sunshine, carefree,

twirling a strand of hair. At
fifty, she's still so girlish.

Life with my father has framed
her face and all her stories.

This look is all I have left

to feel my own connection
to my mother's unclaimed girl.

In Dharka's refugee camp
Pyari Begum lives prepared.

She has packed up everything.

Her *baxas*[i] contain her life:
they've been packed for twenty years.

She arrived at camp aged five
and later got married. Like

my mother, raised four children.

Like my mother, her life spent
stranded; waiting to go home.
At six years old I learnt to
sing: *Pakistan zindabad*![2]

I'd just met my motherland.

I was young, too young to know
Those words would not be enough.

My tongue would learn a language
which would mark me as 'stranger'.

I will not know the red earth

of Sindh, the cool air of Swat,
but in the curve of my cheek,

in the spark of my smile,
I find my stranded motherland.

1 Suitcases
2 Pure land live on! Viva!

oh!

Affection on your own terms –
Something everyone is entitled to.

At 27 I only just found out
I always felt it was for others.

Like marriage was for my parents
Because only they could cope.

saba zai

Affection just for being me –
Feels like a lesson on nuclear physics.

Suddenly I am Ready Brek woman
And I glow like love does, like I imagine love.

Oh! Is what I say as you casually change gear
Oh! Is what you say as I hold your hand and grin.

doreen at 86

I was a seventeen year old virgin when I married your grandfather,
A blushing bride, pure in white and pure in heart.

He slipped that ring on, and with the beauty of it all, the whole
    church wept.

Smiling for the birdie, we cut the cake, drank champagne and
    cheek to cheek
He spun me round the village hall. I knew his first dance was going
    to be my last.

Don't ask me how I knew, it's not as if I guessed the rest, but my
    kidneys can't lie.

I was so brand new for him, he was older, more used up, but I thought
    he was the sea
And he could be cleansed, that he didn't mean it when he said, he'd
    never touch me again.

After 69 years, he left me, widowed and wrinkled.   Too old to
    feel single.

notes on contributors

daniel allan (2002)
Daniel was born and raised in Surrey before moving to Cornwall.
Gaining a first-class degree in English and Cultural Studies at Bath Spa
University College enabled him to apply for the MA programme in
Creative Writing. *The Space Between Waves* is his first novel.

wendy ashley (2002)
Wendy grew up in Cornwall. She has a degree in design and worked as
a theatre designer, bookseller and cinema usher before accepting that
what she really wanted to do was to write. She currently lives in Bath,
where she is working on her first novel, *The Ninth Wave.*

max ashworth (2002)
Max is 24, gets irritated when people say to him, "Please. If you just let
me go, I won't tell the police. Honest." And he is suspicious of people
who say, "Honest," as he should be. He plays bluegrass banjo, watches
banned horror films, hates writing his own biography, listens to Bill
Hicks and Lenny Bruce, drinks to excess, is heavily sedated. That's all
you need to know, he says.

holly atkinson (2001)
Soon after completing her MA, Holly took part in a young writers' six-
month apprenticeship scheme, sponsored by the Arvon and Jerwood
Foundations. She is currently working on her first novel, *The
Accidental Hermit*, which won last year's PFD Prize for the best student
manuscript. She has lived in Bristol for six years but grew up in the
Peak District, which perhaps explains her fascination with isolation,
peculiar people and small village life.

stephanie boxall (2002)
Stephanie has worked in publishing and journalism for many years
and currently works as a sub-editor for a national newspaper. She lives
in Oxford with her husband and cat, and is writing her first novel.

notes on contributors

gloria burland (2002)
Bristol-born Gloria lived in Greece running her own restaurant for fourteen years while writing freelance for various publications, including The Times. She was in Los Angeles interviewing the stars for an Australian 'soap magazine' before returning to do her MA at Bath Spa, and now lives in France.

trudi cowper (2002)
Before Trudi did the Creative Writing MA, she lived in London where she worked as a TV camera operator. She now lives with Daniel in Bath where she is working as a teaching assistant and finishing her novel.

cathy cullis (1995)
Cathy's work has appeared in *The Rialto* and *Tears in the Fence*. In 1996, she received an Eric Gregory award from the Society of Authors. She was also a winner of the Asham Awards for short stories by women and her story appeared in an anthology *The Catch*, (Serpent's Tail, 1997). Cathy won first prize in the New County pamphlet competition and her short collection *Orbital Angel* was published by Flarestack in 1998. Cathy has two children and lives with her family in Cambridge.

barb drummond (2002)
Barb is working on three novels and a biography. She loves old buildings and new music. She once gave a man tea and flapjacks to stop him becoming invisible. She is fond of penguins but has never wanted to be one. She sometimes wishes she were taller.

lucy english (1996)
Lucy was born in Sri Lanka and grew up in London. She has a BA in English and American Literature from the University of East Anglia and an MA in creative writing from Bath Spa. Her novels include *Selfish People* (1998), *Children of Light* (1999), and *Our Dancing Days* (2000), all of which were published by Fourth Estate. Lucy also performs poetry at festivals in Britain, Europe, and the United States.

shane garrigan (2002)
Shane studied creative writing at Ruskin College in Oxford before joining the MA at Bath Spa. He lives in Oxford with his wife and stepson, and is currently writing his first novel, *The Last Laugh*.

yvonne gavan (2000)
Yvonne studied English and Drama with Music as an undergraduate and, after finishing her MA, she worked briefly as an editor before going to Japan to teach English and study Zen Calligraphy. A year-and-a-half later she took up a university teaching post in Thailand, where she taught composition and creative writing at undergraduate level. She travelled extensively in Southeast Asia before moving back to London. She is currently working on a play, a children's book and a first collection of poetry.

sue gibbons (1994)
Sue was born in Bristol, England. She's now a temporary resident of Greensboro, North Carolina, where – thanks to the VIF Program – she's able to teach in American schools. Now that the bug has bitten her, she hopes to continue travelling. She writes poetry and prose.

daniel gothard (2002)
Daniel studied creative writing at Ruskin College in Oxford for a year before joining the MA at Bath Spa. He is currently completing his first novel, *Back to the Light*. He lives and works in Oxford.

deborah gregory (1994)
Deborah began writing seriously after becoming a winner in a South West Arts competition. Her first novel, *The Cornflake House*, was published by Picador in 1999. Her second novel, *The Better Part*, was published by Solidus, a new publishing venture of which she is a founder member, in October 2002.

heather lyn gupton (2002)
Heather holds an honors-level bachelor's degree in English Literature from Saint Andrews Presbyterian College in Laurinburg, North Carolina, and studied for a time at Florida Atlantic College before coming over to finish her MA at Bath Spa.

tessa hadley (1994)
Tessa was born in Bristol, lives in Cardiff, and teaches English and Creative Writing at Bath Spa. Her first novel, *Accidents in the Home*, was published by Jonathan Cape in 2002, and she has had short stories in anthologies and magazines including one in *The New Yorker*. Her book *Henry James and the Imagination of Pleasure* was published by Cambridge University Press, also in 2002.

jules hardy (2000)
Jules wrote her first novel, *Altered Land* (Simon & Schuster, 2002), while studying for her MA at Bath Spa. Her second novel, *Mister Candid*, is due out in April, and *Blue Earth* is her third novel. She is currently studying for a PhD in Creative Writing at Bath Spa.

mo hayder (2001)
Mo lives in Bath with her husband and daughter. *The Treatment* is her second novel.

julie hayman (2002)
Julie lives in Bath but was brought up in Salisbury. She completed a BA in English Literature and Creative Studies before joining the MA course at BSUC, in which she achieved a distinction. She is interested in polar literature and received an award in The Bridport Prize in 2002.

jennifer hunt (2001)
Jennifer lives in West Dorset and has a gallery in Lyme Regis where she paints, draws, makes cards and writes. She graduated (with distinction) from Bath Spa, and has had poems published in several poetry magazines. She will begin a PhD this year, researching Mary Anning, the fossil hunter.

paula hutchings (2002)
Paula was born in London where she still lives with her cat Eric. She completed a degree in English at Southampton University and an MA in Literature at Essex University. *The Duchess* is her first novel.

elizabeth kay (1994)
Elizabeth's books include a book of poetry, *The Spirit Collection* (Manifold, 2002), and two forthcoming children's fantasies, *The Divide* and *The Half-Twist* to be published by The Chicken House. She has had one story adapted for television, and has also won a number of important awards for her poetry and fiction, including the Canongate Prize and the Cardiff International Poetry Competition.

cassandra keen (2002)
Cassandra is an economist (lapsed), and has been an antique dealer in London and Paris. She still appreciates beautiful things. Sustained in Islington by her husband, Robert, and cats, Shirt and Blouse, she has published a short story in a literary anthology, and a poem that won second prize in *Writer's Forum*. She was awarded a distinction in the MA.

simon kerr (1997)
Simon is 31. His first novel, *The Rainbow Singer*, was nominated for the 2003 IMPAC Dublin Literary Award and the 2002 Barnes & Noble Discovery Award. He received his MA with distinction from Bath Spa, and subsequently tutored there for two years. He now lives in Ireland with his fiancée, Caroline.

mike martin (2002)
Mike lives in Somerset with his wife and a designer cat beside him and a career as a consultant to the finance industries behind him. Somewhere in Bristol there are two lively daughters. *Baber's Apple* is his third novel.

vivienne mayer (2002)
Vivienne is currently finishing her first novel, *Normal Proportions*. As an established British newspaper journalist (NCTJ), Vivienne's career to date includes news reporting, national features, and international business coverage. In 2001/2002 she was published by Fodor's (New York), for a series of travel updates and essays. She passed her Creative Writing MA with distinction.

susan mcmillan (2002)
Susan is a documentary producer with BBC television and has written an environmental book for children published by BBC Books.

kate megeary (2002)
Kate was born sometime in 1975, woke up this morning, not sure what happened in between, but she reckons it might have been good!

notes on contributors

sarah menage (2002)
After starting medical school and finishing drama school, Sarah acted in a few fringe plays, did stand-up, wrote songs and learned to type. She later studied photography, journalism, teaching, business ownership and massage. Today she manages a successful team of human-life-sustaining organs and still finds time to love her son.

jan menzies (2002)
Jan is a freelance journalist. Formerly the women's editor of the *Daily Express*, she was also a columnist on the *Daily Mail*. She has published three non-fiction books in the health and slimming market. The Creative Writing MA has provided the opportunity for her to fulfil a long-term ambition to write a novel.

morgaine merch lleuad (2002)
Morgaine claims that her name is the least interesting thing about her. This may even be true. She has been described as an "infuriating cow", as having the "worst dress sense since drag queens were invented", and as "that bloody witch". She has never denied any of these. She writes things. Allegedly.

paul meyer (2002)
Paul was a finalist in last year's National Poetry Competition and has just begun work on a PhD in Creative Writing at Bath Spa. He is writing a novel called *Some Interludes with Charles Mingus* and a related thesis on musical forms in prose fiction.

peter o'connor (2002)
Peter is 41, married, and for that reason says that he says sex "only infrequently". His National Insurance Number is WP10774832291, and his aim is to write good comedy.

helen partridge (2002)
Helen is a mountain bike guide, climber and successful adventure racer as well as a writer and teacher of poetry. She graduated with distinction from the Creative Writing MA at Bath Spa, and came second in the poetry section of The Bridport Prize in 2002. She is currently working on a novel called *The Memory of Water*.

john pemberton (2002)

After running a computer software company for many years, John was aware that his career had relied on the logical side of his brain and he sought to exercise the creative side. He began to research the history of the farm on which he lives and which, in medieval times, was owned by a monastic order. The turbulent and controversial lives of the monks gave him the stimulus to write his first novel.

joanna pocock (2000)

Joanna graduated with distinction from the Creative Writing MA, where she wrote a collection of short stories entitled *Blue Suburban Skies*. She is now in her second year of a PhD at Bath Spa, where she is writing a novel and a thesis based around the life of a nineteenth-century pioneer to Canada and her mysterious links to a twenty-first-century woman. Joanna lives in London where she works as a book designer when she isn't writing.

gilly reeder (2002)

Gilly studied History and Art History at York University and has since spent her time perfecting her skills either side of a bar (sometimes overseas) and stealing time from her employers. As a child of Essex, who now lives in London, her roots can occasionally be said to show. She is currently writing a novel.

sarah rosenfeld (1999)

Sarah is a Canadian writer and editor living in Montreal, Canada. She has worked as the managing editor of a children's magazine, and has published book reviews and travel pieces. She is currently working on a fantasy novel, a poetry manuscript, and works full-time as the associate editor of a travel magazine for Canadian doctors.

julie-ann rowell (1994)

Following the MA in Creative Writing, Julie-ann worked as editorial assistant on the Irish Studies Review and currently works as a freelance editor. She has had many poems published and has won several prizes; her first collection of poetry will be published in 2003. She has also written a novel for young adults called *Sea Change*, published by Solidus in 2002.

notes on contributors

karen sainsbury (2000)
A few weeks after graduating with distinction from the MA course, Karen sold *Powder Monkey* to Weidenfeld & Nicolson as part of a two-book deal. *Powder Monkey* came out in hardback in May 2002. *Maris Piper*, her second novel, is due out in January 2004. Karen is currently working towards her PhD at Bath Spa, where she is writing her third novel, and she also holds local writing workshops.

steve sainsbury (2002)
Steve was discovered in a Sussex wood in 1963. He was about seven years old at the time. He had been raised by badgers and, though able to run at speed on all fours, was unable to walk. He communicated in grunts and squeals. He now writes full time.

susan spencer (2002)
Susan originally hails from Lancashire. She works as a lecturer in further education and has worked as a counsellor and trainer. Susan has always written poetry, more so since a writing holiday in 1995 and, since backpacking around the world from 1996 to 1997, some travel tales. She has two grown-up children and lives in Bristol.

sy standon (2002)
Sy was born in London, where he spent his childhood, and eventually ended up in Bristol, where he has been ever since. He has always had an interest in telling stories and likes to explore the oceans of human emotion, stripping down the story to the bare essentials. He likes to cycle and has started learning to kayak since moving aboard his houseboat. He says: "If anyone finds my message in a bottle, please write back... " The extract here is taken from his novel, *View from a Boxcar*, set in the US in the late 1920s.

mary taylor (1994)
After working for nine years as an NHS dietitian, Mary wrote furiously for two years and surfaced, clutching her MA, in the mid-Nineties. That brainstorm has resulted in many multimedia poetry performances and workshops. Her reviews and poems, with a Celtic and African slant, have appeared all over the place.

mimi thebo (1999)

Mimi hails from Lawrence, Kansas, and published the first anthology of work from the MA course at Bath Spa. Since then, she has won and been placed in numerous short story and poetry competitions, and her novel *The Saint Who Loved Me* (Allison & Busby, reprinted second week of issue) was published in September 2002. She now teaches at Bath Spa, and has just been awarded a bursary to complete her PhD in English and Creative Studies, of which her next adult novel forms a part. Her first of three children's novels for HarperCollins, *Wipe Out*, was published in January, and Mimi writes fantasy under a pseudonym. She had her first child last year and remains happily married to her husband of sixteen years.

neil walker (2002)

Neil was born in Oldham in 1966. He got a chipper bike at the age of eight, but never progressed to a chopper. Neil loathed university and detested work. He lived for six years in the Azores and plans to return with his long-suffering girlfriend, who may be expecting their second child.

tricia wastvedt (2002)

Tricia was born in south London. She moved to Bath in the early Eighties, returned to full-time education in 1998 and then graduated with a degree in Creative Arts. She is working on her first novel.

saba zai (2002)

Saba has worked in a chocolate shop, been a charity worker, a secondary-school teacher and a matron at Cheltenham Ladies College. She is 27 and a poet.